An Army with Banners

The Real Face of Orangeism

William Brown

First published 2003
by
Beyond the Pale
BTP Publications Ltd
Unit 2.1.2 Conway Mill
5-7 Conway Street
Belfast BT13 2DE

Tel: +44 (0)28 90 438630
Fax: +44 (0)28 90 439707
E-mail: office@btpale.com

Website and online sales: http://www.btpale.com

British Library Cataloguing-in-Publication Data.
A catalogue record for this book is available from the British Library.

ISBN 1-900960-24-9

Cover illustration:
'The Twelth of July in Portadown' (1928) by Sir John Lavery (1856-1941)

Who is she that looketh forth as the morning, fair as the moon,
Clear as the sun, and terrible as an army with banners?

Song of Solomon, 6: 10.

'…dedicated to the proposition that all men are created equal.'

(Fragment from Abraham Lincoln's *Gettysberg Address)*

Contents

Acknowledgements and Attributions   vi
Glossary of the Loyal Orders   vii
Foreword   xi

Introduction   1

Section One: Origins of Orangeism

  1.   Protestant Ascendancy versus Radicalism   9
  2.   Peep O' Day Boys and Defenders   14
  3.   James Wilson and the Orange Tradition   18
  4.   The Diamond and its Aftermath   22

Section Two: Objectives of Orangeism

  5.   1795 - 1801: An army whose idea seems to be blood   31
  6.   1801 - 1869: Keeping the Papists in their places   42
  7.   1869 - 1894: Playing the Orange card   55
  8.   1894 - 1914: Irish unionism v. 'little Ulster' unionism   70
  9.   1914 - 1921: Home Rule for the anti-Home Rulers   85
  10. 1921 - 1972: The rise and fall of the Orange State   96
  11. Aftermath: Summation and Sequel   104

Section Three: Ordinances of Orangeism

  12. Orange Religion: Its Relationship to the Reformed Faith   127
  13. Orange Ritual: The Influence of Freemasonry   140
  14. Orange Rights: Marching and Civil Liberties   156

Endgame

  15. Marching backwards from the Future   177

End Notes   184
Select Bibliography   188
Index   191

Acknowledgements and Attributions

Given the extremes of Northern Ireland's religio-politics, the subject and nature of this book could excite many differing sensitivities, emotions and reactions. I therefore considered it wise to minimise the involvement of others, and have refrained from making the usual list of acknowledgements. However, I do owe a debt of gratitude to several people, even to some Orangemen and former Orangemen who gave me so generously of their time. I am, of course, indebted to my sources, and particularly to those fellow radicals from whom I have so liberally quoted. These sources have, I hope, been appropriately acknowledged within the text. But as has already been implied, the final responsibility for *An Army With Banners*, with all its critical assertions, interpretations and conclusions, remains very much my own.

If I forbear from personal acknowledgements, I am happy to make some general attributions to certain formative influences from my past. Much that motivated this book and contributed to its stance and style could be attributed to my background. I came from bible-believing stock, from a people who said what they meant and meant what they said – an attitude that might too readily be regarded as typical of the Ulster Protestant. My upbringing was far from typical. My father was an ultra-dissenter, who, if he had thought of anything so pretentious as a family motto, might well have adapted one from the apostle Paul: 'Prove all things'. The great fundamentals apart, all the elements of my early life seemed open to challenge. It was as though I was nurtured in a school of religio-political argument – with Orangeism on the curriculum.

As my interests broadened, I retained an interest in theology but began to read British and Irish history. I attended lectures in Belfast where I met the late Victor Kelly, an inspirational teacher whose liberal interpretations of Ireland's great historical issues struck a responsibly radical chord and changed forever my inherited understanding of these things. Although many years later I continue to see some value in the Union, I have increasingly come to acknowledge the probability of a new post-nationalist Ireland within the greater Union of Europe. I like to think that such an Ireland may yet realise the vision of the Presbyterian United Irishmen – one, incidentally, that is the very antithesis of Orangeism – a vision of the peaceful unity of Protestant, Catholic and Dissenter in liberty, equality and fraternity.

Far from indicating a political dithering or constitutional neutrality, this arguably is the politics of the future. Such politics postulates that, in the wake of the Good Friday Agreement, Northern Ireland's ancient quarrel will come to be seen as a parochial and sterile one, bound to be overtaken by greater developments in an increasingly global society. If that is so, or even if it is not, there is much that needs to be challenged and changed here – the major reason for my writing this critique of Orangeism. My life-long experience of its influence, and the strongly critical convictions that its attitudes and actions created within me, is the book's *fons et origo*. But beyond that, *An Army With Banners* can be attributed to the desire to see my fellow citizens move forward from an anachronistic past towards a new egalitarian and non-sectarian society.

Glossary of the Loyal Orders

Apprentice Boys

Established in 1714 by a Colonel Mitchelburne who had participated in the siege of Derry in 1689, the Apprentice Boys of Derry is probably the oldest of the Loyal Orders. Its objectives are said to be mainly historical – to commemorate the resistance led by the thirteen apprentice boys who closed the gates of Derry on Catholic King James II, and which eventually led to their triumphant raising of the siege. This event is important in that it was the prelude to James's defeat in the Williamite Wars that followed in Ireland.

Based in Londonderry, the Apprentice Boys are proud of their 'Maiden City' – the maiden that never was taken! They describe their aims as 'mainly cultural and historical', in contrast to those of the kindred Orange Order, which they regard as 'religio-political'. However, their rules clearly require their members to be Protestant and 'at all times to uphold the crimson banner' – a symbolic standard that has strong religio-political, constitutional and unionist connotations.

The Apprentice Boys are reputed to be even more loyalist than the Orange Order, and include the former Orangeman Rev. Ian Paisley MP among their membership. They too are marchers, share Orange facilities, have similar religio-political beliefs, and often associate with Orange parades. In fact around 80 per cent of Apprentice Boys are also Orangemen. Their parade of 12th August 1969, which led to prolonged rioting in Derry, is often regarded as a key point in the development of the Northern Ireland Troubles.

Orange Order

This is the substantive loyal Order that evolved from the tradition of the Orange clubs that were founded by the military classes soon after the Williamite wars. From these came the military-style marching that would later epitomise the Orange-Protestant ascendancy in Ireland.

In the late eighteenth century, when rising Catholic aspirations and the threat of revolution gave rise to Protestant concerns, a militant group called the Orange Boys allied themselves with banditti Peep O' Day Boys in County Armagh and defeated the Catholic Defenders at the Battle of the Diamond in 1795. The victors established the Orange Order – a secret neo-Masonic paramilitary group with a mission to defend Protestant ascendancy.

The founders soon gave way to the Anglo-Irish Protestant gentry, many of whom had British military connections. The new leaders included Establishment clergy, who quickly purged the Order of its proliferating ritual that involved neo-Masonic, pagan and even Catholic Crusader elements. The original system was replaced by two new degrees in the new Orange Order of 1798, but the purge was resisted by ritualistic dissidents, who went on to found the separate but linked Royal Arch Purple and Black Orders.

The politically aware new leadership encouraged the Orangemen to join the government's new Yeomanry. This became an essentially Orange paramilitary force, and did much to put down the Irish Rebellion of 1798. Orange militarism would later provide the manpower for Carson's Ulster Volunteer Force, established to resist Home Rule.

All this would eventuate in the partition of Ireland and in the creation of Northern Ireland in 1921, which for fifty years would be ruled by the Orange leaders of the Ulster Unionist Party. Thus when religio-political Protestant ascendancy was no longer viable in Ireland as a whole, Orange-unionism maintained it in the North by means of what Prime Minister Lord Craigavon ('I am an Orangeman first') could proudly describe as a 'Protestant parliament for a Protestant people'.

Royal Arch Purple

The attempt by the Orange leadership to rid the Order of its ritualism circa 1798 was opposed by traditionalists who wished to retain the original degrees. Unlike the now independent Black Order, these traditionalists covertly worked the old ritualism within Orangeism in defiance of Grand Lodge. This 'Order within the Order' became known as the Royal Arch Purple, and was eventually integrated into Orangeism in Scotland and elsewhere throughout the British Empire, but not in Ireland. That is still the official position.

Failing to gain official legitimacy within Irish Orangeism in 1909, the Arch Purple formally established itself as 'independent'. However, this proved to be something of a device, for about 95 per cent of all Orangemen now graduate to it, while remaining Orangemen. Its membership therefore overlaps with the Orange Order, and in that sense it remains integral to Orangeism. In fact, it 'shadows' the Orange at all levels, sharing the same venues and meeting just before or after Orange lodge meetings, which are 'raised' to Arch Purple level to facilitate this circumvention of the official and still extant Orange rules. The rules continue to regard the Arch Purple as illegal, but this seems to be treated as a mere technicality.

Royal Black Preceptory

Black Lodges existed from the earliest days of Orangeism, but although associated with the Orange Order these Lodges were usually frowned upon. However, the Royal Black Preceptory now regards itself as the highest of all the Loyal Orders, elitism being the main reason behind its formal declaration of independence in 1846.

More independent of the Orange Order than is the Royal Arch Purple, yet it too remains closely linked to the Orange Order in that all its members are drawn from it via the Royal Arch Purple, and by invitation only. All Blackmen must therefore be Arch Purplemen, and Arch Purplemen must first be Orangemen, so that expulsion from one Order leads automatically to expulsion from the others. This ensures close structural linkage between all three Orders and maintains a common religio-political status. It is estimated that 40 per cent of Irish Orangemen/Arch Purplemen are also in membership of the Royal Black Preceptory.

Black degrees were worked within Orangeism from an early stage in defiance of Grand Lodge, which in 1798 sought to rid the Order of a proliferation of neo-Masonic and other home-spun degrees. The Black Order is so called because its adherents are said to be in symbolic mourning for 'brother Joseph', the son of Jacob who according to the biblical story was cruelly sold by his brothers into slavery in Egypt. This example of its symbolic ritualism is typical of a far-fetched esoteric system that involves eleven stages culminating in its final Red Cross degree.

The Black Order claims a long heritage, regarding itself as a chivalric brotherhood with antecedents in the feudal knighthood of the Middle Ages. Blackmen address one another as Sir Knight and, despite an avowedly Reformed religious credo, the Royal Black Preceptory claims, like the Freemasons, to have inherited much of its ritualistic tradition from the medieval Crusaders. Yet incongruously from the standpoint of an allegedly Protestant Order, the Crusaders were the Catholic soldiers of the Holy Roman Empire who, by direction of Pope Urban II, fought under the banner of the Cross to recover Jerusalem and the Holy Sepulchre for Roman Catholicism.

Independent Orange Order

Known as the 'I Double O', this Order was established in 1903 following a schism within the Orange Order. Tom Sloan, a Belfast shipyard man and Protestant preacher, was a working class ultra evangelical who distrusted the leadership of Orange-unionism – an elite he saw as suspect in its religious convictions and compromising as to its Protestantism. Sloan, who in July 1902 had publicly heckled the Orange-unionist leader Col. Edward Saunderson for not supporting legislation to control Roman Catholic laundries, stood as an Independent in a South Belfast by-election shortly afterwards and defeated his official unionist opponent and fellow Orangeman. These actions led to Sloan's suspension from the Orange Order.

He and his fellow activist Lindsay Crawford, who was also strongly anti-Catholic and zealously opposed to ritualism in the Church of Ireland, retaliated by creating the IOO in 1903. The new Order saw itself as representing the Protestant working class, although its politics were more ultra-Protestant than class based and religio-sectarian rather than definitively socialist. Crawford, who had greater political potential than Sloan, presented his Magheramourne Manifesto to the IOO in July 1905. This was to advocate an approach to the Irish problem that was reminiscent both of the United Irishmen and Gladstonian Home Rule liberalism. Tom Sloan soon broke with Crawford on these issues and in 1908 Crawford was expelled from the IOO. Sloan then lost his parliamentary seat, at which point the Order went into steep decline, a condition in which it remained for many years. At this time Lindsay Crawford emigrated to Canada, where he eventually embraced Irish republicanism.

The upsurge of Paisleyism in the 1960s made for a new beginning in Northern Ireland's extremist politics, and the Independent Order now began to attract a new wave of 'Sloanite' evangelical and ultra-Protestant elements. In any event the post-Crawford IOO had long reverted to its original fundamentalism. This made it popular with the ultras, all of which paved the way for a minor revival in its fortunes. The Independent Orange Order is now estimated at one thousand strong.

Like the Rev. Ian Paisley MP who gives it his patronage, this quirky Order is slightly leftist on social policy, strongly rightist on constitutional politics, and staunchly fundamentalist on matters of religion. Whilst adhering to the two official degrees of Orangeism, the Independent Orange Order continues to include the old neo-Masonic and ritualistic Royal Arch Purple degree in its ceremonial practices. This is most surprising given the rigour of its professed evangelical fundamentalism, to say nothing of its original Sloan-Crawford legacy of anti-ritualism.

Foreword

A recent writer on Orangeism, Kevin Haddick-Flynn, observes that it is a subject which 'curiously, has received only sparse and spasmodic attention'. This should hardly surprise us. On the one hand, many people nowadays cannot even begin to comprehend Orangeism's eighteenth century philosophy and eccentric marching practices, and are therefore sufficiently disinterested, if not alienated, to feel no need for further enquiry. On the other hand, the loyal adherents of the Orange Order, essentially a secret and exclusive society,[1] normally adopt a withdrawn and defensive stance on the subject, and certainly do not encourage the prurient investigation of outsiders. Given such attitudes, 'sparse and spasmodic attention' was probably inevitable. Yet despite this, Haddick-Flynn was soon to find that the publication of his *Orangeism* almost coincided with Ruth Dudley Edwards's *The Faithful Tribe*.

Thus, after the dearth, two substantial works have virtually come out together, which seems to indicate that Orangeism is now receiving some fresh interest and attention. Paradoxically, despite my suggested explanation for the earlier paucity, this development might in another sense have been expected given the controversy and adverse publicity the Orange Order has attracted during recent years. But more than that, the ending of the dearth also coincides with the recent important changes in Northern Ireland's political climate, and this new interest could therefore suggest that some minds are at last beginning to realise the real strength of the connection between Orangeism and our deeply troubled past. However, that past is one which is very much in keeping with what St. Augustine described as 'the past in the present', for as recent sectarian events illustrate all too clearly Northern Ireland still has a very long way to go in terms of its required political progress.

This new interest in Orangeism is both welcome and timely, not only because the subject is important enough to justify investigation, but because conflict resolution requires that greater understanding which can only come with sufficient information. This is not to suggest that hitherto there was a dire lack of knowledge here, but rather that until recently the material was largely of a fragmentary nature. With the exception of the histories of Senior and Sibbett, and of some local Orange apologists, writing on Orangeism has been confined to the general works on Irish history, and to vignettes within works on related political subjects covering the last two hundred years. As such, the material required much sifting, sorting and synthesising. But this is now well on the way to being remedied, Dudley Edwards having produced an interesting if revisionist apologia, and Haddick-Flynn a quite excellent and objective history.

My own work proffers a critique of Orangeism as a religio-political credo or belief system and, as such, may be seen as something of a counterweight to the Orange apologists, among whom Ruth Dudley Edwards is the most recent. In *The*

Faithful Tribe she assays to get close up and intimate with Orangeism so as to inform us that Orangemen are 'just people'.[2] Much more anecdotal than analytical, she treats us to graphic accounts of folksy parades, frolicsome picnics and frigid lodge meetings, which served to familiarise her with Orange sub-culture and provided opportunity for fellowship with good-natured Ulster folk. But her story involves an underlying agenda – to show that the majority of Orangemen are good human beings, who are 'much less bad than they seem'.[3] This objective has significance for the quality of the argument, which does little for revisionism and reveals something of what another writer has described as the 'irritating zeal'[4] of the proselyte. Revisionism is not necessarily a bad thing, but in challenging old ideas on the basis of apparently new information it can sometimes lose a sense of proportion and occasionally may throw out the baby with the bath water. As for zeal, there is no obvious need to elaborate on the decency of the mass of the ordinary people involved. Decency is not at issue here. Indeed, no informed Ulster writer would feel a particular need to defend the character of the generality of people who make up the ranks of Orangeism.

Why then the special pleading? Dudley Edwards' case is that, like the people concerned, Orangeism is much less bad than it seems – something that does not necessarily follow. Her apologia typifies a revisionism whose loathing of IRA violence leads it, on the one hand, to diminish important criticism of Orange-unionism and, on the other, to view it through zeal-filtered glasses. This produces an unfocused and unbalanced perception. But be that as it may, the proposition that Orange folk are decent human beings does not mean that Orangeism is a good and wholesome thing. That is another question altogether.

Neither movements nor institutions should be assessed by recourse to the common human qualities of their individual members, nor indeed by inevitable lapses in these. Movements must be evaluated, not by what they have in common with others, but by what distinguishes them. Normal personal traits tell us nothing of the distinctive principles or politics of the group to which the good or not-so-good person may belong, and subsequent political discovery can often give rise to great surprise. The fact that Orangemen at the human level are decent people makes no contribution to questions about those moral or political values for which their institution stands. Such questions must be determined by recourse to the distinctive principles that make Orangeism what it is. In that sense Orangemen are more than 'just people', and that 'more' involves the real issues which need to be addressed, for Orangeism amounts to more than the personal attributes of individual Orangemen, some of whom may know only a little about what it really stands for, and who joined the Order merely for family or traditional reasons. More than a collection of 'just people', decent or otherwise, Orangeism is a culture that involves a long tradition with a powerful canon of beliefs and attitudes that have had a profound and often far from benign bearing on Ireland, and more especially on Northern Ireland's politics and religion.

It is therefore arguable that Dudley Edwards' rather bland and personalised approach provides Orangeism with far too much comfort, especially given the Ulster Protestants' predilection to political self-righteousness in their long-standing cause 'for God and Ulster'. If God is on your side, your opponents are obviously in the wrong – an attitude that never was more strong in Northern Ireland than it is today, when Orange-unionists are pinning the blame for almost all the wrongs of the Troubles on republicans and nationalists. Yet, on the face of it, this cannot be right given that unionism was in charge of Northern Ireland for nearly fifty years when things started to go so terribly wrong. One therefore feels that the work of peace and reconciliation in Northern Ireland would be better served if, instead of being preoccupied with the sins of others, Orange-unionism could be encouraged to question its sense of moral superiority, and to reflect on its own not insignificant contribution to our deeply troubled past. Such is the chief consideration of this book.

For that reason the book is far less interested in the socio-organisational elements of the Orange Order than in those collective beliefs and attitudes that make Orangeism what it is – an ism that is deeply pervasive of Northern Ireland's Protestant society, that makes us what we are and explains what we do. That ism is wider than the membership of the Order itself, what is described as Orange-unionism being its prime example. Thus *circa* 1912 we find British statesmen such as Asquith, Churchill and Lloyd George using words like 'Orangemen' or the 'Orange army' as aphorisms for the Ulster opponents of the third Home Rule Bill. Such usage, then as now, was not always quite accurate, but can usually be appropriate if the people, precepts or practices in question derive from, or are in general accord with, the principles of the Orange fountain from which Irish unionism largely sprang.

The extent of Orange influence is beyond question. The Unionist Party, which held power for fifty years in Northern Ireland, evolved from the Irish Conservative and Orange Party at the turn of the century. In the days of its power every unionist prime minister was an Orangeman, and throughout its history 95 per cent of all its MPs and councillors have been Orangemen. The Order sends 120 delegates to the Ulster Unionist Council, the governing body of the Ulster Unionist Party, even though the large majority of the other 700 delegates are also Orangemen. The local Orange hall, of which there are about 900 servicing a fluctuating number of up to 100,000 Orangemen across Northern Ireland, is more than just a meeting house for Orange Lodges, or for the gospel missions of fundamentalist preachers. It is also the engine room of the Ulster Unionist Party, the local centre of Orange-unionism's social, political and other related activities. In the past Orange halls were used for the recruitment and drilling of the illegal Ulster Volunteer Force, which metamorphosed into the B-Specials who also drilled there. More recently there have been reports of the unofficial use of Orange halls by the terrorist Orange Volunteers. Thus many aspects and elements of unionism and therefore of Northern Ireland's Protestant political life, both ancient and modern, the good and the bad, have been shot-through with Orangeism.

Given that for over two hundred years Orangeism has been so pervasive and influential in Ireland's history, and during more recent times in the tragic events of Northern Ireland, it is suggested that the time has come for Orange-unionists to take stock. We should take a long hard Cromwellian 'warts and all' look at ourselves, at our history, our attitudes and behaviour, as well as at those objectives and beliefs that motivated us and made us what we are. There is a sense in which 'we are what we believe', and if there is now much about Orange-unionism that is detrimental, dysfunctional and in dire need of reform, it is not unreasonable to conclude that this is deeply rooted in our Orange psyche and in its atavistic belief system. An examination of this will tell the story of the development of the politics of Orange-unionism and of its religious principles, which will be compared with the generally accepted standards of Christianity and the Reformed Faith. It is hoped that the exercise will prove profitable, especially for those who are perplexed by Northern Ireland's current and recurring sectarianism, and by the bitter internecine strife within Orange-unionism. Self-examination is the necessary starting point on the long hard road to reform leading to a better and more peaceful future for us all.

Introduction

Background

This book tells a story and proffers explanations of Orangeism's late eighteenth century origins and developing objectives, both political and religious, during the two hundred years of its history to the present day. The Orange Order was conceived and cradled in Ireland at a time of great fear and uncertainty – things that were by no means confined to Ireland at that time. At the beginning of the century the British crown had just been won by the Protestant Prince of Orange, a revolutionary change that underpinned the British Protestantism which had struggled for ascendancy since the time of Henry VIII. From then onwards the British people gradually coalesced into something approaching nationhood, cemented by what might be described as a form of pan-Protestantism. This, as Linda Colley has shown in her book *Britons*, was not a Protestantism of strong political, religious or even cultural consensus, for it harboured much diversity. Rather it was the catalyst of a developing sense of identity, as the eighteenth century British began to regard themselves as one people, defined by their Protestantism in reaction to the Catholic enemy just beyond their shores – the Protestant 'Us' struggling for survival against the alien Catholic 'Them'.

That enemy had previously reared its head during the first half of the century when the Jacobites rebelled in an unsuccessful attempt to bring back the Stuarts and thus restore a Catholic monarchy. Now, at the end of the century, Protestant Britain was embroiled in a long and dangerous war with Catholic France. The British were therefore united in their watchfulness. Catholics were often regarded with suspicion, and until as late as 1829 were not allowed to vote or to hold offices of state, and were excluded from both houses of parliament. In Ireland the situation was politically and morally different, more internally volatile because of Catholic numbers, and therefore potentially more extreme. Here Protestants had greater cause for fear. Unlike the British, who as a large national entity included Dissenters and Nonconformists, the Irish 'nation' was an exclusive minority that represented about only one-eighth of the population, limited to members of the established Church of Ireland. Not only Catholics, but the dissenting and dangerous Presbyterians who were strong in the North were effectively excluded. Thus although this minority Irish 'nation' defined itself as the 'Protestant ascendancy', this was more like a colonial garrison in a conquered Ireland – the Ireland that should have been the nation. It was this that constituted the moral and political difference referred to above. But the outbreak of war in 1793 between Britain and France revivified Protestant fears of a French invasion by the 'back door' of Ireland – an invasion that could conceivably be augmented by a republican uprising by both 'United Irish' Catholics and Presbyterians. It was in such a volatile atmosphere that the Protestant ascendancy-supporting Orange Order was founded in late 1795.

1

Methodology

In telling the story of Orangeism we shall re-visit many old landmarks such as the Battle of the Diamond, the 1798 Rebellion, the Act of Union, Catholic Emancipation, Disestablishment of the Church of Ireland, Home Rule, the creation of Northern Ireland, the partition of Ireland, and many others. It should be understood, however, that these excursions into history do not purport *per se* to provide a history of the Orange Order, nor indeed any other kind of history. Given that by their very nature such thematic historical excursions have to omit or pass over so much, their deployment should be regarded primarily as a back-cloth against which we seek to unfold, illustrate and examine the various principles and beliefs that lie behind Orangeism's origins, its ongoing objectives and ordinances. We shall explore Orangeism's *raison d'être* – what does its belief system involve in terms of politics and religion; what are its aims and objectives; how successful have the Orangemen been in achieving these; and has Orangeism over time been a force for good or ill to the people of Ireland? In pursuing these issues, the chosen methodology is to tell a story and provide a commentary and critique – a general approach that the ancients might have described as an *historia*.

Political Objectives

Arguably the most significant and far-reaching of Orangeism's religio-political principles is that of conditional loyalty to the Crown, subject to the maintenance of a Protestant ascendancy. That principle was to have a profound bearing on Northern Ireland's tragedy – a place that one writer rather colourfully and not inaccurately at the time described as the 'Orange State'.[1] We shall examine the powerful influence that Orangeism, pursuant to its political objectives, has had both on our politics and on our society. Nobody could have put it higher, or more plainly, than Northern Ireland's first Prime Minister, Sir James Craig the later Lord Craigavon, when after over a decade of Orange-unionist power he famously said, 'I am an Orangeman first and a member of this parliament afterwards . . . we have a Protestant parliament and a Protestant state'. The collapse of that parliament and state in 1972, after fifty years of unbroken Orange-unionist power, was due to many things that will be examined and questioned in the course of the book. But in the end perhaps the most pertinent question is whether the collapse of exclusive Orange-unionist government was down to the unfeasibility of ascendancy politics in the context of an emergent social democratic Western world.

Thirty years on nothing more sharply indicates the changing nature of our times than Ulster Unionist leader David Trimble's stated aspiration to 'a pluralist parliament for a pluralist people'. That aspiration is obviously the antithesis of Craig's old ascendancy philosophy and also, as we shall see, of Orangeism's political doctrine from the beginning. It is therefore not surprising that this aspiration to pluralism is not currently shared by the Orange Order, even though it was supported by many individual Orangemen and by over seventy per cent of the Northern Ireland electorate in the 1998 Referendum.[2] Interesting questions arise as to why and how this change has come about, and what lies behind Orangeism's continued opposition to it. It seems evident that Orange-unionist ascendancy power, which in many respects came to an end with the demise of the old Stormont parliament in 1972, can have no place in anything approaching a pluralist polity. Orangeism therefore has to confront the reality of its greatly diminished influence, and to recognise that so long as its anti-Catholic and supremacist belief system remains unreconstructed it will virtually exclude itself from major political influence in anything remotely purporting to be a pluralist polity in a new Northern Ireland.

Religion and Culture

We shall examine Orangeism's ordinances, by which we mean its religious rules, beliefs and ritual, in order to assess the nature of what it regards as religion. Critics are sometimes sceptical when, in the context of a disputed parade, Orangemen protest that marching is an integral part of their religion. These critics might well point to the words of Jesus who gave very precise instructions to his disciples on how to behave if, on their mission walking tours, they found themselves in places where they were not welcome. His approach was the very antithesis of confrontation,[3] and certainly unlike that described by Jeremy Paxman as 'those booming, swaggering marches every 12 July'.[4] And yet, spite of all and specifically because of its religious claims, the critics might well expect Orangeism to be strong on Christian standards of citizenship, and to be at the forefront of the quest for peace, love and reconciliation in our society. We shall therefore examine its position on this matter, for whatever our view, fair enquiry demands that its religious claims be taken seriously. It may well be that Orangeism's ordinances could reasonably be regarded as a form of religion in its own right, with its own ceremonies, rituals and faith claims. However, the real question here is whether, or to what extent, Orange religion is compatible with that Christianity and Reformed faith it professes to represent.

As though acknowledging the query against its religious claims, many now speak of their Orangeism as 'Protestant culture'. Given that Protestantism is a global culture this usage seems far too broad a description to fit what Orange sub-culture really stands for in its native and narrow Northern Irish context. It is sometimes tempting to think that this use of the term could be no more than a useful bolt hole, for it is when Orangeism comes under criticism for things associated with its marching demonstrations that it seems most keen to describe itself as a culture. In quest of a better PR image, it has adopted what has been described as 'modern multi-culturalist logic' by positing equivalence between Orange marching and 'other' widely recognised cultural expressions such as the Irish language and Irish dancing. Thus in the aftermath of Drumcree 1996 and all its violent upheaval we find the Orange-unionist leader David Trimble rationalising Orange behaviour as an affirmation and demonstration of identity and culture.[5] This approach appears to argue that since Orangeism is a culture it must *ipso facto* be regarded as wholesome or benign – culture thus providing an attractive cover for its baggage of sectarian axioms, attitudes and actions that, like Pilgrim's burden, nevertheless remains strapped to its back. Afrikaner apartheid, Nazi fascism and Ku Klux Klan wasp philosophy have all in their time vainly carried the concealing concept of culture. However, the extreme nationalism and racism obviously involved in those belief systems were never regarded as morally worthy of toleration by democratic societies.

In their recent petition to the Northern Ireland Parades Commission on the Orange Order's right to march despite opposition or violence (June 2002), moral considerations such as these apparently could not prevent the Orange-unionist petitioners from citing American case law that upheld the right to public demonstrations by the Ku Klux Klan and the American Nazi Party. It seems incredible that an Order that sometimes claims to be Christian should be so interested in its own alleged rights as to be impervious to its responsibilities and to the obvious moral argument here. It is clear that this use of culture is no more than a device to conceal sectarianism. Cultural claims do not necessarily have *carte blanche* legitimacy, but should pose questions as to the essential nature of that culture, what exactly it entails, and what are its effects and consequences on society. Legal considerations and rights issues are certainly relevant here, but so too are the greater issues of peace and public order, of good citizenship, equality and moral responsibility towards our neighbour.

Marching

Marching has always been the important public manifestation of the Orange Order's politico-religious culture and ordinances. Without this ongoing activity Orangeism might hardly even exist in the public mind nowadays, but it is this that makes it most controversial – and at times also most dangerous. In the relatively small territory of Northern Ireland there are almost three thousand Orange marches every year. We therefore need to know what this marching is all about. Some critics, by recourse to two hundred years of history, regard it as an expression of a militaristic 'frontier' tradition designed to quell the enemy. Thus considered it is often seen as aggressive and triumphalist. Some Orangemen, with scant regard to political correctness, would frankly admit to that, but others deny it strenuously and speak of their Twelfth of July marching celebrations in terms of 'the largest Folk Festival in Europe'. It is therefore important that we examine the nature of Orange marching. Is it really a benign, Mardi Gras style religio-cultural celebration, or has it much more serious, even sinister connotations and motivations? These questions will involve larger political, cultural and religious issues relative to liberty, human rights, respect and toleration. We shall therefore discuss the question of the right to march through disputed territory, and whether it is reasonable to expect the Catholic-nationalist people, upon whom that marching sometimes quite deliberately impinges, to acquiesce with it in a spirit of liberal toleration.

Although the Orange Order has now lost much of its power, it has a tradition of over two hundred years behind it and a membership which until relatively recently fluctuated from *circa* 75,000 to 100,000 men. It still has to be taken seriously, for in a wider sense the Orange ethos continues to wield religio-political influence in Northern Ireland. It is heavily involved in the battle now being fought for the mind of the Ulster Unionist Party in relation to the Good Friday Agreement. It is also engaged in a struggle for the heart and soul of some of the churches in regard to questions such as sectarianism, the peace process and reconciliation, and as to what constitutes true Protestantism. Such serious issues indicate the relevance of examining Orangeism's belief system. Beliefs are always important, but particularly so in Northern Ireland. The things that motivate and sustain Orangeism, and confirm it in its attitudes and actions regardless of cost or consequence, are the things which despite its arcane secrecy can reveal what it is all about. And those beliefs constitute the standard against which it must ultimately be judged.

Section One:
Origins of Orangeism

1.

Protestant Ascendancy versus Radicalism

The circumstances surrounding the origins of a movement may tell us something of its essential nature and *raison d'être* and therefore shed light on its foundation beliefs and objectives. But in Orangeism's case those immediate circumstances would of themselves be insufficient fully to explain these things. The fact that the Orange Order emerged in 1795 in the early aftermath of a gun-battle in County Armagh between its incipient members, traditionally known as the Peep O' Day Boys, and the Catholic Defenders is telling enough, but there was much more to its origins than that. It is important to note that in Ireland the latter part of the eighteenth century was a time of prolonged and violent political activity in a situation involving acute socio-religious and economic tensions, especially in the North. As a product of that situation, Orangeism did not fall out of the sky, nor was it just the sudden outcome of a small local disturbance. We later describe the actual circumstances and events associated with the founding of the Orange Order, but first we sketch out the major contributory and background forces which had already been long at work.

When we bear in mind that the Orange Order was founded just three years before the rebellion of the United Irishmen in 1798, it will be appreciated that this occurred during one of the most turbulent and complex periods in Ireland's history. A mighty political spirit was moving on the face of the waters, and there were signs and fears that the great levelling which so recently had produced the republican revolutions in America and France might be replicated in Ireland. Long before those revolutions the Anglo-Irish Protestant ascendancy had discriminated against Catholics by means of penal laws that were much more stringent than those in Britain. But unlike the British, and for its own reasons, the ascendancy also discriminated against the Nonconformists and Dissenters. Earlier in the century Irish Catholics and Dissenters had remained largely quiescent when the Jacobites rebelled in Britain. Even now, when some Irish dissidents began to espouse radical and republican ideas, reform remained the preferred option for the majority of the Irish people.

Radical ideas spread by the Enlightenment and by the then recent foreign revolutions were naturally fuelled by the oligarchic attitude of the Anglo-Irish ascendancy. Thus an even more volatile situation ensued in 1793 when war broke out between Britain and Catholic France. It was only to be expected that a British government should regard the situation as a serious emergency. Sadly, however, it did not come naturally to an imperialist British government to acknowledge its own contribution, even if this were to some extent one of neglect, to the creation of the serious situation that for so long had been smouldering in Ireland, and which modest reform might have averted.

The United Irishmen, in the North led by radical Dissenters who were largely Presbyterian, sought to reform what the vast majority of the Irish people saw as the oppressive government of the ascendancy class that administered Ireland from Dublin Castle. That ascendancy, which was the preserve of members of the Anglo-Irish Church, included the Castle civil service, the Irish parliament and the established Church. The ascendancy was in all its parts widely regarded as corrupt, and the Church of Ireland by no means least in that respect. There were particular reasons for this, though doubtless the bribery and jobbery that characterised the Irish ascendancy were not uncommon to other ruling classes and governmental institutions of the time. But what distinguished the Protestant ascendancy in Ireland was the nature and extent of its powers and their attendant corruption, such as to epitomise Lord Acton's later and famous dictum that 'absolute power corrupts absolutely'.

This ascendancy power was under-pinned by four principles, which may be described as chance, cause, calling, and conquest. To some extent the chance to benefit from corrupt power derived from devolution and distance from the imperial parliament in Westminster. Its cause owed much to what Edmund Burke described as the 'fearful arrogance' of a garrison mentality, for the minority Anglo-Irish ruling class could feel they had greater cause than the British to be fearful of the Catholic enemy and the potential invader from France. But it was an arrogant mentality because of the vast moral difference between the two situations given that, unlike Britain, Ireland was a Catholic country, and where colonialist minority fears were expressed through vicious laws designed to keep the vast majority of the people in abject subjection. The 'Protestant nation' justified itself in these matters by its sense of providential calling – a providence that had placed the bearers of the true religion, the chosen few, in ascendancy over the native heathen. This ruling elite enjoyed the wider support of the ordinary Protestant and nominally Church of Ireland people, but even taken as a whole the extended ascendancy class represented only about one eighth of the whole population.

Finally, there was the decisive factor of conquest. The ascendancy mind considered itself to have been fully entitled and empowered by the triumphs of the Prince of Orange, who was understood to have charterised the Protestant ascendancy when in replying to the Bishop of Meath in 1690 he famously said:

> I am come hither to deliver you from the tyranny of popery and slavery, to protect the Protestant religion, and restore you in your liberties and properties; and you may depend upon it.[1]

Unfortunately, deliverance from one kind of tyranny was understood by the ascendancy to require the imposition of another, for William's 'deliverance' served to underpin the position of the small Anglo-Irish ruling minority. Its terrible concomitant was the subjugation of the vast majority of the people of Ireland by what Edmund Burke later described as 'a sort of colonial garrison to keep the natives in subjection'.[2] But although William held strong Protestant convictions, this subjugation flew in the face of his also strong natural instincts for toleration.

He had family links with Catholicism, and was not above doing political business with the Pope. Penal subjugation was therefore contrary to his best judgement, and during the early 1690s he tried to ameliorate the position of the Irish Catholics and Dissenters. However, he was soon to find his efforts so frustrated by his ascendancy followers, who were forerunners to the Orangemen of a hundred years later, that his biographer Nesca Robb could write:

> It was small wonder that William began to give up hope of the crazy island and to push its tiresome affairs ... into the background.[3]

That craziness was the product of those who wielded power – the Protestant ascendancy. In Ireland's dream of a glorious summer of liberty King William was as a lone swallow. The benefits of the Williamite new beginning, with its great principle of civil and religious liberty, would soon be seen to be of exclusive application to an elite class, for Protestant ascendancy and Protestant liberty were understood to necessitate the keeping of Papists and Dissenters in their places. The main objective and interest of the small ascendancy class was essentially the protection of its own liberties and property. This it ensured by further restricting the rights and liberties of the large majority of the Irish people, both Catholic and Dissenter, by a raft of draconian penal laws enacted during the period from 1695 to the 1720s.

Catholics suffered by far the most under these laws. They were forbidden to carry weapons (a normal citizen right), or to own a horse worth more than five pounds. Education was forbidden unless in a Protestant school. Bishops, monks, nuns and friars were banished and Catholic religious assemblies banned. Catholics could neither inherit nor purchase property, nor could they lease land for longer than 31 years. They also were forbidden entry to the professions or to apprenticeships, and could neither vote nor be elected to parliament. Thus for generations before the days of the United Irishmen the ascendancy had the legal power to rule with a rod of iron, even though it mercifully did not always apply the penal laws to their fullest extent.

There was no need to do so, for what Edmund Burke described as the 'vicious perfection'[4] of the penal system was more than enough to ensure that the Catholics, who only with exaggeration could have been described as third class citizens, were as non-citizens and aliens in their own land. Thus to all intents and purposes the Protestant ascendancy, despite its defining principle of civil and religious liberty, had succeeded in ensuring that the Irish Catholics and Dissenters had no such liberties and no legal status within 'the Irish nation'. These penal policies vied with the worst kind of colonialism and created a situation that was a far cry from the days before 1641 when Catholics owned 60 per cent of the land of Ireland, whereas under the ascendancy's penal laws of the early eighteenth century Catholic ownership had declined to just 5 per cent.

Dissenters such as Presbyterians and Quakers were also penalised, although not to the same degree of severity. Certainly they were treated as second class citizens, were prohibited from taking university degrees in Ireland, and their ordained ministers from officiating at marriages, burial services and the Lord's Supper. In quest of either liberty or opportunity, or both, thousands of Irish Presbyterians had by the 1750s immigrated to America, where they made an indelible mark and established their own religious and political principles. The American census of 1790 showed 44,000 persons of Irish birth, many of them frontiersmen and most of whom were from Ulster. In regard to religion, it was a very early Ulster émigré, Francis Mackemie, who founded the first American presbytery and became known as the father of American Presbyterianism. These people were therefore strongly Protestant and there is evidence that some of them continued to regard King William as a folk hero – probably because of his associations with 'liberty', despite what happened in Ireland after him and which was often done in his name. Politically they were ruggedly independent and naturally given to democratic and republican ideas, which were often sympathetically received when communicated back to their kith and kin in the North of Ireland. In fact, eight men of 'Scotch-Irish' descent were later to be signatories to the American Declaration of Independence, and over the years no less than twelve Scotch-Irishmen would become President of the United States.

One effect of the penal laws was that young Irish Presbyterians in quest of higher education had to go to the Scottish universities. Here they came under the influence of the radical political philosophy of the European Enlightenment as taught there by brilliant academics like David Hume and Francis Hutcheson. The latter was a Presbyterian Ulsterman and a son of the manse, but he was now professor of moral philosophy in Glasgow University. Hutcheson's ideas influenced men who were to become much more famous than he – men like Jeremy Bentham and Adam Smith, the former borrowing and developing Hutcheson's notable axiom of 'the greatest good for the greatest number'. The republican-minded Hutcheson believed strongly that governments should be accountable to the people they governed. He carried this heady doctrine even further by asserting that if the rights of the people were spurned by those in authority then the people could with justification take action to defend themselves against that abuse of power.[5] In the then prevailing political climate in Ireland these Enlightenment ideas could readily provide a credo for a democratic and even militant republicanism. And they did.

Some of these Ulster Presbyterian graduates, among whom was the young medical doctor William Drennan, subsequently brought this radical republican politics back home to Ireland. Drennan would quickly become a leading light within the new Society of United Irishmen in Belfast, whose founding committee was entirely Presbyterian. This committee soon associated with Wolfe Tone, who was later to be regarded as the prophet of Irish republicanism. On the proposal of Drennan the new 'brotherhood' agreed to adapt a ritualistic Masonic model for the purposes of identification, association and secrecy. This involved more than mere adaptation. Freemasonry, which had now developed an affinity with both the United Irishmen and a military movement known as the Volunteers, was not unsympathetic to the non-sectarian political radicalism that was popular at the time. Masonic Lodges were therefore a useful meeting ground, perhaps the only one then available for fellowship between Protestant,

Catholic and Dissenter. But as we shall see later, other very different political groups and secret societies that did not enjoy similar Masonic sympathy would also adapt certain aspects of Masonic rites and ritual for their own recognition and organisational purposes.

The Volunteer Movement, which initially was led by public-spirited Protestants from the middle and upper classes who tended to support the ruling ascendancy, was founded in 1778 for civil defence against the threat of a French invasion. But the Volunteers were, or would become a *mixtum gatherum* with mixed motives. Some of them just enjoyed the showy aspect of military uniforms and armed parading. Many held to Williamite political ideas, although as already touched upon these could mean different things to different people. Some of liberal disposition might rejoice in William's 1688 policy of liberty and toleration, while others of conservative persuasion could glory in the victory of 1690 and the putting down of popery and the papists. But now in the wake of the French Revolution many Volunteers were beginning to adopt radical and egalitarian ideas such as Catholic emancipation. By the early 1790s some Volunteer Corps had even developed links with the United Irishmen, a number of whose most prominent leaders were now enlisted in the ranks, and these Corps had become so radical as to admit Catholics. There was often a strong correlation between the diverse Volunteer views and the prevailing politico-tribal balance in any given geographical area, especially in Ulster, a subject we shall return to later.

Whilst the Volunteer Movement of the early 1790s could not be regarded as thoroughly republican, substantial sections of it were now moving in that direction. The republican mind could readily idealise the Volunteers as the good citizen militia that might oppose arbitrary government and ensure that private and sectarian interests were subordinated to 'civic virtue'. Such virtue was understood as seeking the general good of all citizens, as opposed to the prevailing political self-interest and corruption that characterised governments at large and the Irish ascendancy in particular. These powerful ideas rang true to many minds in the prevailing political circumstances of that time. Indeed, enough Volunteers had become sufficiently radicalised for the ascendancy now to regard them as a serious threat. Thus when war with France broke out in 1793 the government stepped in and disbanded the entire Volunteer Movement, declaring it 'unlawful'. This action would have important implications for the United Irishmen and for the incipient Orange Order, as will be shown in a subsequent chapter.

2.

Peep O' Day Boys and Defenders

In Ireland the late eighteenth century was a time of political radicalism and of strong pressure for change. The draconian penal laws were gradually being ameliorated, albeit for reasons of expediency and despite the reluctance of the Protestant ascendancy oligarchs. But the philosophy of religio-political ascendancy, then as now, always inheres a zero-sum approach to politics. And so it was hardly surprising that the relaxations in the Penal laws, some of which will be described below, should create a violent reaction among mid-Ulster Protestant elements who believed that any improvement in the position of Catholics, however small, had to be at the expense of Protestants. As a result, some of these formed themselves into a militant anti-Catholic banditti that, because of the nature and strategy of its activities, became known as the Peep O' Day Boys. These provided an early example of the Protestant rioter's tactic of deliberately breaking the law in order to compel the authorities to act consistently and 'even-handedly', and thus enforce the law against Catholics, who to all intents and purposes were legally at a much greater disadvantage. The Catholics in turn established a counter organisation called the Defenders, a development that was to have far-reaching consequences in Ulster.

The background to this is interesting. Violence was of such common occurrence as to be almost endemic in eighteenth century Ireland. Faction fighting at fairs between rival gangs armed with sticks was a regular country sport, and determining the strongest fighting gang in the locality provided much interest as well as social prestige for the victors. Originally these gangs, or 'fleets' as they were called by allusion to the great contemporary naval battles that had caught the public imagination, were religiously mixed. However, because of the religio-political and socio-economic factors then at work in that part of Ulster, faction fighting had by 1785 taken on a fiercely sectarian character. It all began trivially enough when two leading County Armagh gangs, the Nappagh Fleet and the Hamilton's Bawn Fleet, hitherto religiously mixed, decided to realign themselves in the aftermath of a fist-fight between two Protestants. The 'second' to one of the protagonists happened to be a Catholic who allegedly had interfered in the fight to provide his man with an unfair advantage. This gave rise to rival sectarian feelings, in consequence of which opposing groups of Protestant Peep O' Day Boys and Catholic Defenders came into being.[1] The Defenders would later, under instruction from the United Irishmen, struggle to quell their sectarianism, though often unsuccessfully. But the Peep O' Day Boys, whose objectives were inherently and expressly sectarian, would have no such qualms. They believed that it was the papists who constituted the real and ever present threat to their welfare and that of the entire country. In fact, they believed that by carrying a sectarian fight to the enemy they would compel the authorities to get off the fence and enforce the law – especially the residual penal laws against Catholics, and particularly those laws pertaining to the holding of arms, forbidden in their case.

These tactics led to further sectarian activity, and country stick fighting soon developed into more dangerous practices. This was more than a simple escalation in tit-for-tat violence. The right to bear arms, which at that time was regarded as an important badge of citizen-right, and therefore exclusively a Protestant one, was something to which Catholics, desirous of emancipation and certainly of their own defence, now increasingly aspired. William Drennan believed that these local disturbances were motivated by 'an instinctive desire for arms',[2] the corollary so far as the Peep O' Day Boys were concerned being to keep the arms out of Catholic hands. Indeed, the quest for arms had become a new cause, and an additional source of violence, as the homes of 'the other sort' were nocturnally raided for the purpose of seizing guns and ammunition. This would lead to further violence, for the acquiring of guns was more than a token or rights issue, but became the means to much more serious ends.

Arising from the reforms of the 1780's mentioned earlier, Catholics were now permitted to compete on an equal basis with Protestants in the buying and leasing of land. This easement in the Penal Laws was tactically designed by the government to dampen down incipient revolutionary tendencies, and to encourage the then necessary recruitment to the British army. In the context of reform, military considerations were always very important, but it would take another forty years before a British government would introduce Catholic Emancipation. When finally this was achieved, it was significantly at the hand of Wellington the Anglo-Irish soldier-statesman who had defeated the European Catholic threat at Waterloo and who, more than most, knew the value of Irish and Highlander Catholic soldiery. As ever, the British and the Irish ascendancy were nothing if not expedient. However, now encouraged by reform, many Catholics began to migrate northwards into mid-Armagh in search of land, but the effect of this, as of all such reforms ever since, was the creation of a sectarian backlash. Since the Plantation of Ulster, land had always been a contentious issue, and the Armagh Protestants regarded this re-entry of the 'encroacher' Catholics into the land market as a dangerous and unwelcome intrusion. Although the land in question was not fertile, it was well enough suited to the important cottage linen industry in what had become known as the 'linen triangle' that lay just to the south of Lough Neagh.

Many of the younger members of the Protestant farmer-weaver community were prominent among the Peep O' Day Boys, one of whom complained that 'some of us refusing to pay the extravagant rent demanded by our landlords have been turned out, and our lands given to papists, who will pay any rent'.[3] Competition among land-hungry factions therefore provoked strong sectarian rivalry, which was always even more likely in a locality of high and mixed population such as County Armagh, for its size then the most populous county in all of Ireland. At that particular time these problems were greatly exacerbated by the world recession in the linen trade caused by the collapse of the American market in the aftermath of the recent American War of Independence. Thus in mid-Ulster the discontent surrounding the land issue, the economic recession and the endemic sectarianism all imploded together in bitter sporadic violence in which rival heads and linen looms were regularly broken, and homes sometimes wrecked or burned.

This was therefore a time of rising expectations, of growing political awareness throughout Ireland, not least in the North, and yet it was also a time of disaffection, reaction and counteraction. In such a situation Dublin Castle was subjected to increasing political scrutiny and criticism. This was notably led by the philosopher-statesman Edmund Burke, who flayed the ascendancy mercilessly as the very epitome of oppression and corruption. By the 1790s, the United Irishmen had become strong in Presbyterian Belfast, Antrim and Down, and were beginning to constitute a threat to the Protestant ascendancy government. A coalition of radicals and revolutionaries, they were inspired by the American and French Revolutions and by the republican ideal that aspired to the unity of Catholic, Protestant and Dissenter in a reformed polity for Ireland. Should reform fail, they would look to revolution and separation, albeit with reluctance, as the only means left to them of achieving their goal of liberty, equality and fraternity. The United Irish coalition included the Catholic Defenders who, because of the religio-political nature of the ancient conflict with their oligarchic Protestant rulers and their ongoing fracas with the Peep O' Day Boys, naturally tended to see the struggle in straightforward sectarian terms. It was a very difficult business for the United Irishmen to control.

Despite the British government's foreign difficulties and the dangers of the war with France, many like Edmund Burke felt that these things could not excuse what was being allowed to happen in Ireland under the stewardship of the minority Protestant ascendancy. The Irish situation was certainly complex and confused, but when the United Irishmen offered an inclusive and non-sectarian solution to the problem the ascendancy chose instead to sponsor an exclusive and sectarian one – a policy that historian Kevin Whelan poignantly describes as 'a deliberate effort to create disunited Irishmen'.[4] We shall see the significance of this as the story of Orangeism unfolds in later chapters. Instead of addressing the issues Dublin Castle, after some agonising, chose to exploit the conflict first by encouraging sectarianism and then by tapping into it in taking those measures it considered necessary for the defence of the ascendancy's oligarchic privilege. And because of the world events already referred to, those measures could be presented as essential to the defence of the state itself, measures that included censorship, the repression of the United Irishmen, and the initial encouragement followed indeed by the management of the fledgling Orange Order. In what follows it will be shown how that Order would in one massive paradox provide the ascendancy with a magistracy, a legally armed but partisan yeomanry and even, if circumstances so conspired, a terrorist organisation.

It was a great irony that these things were taking place at the time when the radical and non-sectarian ideals of the United Irishmen were at their zenith. The irony is explained by the fact that then as now radicalism evokes reaction, even as the quest for unity always provokes sectarianism. It is significant, however, that the forces of reaction and sectarianism were more in evidence in some parts of Ulster than in others. A.T.Q. Stewart suggests that this was often due to local factors and depended upon the demographic balance of population between Protestant and Catholic in the local area.[5] Where the Presbyterians were comfortably in the majority they could adopt liberal attitudes toward their Catholic neighbours; but where the demographics were approaching balance the now upwardly mobile Catholics were perceived as a threat. Given the situation as described, this explains in part why religiously mixed County Armagh together with adjacent areas of Tyrone became the cockpit of sectarian strife between the Protestant Peep O' Day Boys and the Catholic Defenders. After more than two hundred years this part of Ulster, which encompasses the Orange marching flash-point of Drumcree near Portadown, is still such a cockpit.

Following the demographic argument, it may be significant that this area fell within the escheated counties of the Ulster Plantation.[6] Although it had a substantial and, as we have seen, a growing Catholic population, it had been heavily 'planted' by English Protestant settlers of particularly tough colonial attitude. These tenacious planter people identified at least nominally with the established and 'Anglican' ascendancy Church of Ireland and remained strongly imbued with loyal and British imperialist views. On the other hand, the dissenting settlers of Antrim and Down, which had relatively low Catholic populations, were predominantly of Scottish Presbyterian origin and were of a rather different religious and political disposition. Broadly speaking, therefore, this distribution of Catholic, Protestant and Dissenter populations was to express itself in the differing political attitudes and responses that prevailed locally. And so mid-Ulster would become the cradle of Orangeism, and east-Ulster that of the United Irishmen.

3.

James Wilson and the Orange Tradition

There were some important exceptions to the broad-brush religio-demographic analysis of the previous chapter. For example, some Presbyterians in mid-Armagh and the adjacent areas of Tyrone, whilst not overly sympathetic to their Anglo-Irish ascendancy landlords, were most decidedly not well disposed to the increasingly assertive Catholics who had recently moved into the area. These Presbyterians were of a politically less liberal and radical disposition than their brethren in Belfast, Antrim and Down where the Catholics were in a weak minority position and therefore not perceived as a serious threat.

After the standing-down of the Volunteers, and as the situation in mid-Ulster polarised, people became more territorially aware. Vigilante groups were set up to defend local areas, but then as now vigilanteism slipped all too easily into paramilitarism, based on the adage that the best form of defence is attack. This gave rise to increasing engagements between rival sectarian gangs of Protestant Peep O' Day Boys and Catholic Defenders. Early in 1793 James Wilson, a Presbyterian farmer and noted Freemason from the Dyan in County Tyrone, emerged as a leading local Protestant activist when he established an Orange club 'to maintain the Royal Order of His Majesty George III in person, Crown and dignity against all enemies and oppressions whatsoever'.[1] Wilson was a big, ruddy and full-bearded man of strong personality and conviction, who was intensely proud of the fact that his ancestors had fought for the Protestant cause at Derry and with King William at the Boyne. His leadership potential was enhanced by the fact that he was a dashing horseman, which was of considerable organisational and communications advantage to a man of his ilk in the rural Ireland of that time. Indeed, the Irish poet Dominic Behan once facetiously but graphically defined ascendancy as 'a Protestant on a horse'.

On 24th June 1794, the Defenders perpetrated a drunken outrage against Protestant homes in the village of Benburb after attending the funeral of one of their supporters. James Wilson, whose Masonic lodge happened to be meeting in the village at that very time, swiftly retaliated by organising an action group that soon ejected the intruders. Immediately afterwards he tried unsuccessfully to persuade his local Masonic lodge to establish properly organised defence arrangements for future protection against the Catholic Defenders. However, as Freemasonry was neither religiously exclusive nor party political, it was ideologically quite unsuited to the task that the staunchly Protestant Wilson had in mind for it. So when the Masons rejected his idea he angrily mounted his horse, vowing to 'light a star in the Dyan which would eclipse them forever'. Soon afterwards, he founded his alternative defence organisation, a local association called the 'Orange Boys', membership of which included Peep O' Day Boys from the Blackwater Valley and involved oath-taking, initiation rites, secret signs and rituals which Wilson adapted from his Freemasonry and other sources. Many of these rites still exist within Orangeism today, as we shall see later.

The idea of Orangeism has what might be described as a pre-history in that it belonged to the long-standing ascendancy tradition in Ireland, which believed it owed everything to William of Orange. That Protestant ascendancy tradition commemorated the religio-political victories of King William III by various means. There was the large equestrian statue in College Green of William the conquering hero, which in 1701 the City of Dublin unveiled on 1st July (now the Twelfth). There were also the great tapestries that were hung in 1733 in the nearby Parliament House, one of which depicts the triumphant William crossing the Boyne. In fact, long before the founding of the Orange Order, William's birthday on 4th November was a state occasion in Ireland, which involved large ceremonial parades to the King's decorated statue, and all celebrated in great style by the administration at Dublin Castle. Throughout Ireland some local commemorations were held on 1st July each year, when Protestants wearing cockades, ribbons and floral emblems such as orange lilies or sweet william marched in military style to bands and drumming parties in noisy celebrations, which occasionally included the firing of shots into the air.

This kind of thing began early in the eighteenth century after the Williamite Wars, when groups of ex-service officers formed themselves into secret Boyne societies and ascendancy-supporting clubs. An early Apprentice Boys of Derry club was formed to commemorate the raising of the siege. In the city of Dublin the Aldermen of Skinner's Alley was another such Williamite club. Protestant victories were celebrated annually in the sham fight at Bandon in County Cork, a triumphalist folk tradition that continues to this day in the annual Orange Festival at Scarva in County Down. Thus an early Orange folk culture was expressed through a variety of Protestant ascendancy organisations, some of which had traditional connections with Williamite militarism and with military-style marching – all long before the founding of the Orange Order. Variously calling themselves 'Orange', 'Orange & Blew', or 'Boyne Men', many of these clubs plagiarised their formal structures and rites from Freemasonry, as was not uncommon at the time. Like their political leaders, they regularly celebrated their own versions of William's 'Glorious Revolution', but the activities of the Orange clubs were more than merely commemorative. They in fact made a very substantial contribution to what has been described as the 'Protestant defence tradition'. Over the years this military tradition would be variously expressed through the local Militia after 1715, the Volunteers after 1778, and the Yeomanry after 1796. However, the most enduring and most significant contribution to that defence tradition would undoubtedly be made by the 'army with banners' – the Orange Order after 1795.

Orange tradition has gradually elevated King William III into something of a cult figure. In stark contrast to W.E. Gladstone's popular acclaim as 'the people's

William', the Prince of Orange would privately be claimed by the Orangemen as 'our William' long after his death. Thus in that partisan sense his memory has been taken over and venerated by the Orange Order with a view to serving its own narrow and sectarian interests. But although William of Orange was a committed Calvinist, he was in many respects an inappropriate icon for the Orange Order. He was certainly not an anti-Catholic religious bigot. Attention has been drawn to his relative toleration, and to his natural antipathy towards the Protestant ascendancy's already overt extremism in Ireland, an attitude that owed much to his European republican background. Indeed, by the subsequent standards of Orangeism he was not even a fully-fledged royalist, for prior to ascending the British throne he was not a hereditary 'prince of the royal blood'. The Prince of Orange was a republican stadholder (a kind of political lord lieutenant) to the Dutch Republics, and his claim to the British Crown – in a sense a rather tenuous one – was primarily through the female line. William's mother was the daughter of Charles I whom the Cromwellians had beheaded, and his wife the daughter of Catholic James II whom he would fight with the full blessing of the Pope at the Battle of the Boyne. However, these and other important matters that could be pertinent to the question of William's suitability as an Orange icon are in another sense irrelevant, for cult figures are largely of cult invention, selected elements being moulded in the cult's own image, with all contrary factors conveniently screened out. Be that as it may, it is doubtful if anyone of William's religiously mixed maternal and matrimonial connections, to say nothing of his naturally wise toleration, could nowadays be admitted into membership of a Loyal Orange Lodge of Ulster. Indeed, the seventeenth century liberalism of the Prince of Orange was decidedly of a more advanced order than that of many twenty-first century Ulster Orangemen.

It has been shown that Orangeism has a pre-history in the long-standing Williamite tradition going back to the Boyne – a Protestant cult involving social and drinking clubs, with associated militarism, colours, marching, symbols, rituals and commemorative ideas that were developed for the cohesion and protection of the minority Protestant ascendancy. All this eventually provided a ready model for James Wilson's Orange Boys. But equally there is no doubt that the events Wilson inspired in County Tyrone in the early 1790s proved to be a significant new beginning for the cult of William. His new brand of militant, organised Orangeism would be the forerunner of the Order he helped to establish in 1795, as we shall now see. Indeed, it is interesting to note that Wilson's Orange Boys were marching in the Drumcree area of Portadown in the months before the Orange Order was formally established. However, despite Orangeism's pre-history, it is equally significant that what are now universally recognised as the Twelfth of July Orange demonstrations – the massively and formally organised marching celebrations of the Battle of the Boyne – did not take place until nearly a century after William's death. As such, the Twelfth as we now know it has been something of an afterthought, a belated invention and political appropriation to meet the particular needs of the Protestant ascendancy in the situation that developed in the late eighteenth century.

Having struck the spark, if not exactly lighting a star, the hustling Wilson's men joined forces with other Peep O' Day Boys during the summer of 1795 and engaged in several skirmishes with the Defenders. Some of these fights took place near the Diamond, a clachan of farmer-weavers' houses close by Loughgall. Here Dan Winter, who was a hearty Protestant of Quaker stock, a Freemason and a noted cock-fighter, was well known as the local spirit grocer and innkeeper. Religiously speaking, the redoubtable Winter had obviously lapsed fairly dramatically, but he was intensely proud of his nickname 'Orange Dan' and was related to James Wilson. By the early 1790s he had become the ringleader of the local Peep O' Day Boys, some of whom met from time to time with Wilson and the Orange Boys in Winter's pub, the signboard of which depicted King William crossing the Boyne. At one stage a local magistrate Richard Abbot had reason to advise that Winter's liquor licence be revoked, but it is hardly surprising that Winter seems to have had sufficient leverage with men of influence to find means of preventing this. It is clear that Orange Dan's inn-house was attracting considerable notoriety, and had become a special target for the Defenders. The adjacent Diamond Hill and nearby crossroads were now of strategic interest and the scene of recurring sectarian skirmishing.

The authorities were far from even-handed in their approach to these affrays. On one occasion two Protestant magistrates arrived on horseback accompanied by a platoon of militia, and each arrested a rival group. One of the magistrates, on learning that his prisoners were Protestants, promptly released them; but the other consigned his Catholic prisoners to Armagh jail. It was precisely that kind of partiality and inequity which lay at the root of the problem and, as subsequent events would show, the Protestant magistracy was to play a leading part in perpetuating this. The unrest smouldered on and serious trouble flared in September, when both factions were suddenly reinforced by new insurgents. After days of disturbance and sporadic shooting in the general area of the Diamond, truce negotiations took place on 18th September between Protestant magistrates and Catholic priests. During these talks the magistrates, who earlier themselves may have participated in the stand-off, stated that whereas the Protestants had the right to bear arms the Catholics had not. This angered the Defenders, but a truce was eventually agreed and the combatants gradually withdrew from the immediate battle zone. It was to be an uneasy and short-lived peace.

4.

The Diamond and its Aftermath

During the two days of cease-fire created by the truce of 18th September, fresh groups of Defenders arrived and took up position on nearby high ground. Seeking action and considering themselves not bound by the earlier truce, they proceeded sporadically to fire down upon the Protestant houses. But the truce eventually took effect, producing an uneasy peace that lasted until the early hours of 21st September. Suddenly Dan Winter's inn was attacked. The besieged Winter and his sons held off their attackers for a time, but had to flee for their lives when the inn's thatch was fired. The inn was soon invaded, looted and burned, but in the ensuing confusion the fleeing Winter and sons managed to link up with Wilson's men, who were now quietly entrenched in military fashion on top of the hill that lay just behind the burning inn. As James Wilson had shrewdly anticipated, the emboldened and high-spirited Defenders eventually came looking for Dan Winter, at which point the Orange and Peep O' Day Boys, waiting for the critical moment, drew them into an ambush. The Orange historian Rev. John Brown tells us that some of the Protestants who had been in the Volunteers then 'stepped out, dressed their line according to the drill-book, and fired a destructive volley from their commanding position and from close at hand directly into the mob of Defenders. This won the battle'.[1] The battle, which lasted for only fifteen minutes, was a total rout and it was later discovered that more than forty Defenders had been killed.

John Brown's terminology and description here is not untypical of the Orange historians who usually endeavour to depict Protestant activity, even when involving banditti elements, as legal, disciplined and defensive in contrast to that of the illegal and rebellious Catholic 'mob'. Ruth Dudley Edwards, in similar vein, goes even further in rejecting the traditional belief that it was the Peep O' Day Boys who founded the Orange Order after their victory at the Battle of the Diamond.[2] She chides historian Jonathan Bardon for reiterating the point, and asserts that it 'does not bear scrutiny', claiming that new research shows the main founders to have been Volunteers. However, as we have just seen, there is nothing new in this idea, for John Brown and others have alluded to the presence of 'some' Volunteers at the Diamond. It is of course natural that apologists should do their best to gloss over the tarnished image of the Orange Order's reputed Peep O' Day Boy origins, although it has to be said that these efforts have failed by and large to convince even the Orange historians.

Traditional beliefs obviously have stood the test of time, usually for good reason, and there is strong evidence to support the traditional view followed by Bardon and others that the Peep O' Day Boys were prominent among the early foundation members of the Orange Order. Prior to the Order's founding there were several similarly militant Protestant groups, some of which had broadly common interests and some of which were disparate and loosely organised. It is therefore likely that most of these groups if not all of them contributed to the early membership of the rapidly growing Orange Order, so it is probably unwise to draw sharp distinctions or make specific or dogmatic assertions in regard to its original composition. Nevertheless, by common consent James Wilson's original organisation of Orange Boys drew many of its members from the Peep O' Day Boys, among whom Dan Winter, his relative and fellow-founder of the Orange Order, was perhaps the most notable ringleader.

The Orange Boys and Peep O' Day Boys had overlapping membership and, as some Orange historians have recently acknowledged, 'their main purpose was similar and in the eyes of the public, the authorities and gentry they were grouped together.'[3] That perception is supported by the fact that both groups were working together in common cause, by dint of their cross-memberships, and under the leadership of the close acquaintances Wilson and Winter. There is therefore no reason at all to doubt that the Peep O' Day Boys were prominent among those who formed the nucleus of the original Orange Order. Dudley Edwards eventually does admit their involvement, albeit only in a footnote where in effect she argues against herself when she states, 'It flies in the face of common sense to believe that there was no cross-over in membership'.[4] And yet even this admission is unsatisfactory, for in acknowledging the 'cross-over' that perforce involves the Peep O' Day Boys she undermines and qualifies her strong assertion that it was the Volunteers and not the Peep O' Day Boys who were really the main founders of the Orange Order.

As was shown in an earlier chapter, the Volunteers were founded in 1778 for national defence against the threat of a French invasion. They were both Protestant and Masonic, and although politically mixed, substantial numbers of them were gradually becoming politically independent of the ascendancy government. Despite their origins, many sectors of the Volunteer Movement had begun to adopt democratic ideas, and during the 1780s enjoyed the support of Catholics, many of whom were Freemasons who had found the Masonic lodges conducive to social intercourse with Protestants; probably there were precious few other such venues available to them. The democratically minded Volunteers now campaigned enthusiastically for free trade and also for the parliamentary reform that produced Grattan's Irish Parliament. This kind of politics led to the growth of even more radical ideas, which gave rise to much mutual admiration and cross-fertilisation between the Volunteer Movement and the republican United Irishmen, whose leaders Drennan, McTier and Neilson were members. Even their most famous leader Theobald Wolfe Tone would become an honorary member of the Belfast Volunteers in 1791, while another leading United Irishman, the Presbyterian Jemmy Hope, would later proudly acknowledge that his 'connection with politics began in the ranks of the Volunteers'.[5] Some Volunteer companies were therefore now quite open in their support for the United Irishmen, and although the broader Volunteer Movement stopped short of adopting an all-out republican agenda, Volunteer radicalism was much on the increase. On the eve of war between Britain and France things had reached the point where the Volunteer Movement was advocating civil rights for Catholics, many of whom they now began to admit into their (armed) ranks.[6]

On a broad brush approach all these elements together provide a description of the Volunteers of the 1790s as increasingly liberal, non-sectarian, reformist and radical, with some of their leaders and corps even tending towards the revolutionary. It is a therefore a picture that is the very antithesis of the Orangeism which the Volunteers are alleged to have founded in 1795. And yet, for all that, it is only right to acknowledge that the Volunteers were to an extent still something of that *mixtum gatherum* referred to earlier. The description of Volunteer radicalism is therefore a generalised one and not entirely the full picture, for not all Volunteers were involved in that radical or republican trend. Not for the first time it has to be pointed out that in parts of mid-Ulster things were different. Here there were some Volunteer contingents that continued to refuse membership to Catholics and from time to time marched the Armagh county highways to the 'Protestant Boys' and other sectarian tunes. Indeed, with some deference to the Dudley Edwards argument, it is acknowledged that there were Armagh Volunteer contingents that included local Peep O' Day Boys who, according to the historian David Miller, had joined the Volunteers for the express purpose of obtaining new arms.[7] Membership of the Armagh Volunteers therefore did not preclude the possibility, and perhaps even the probability, of those Volunteers also being Peep O' Day Boys. And so it follows that the argument about the status of the founding fathers of the Orange Order involves the principle of synthesis rather than the defensive antithesis that Dudley Edwards seeks to draw. In this regard it would be pertinent to observe that it hardly dignified the Armagh Volunteers to be so out of step with the non-sectarian radicalism of their Movement at large that some of them should be doubling-up as prowling Peep O' Day Boys. Such a *cv* would hardly enhance the Volunteer status of the people concerned, nor would it dignify those alleged to have been the 'Volunteer' foundation members of Orange Order, even if that were the end of the story.

But the matter cannot rest there. The simple fact is that the founders of the Orange Order could not have been Volunteers, nor even renegade Volunteers, because the Volunteer Movement had been disbanded by the ascendancy government in 1792, more than three years prior to the founding of the Order. There were no Volunteers in 1795. The government had disbanded them, not because they were Orangemen in the making, but for precisely the opposite reason – the Volunteer Movement at large was regarded as a threat to the ascendancy and therefore to national security. Because of its radicalism and its associations with the United Irishmen, it was now perceived as representing the very antithesis of sectarian Orange-style ascendancy-supporting loyalism. And so it had to go. We shall see later how the ascendancy would soon take up the new Orange Order for explicitly sectarian and paramilitary purposes – and for the suppression of that very radicalism for which the Volunteer Movement had broadly speaking taken its stand.

Just after the Battle of the Diamond in September 1795, the victorious leaders, who included James Wilson, James Sloan, Thomas Sinclair, Dan Winter and an important politico-military figure from Dublin, Captain John Giffard – all of them Freemasons – held a meeting at which it was decided to form a properly regulated paramilitary defence organisation. Giffard, who was a Captain in the Dublin militia, had a strong reputation in that city as an ultra-Protestant zealot vehemently opposed to the United Irishmen. He was also a government agent, probably on a special reconnaissance mission to the troubled Armagh area at that time. This could indicate that special politico-military activity was afoot, and suggests that some pro-active and defence-minded people in Dublin Castle were beginning to think like James Wilson. It will be recalled that Wilson had long recognised the need for an armed organisation of local loyalists, with secret Masonic-style methods of recognition and assembling, the prototype of which he had already established and in place within his own organisation, the Orange Boys of the Dyan in County Tyrone.

It is quite clear from all this that the Orange founding fathers – a collection of vigilantes, cock-fighters, publicans and Protestant militants, all of whom were Freemasons – had absolutely no notion of creating any kind of Christian or para-church organisation. The new Orange Society was to be an organised, oath-bound and armed band, bonded by a neo-Freemasonry, and initially comprising local militants such as the Orange and Peep O' Day Boys and other gangs of fighting men like the Bleary Boys, of which there were many throughout the countryside. It was to be a society for defence. In an early version of its Rules, the Orange Order pledged to defend King George III and his successors 'so long as he or they support the Protestant ascendancy, the constitution and laws of these kingdoms'. This rule reiterated the substantive first and most important of the four 'General Principles' of Orangeism that James Sloan announced in 1797.[8] Yet the Rev. Dr. M.W. Dewar, an Orange Grand Chaplain, has recently written that 'Protestant ascendancy' has been misunderstood to mean dominance over Roman Catholics whereas it was just the name of the Anglo-Irish ruling class. This is quite disingenuous, rather like arguing that the 'Western democracies' is a name for a bloc of countries, and bears no reference or relevance to the principle of democracy. The term was not just a mere title or technicality, but was an eponymous description of the inherent nature of that ruling class in Ireland. It was so described because it was constitutionally 'in the ascendant' with attitudes and policies to match, and also because its whole *raison d'être* was to maintain its dominance in Ireland, not just over Roman Catholics but over Dissenters and Nonconformists as well.

The new Orange Society was established with its headquarters in James Sloan's Inn in Loughgall, where a Masonic-style initiating ritual known as the 'Orange degree' was administered, in which oaths were sworn, and secrets and recognition signs promulgated. Captain John Giffard assisted the leaders in this work, but the initial degree arrangements were soon felt to be inadequate. And so later the following year Wilson, Winter and Sloan were invited into a Masonic room in Portadown, where they received the expert assistance of a certain John Templeton, who was both a Mason and an Orangeman, in devising a new progressive degree called the 'Orange Marksman'. About a year later a third and more advanced degree was similarly devised, probably by the same people and in the same Masonic room, which became known as the 'Purple Marksman' degree. So the Order now had three degrees – the original initiatory Orange degree, the progressive Orange Marksman degree, and the advanced Purple Marksman degree, this structure coinciding with the Masonic model's three primary degrees. In the course of time, because of the association of these degrees with the founding fathers, they became fondly known as the 'Diamond system', so called after the

Battle of the Diamond. Likewise, because of its origins and associations, the Diamond System has always been perceived as closely linked with Freemasonry. In referring to the Masonic room where the second and probably third degrees were devised, the Orange historian Colonel Wallace observed entirely uncritically that 'the influence of the place and its associations can be discerned in the results'.[9]

The gentry and clergy soon began to join the new Order in numbers and quickly assumed positions of leadership. In fact, when the new leaders began to make themselves felt the founding fathers Wilson, Winter and Sloan suddenly, in the words of the Orange historian John Brown, 'retired from notice'. A ruling Grand Lodge of Ireland with headquarters in Dublin was established early in 1798, and one of its first actions was controversially to abolish and replace the 'Diamond' degree system. In addition to the original three degrees a general proliferation of homespun degrees were also being 'worked' within the Orange Lodges on a *laissez faire* basis at that time. There was therefore a perceived need for regulation and control. But there were more important reasons for this. The original Diamond System bore such a close resemblance to Masonic ritualism that it was now regarded as neo-Masonic and objectionable to incoming Churchmen. Also, due to the political situation, the Protestant ascendancy government was now taking steps to discourage any semblance of Freemasonry, because of the Masonic Order's associations with the former Volunteers and the United Irishmen. Abolition was therefore not only because of the need for internal discipline and control, but also for reasons of religious orthodoxy and for important politico-security considerations.

Some time later the original Diamond degree system was revived, albeit unofficially and surreptitiously, in circumstances of extended controversy. Indeed, the old system still survives to this day in a modified form within the ritualistic Royal Arch-Purple Order which, though in one sense separate, yet remains powerfully linked to the Orange Order, as we shall see later. The even more ritualistic Black Order has also adapted some of those early and outlawed degrees, which have been incorporated into the highly elaborate degree system of the Royal Black Preceptory – also an independent body though in a direct and meaningful sense still linked to the Orange Order.

Despite the reforms of 1798, the founding fathers of Orangeism had started something quite significant, and warrants were soon being issued for new Orange Lodges throughout the country. As regards originating accreditation – still an irksome subject to some Armagh Orangemen who like to think of Portadown as the Orange Citadel – it is notable that the first four warrants were issued to those districts which had been covered by the original Orange Boys centred on the Dyan in County Tyrone. There is therefore no room for doubt that it was the militant and Masonic James Wilson's initiative, energy and early contribution which were of crucial impact and importance in the creation of the Orange Order in 1795.

Whilst the immediate origins of Orangeism owed their impetus to the working class sectarian strife that was in danger of engulfing mid-Ulster in 1795, there were other strong forces at work. At the confluence of all these contributory forces the mainstream was undoubtedly politics. It was those political developments such as Presbyterian radicalism and the resurgence of Catholic aspiration that served greatly to exacerbate the 'garrison mentality' of the ascendancy in its defensive reaction to these developments and to those beyond Ireland's shores. That growing political mainstream would soon become the turbulent maelstrom that would disgorge the Orange Order.

Many take the view that the circumstances of the 1790s were such as to render the creation of Orangeism both inevitable and justifiable, but this is doubtful. Those who supported or approved of Orangeism in its earlier years were not representative of Protestantism as a whole if we include the even more protestant Presbyterians. The ascendancy constituted only a tiny minority of the people of Ireland. They were a minority even in Ulster where the Catholics formed half the population, and where numerically strong Presbyterianism was for the most part either opposed to Orangeism or ambivalent towards it. There were some Presbyterians like James Wilson who lived in areas of pronounced sectarian conflict, who were in the Order from the beginning, but as the historian Hereward Senior has pointed out, 'there were no dissenting clergymen or prominent Dissenters among the early patrons of Orangeism'.[10]

In those early days the membership of the Orange Order was predominantly Church of Ireland at least in a nominal sense, and its leadership almost entirely so. Therefore, by opting to support the Protestant ascendancy of their ultra-conservative Castle rulers, the Orangemen supported the few against the many. They participated in the creation of a society of divided Irishmen, rather than of united Irishmen. They not only opposed the Catholics they regarded as their natural enemy, but raised their hand against the enlightened ideas of a substantial number of their Presbyterian neighbours who stood for the noble ideal of the unity of Protestant, Catholic and Dissenter within a new, liberated and egalitarian Ireland. Had such been achieved, and especially by means of the political and parliamentary reform originally intended, this could have been to the lasting benefit of the people of Ireland.

Although in the minority in 1795, the Orangemen were soon to succeed beyond all imagination. They succeeded because of the power and influence of the new leaders who rapidly attached themselves – leaders who would soon see the opportunity to use the burgeoning new institution as a paramilitary means of securing their now threatened privilege. It might have been otherwise, and something much better could have been possible if enlightened people like Edmund Burke, the United Irishmen and the vast majority of the people of Ireland had had their way. Instead, egalitarian and liberal politics would be virtually silenced by an institutionalised sectarianism that would scourge Irish history and politics for the next two hundred years. The ascendancy ruling class was the chief factor in the growth of Orangeism, providing influential and representational links into all areas of the Establishment – the judiciary, military, the Established Church, Dublin Castle, the British government, and even the British Royal House itself as we shall see later. But it is precisely because the new Orange leadership would prove to be powerfully manipulative and managerial that this aspect will be considered in our next section, where we examine, against the back-cloth of British and Irish history, Orangeism's essentially political objectives and how it set about achieving them.

Section Two:
Objectives of Orangeism

5.

1795 - 1801
An army whose idea seems to be blood

As indicated earlier, the stated objective of the Orange Order under its early rules lay in its pledge to defend the King and his heirs 'so long as he or they support the Protestant Ascendancy, the constitution and laws of these kingdoms'. That pledge at once epitomised the paramilitary and frontier spirit of the new Order, and indicated that its primary objective held the notion of a contractarian oath of conditional loyalty to the Crown. The Order's loyalty to the King would be subject to the continuance of a distinctive Protestant polity in Ireland, predicated under what was presumed to be an unchanging constitution. This indicated a fixed and inflexible approach to constitutional politics that, in conjunction with conditional allegiance, would become the formula for unstable political dynamite. Indeed the contractarianism that privileged one group at the expense of others – especially when the others were demographically strong – would eventually become incompatible with a broadening polity in an incipient democracy. Contractarianism said in effect: 'We remain loyal to our contract, however impolitic or out of date you may deem it to be, but we will be loyal to Britain only so long as that contract continues to be honoured in full'. This was a signpost on a road to rebellion. As one 'loyalist' recently expressed it: 'My loyalty is to the British Throne being Protestant. I have no loyalty to any Westminster government'.[1] But the direction in which Orangeism was headed became even more dangerous when contractarianism mutated into the religious concept of covenant. This would produce an equally unworkable and even more contradictory formulation of covenant-contract political theory – a theocratic idea that Norman Porter explodes in his *Rethinking Unionism*.[2]

As Porter argues, contractarian government is based on the idea of popular sovereignty. The contract is founded on the secular consent of the people as citizens, as opposed to government by a sovereign based on divine right. By logical extension, and over time, the contractarian theory leads us to the concept of democracy – government by the consent of all the people via the ballot box and parliament. However, it is precisely that logic with which ascendancy and privilege-supporting Orangeism has often been at odds, having over the years opposed both democratic opinion and the will of the sovereign parliament. It is therefore significant that when

Orange-unionism ultimately threatened armed rebellion against the Crown in parliament in 1912, it should at that time decide to crossbreed its unworkable political contract theory with another untenable notion of a covenant with God. This was the Ulster Covenant, as we shall see in chapter 8. The covenant theory has three main strands. First, God made a covenant of blessing with his people (Protestants) subject to their continued faithfulness. Second, the sovereign in the coronation oath has sworn to maintain the Protestant religion as established. And third, Protestants must obey the sovereign and the laws of the state insofar as these continue to reflect the true religion. This kind of privileged thinking would later produce, among other things, Orange-unionism's high-handed attitude to the rule of law circa 1912, and later would give rise to its 'Protestant Parliament for a Protestant people'.

This hybrid theory is at once contradictory, subjective and arbitrary. It is contradictory since it creates a clash between the consent-based contractarian democracy of a whole citizenry and the covenantal exclusivism of a privileged Protestant group. It is subjective in that it rests on nothing but a blind belief that cannot be sustained on any politico-legal or theological basis. And it is arbitrary because no democratic British government has ever regarded itself as party to any such religio-political covenant-contract – a notion that, as Norman Porter says, 'fails to raise the merest flicker of recognition at Westminster'.[3] If it ever did, that flicker would be a rather derisory one.

In a rapidly changing world, and especially under the British constitution, there were bound to be ongoing problems with a contracted and conditional loyalty to what Orangemen continued rather vaguely to regard as 'whatever it was King William had established'.[4] A contract of loyalty to what was regarded as fixed and immutable could not with any political coherence survive indefinitely within an unwritten constitution that was designedly flexible, progressive over time, and by its very nature changeable by the will of elected parliaments. Legal and political problems would inevitably arise from the Orangemen's self-arrogated claims. But a bad situation would be worsened by the additional notion of a covenant with God. With God on your side, and a gun in your hand, why worry about British parliamentary democracy?

This doctrine had two serious implications for the Orange Order. First, it gave it a self-importance that 'tends to put itself in the place of law'.[5] It conferred to the sons of William such an arbitrary sense of power that they became 'the bearers of a particular attitude toward authority'.[6] William Blacker, an early Orange leader, exemplified this when he refused to instruct Orangemen to obey a law on the grounds that it was made by the Whigs, who had made many laws which ought not to be obeyed. This would prove to be typical of Orangeism's arbitrary attitude towards any liberalising government's laws, and reminds us for example of its stance on the Parades Commission. (When we come to consider its religious ordinances, we shall see that its political arbitrariness is underpinned by its ultra-Protestant concept of religion – one that can hardly be squared with the Christian doctrine of citizenship.) Secondly, these covenant-contract theories tended to set in stone notions as to what the King and his heirs must or must not support, as though the British constitution were an irrevocable and once-for-all transaction.

They would increasingly become a dangerous Orange-unionist doctrine that, when aided and abetted by the British Tories, would encourage rebellion against democratic change in a world now utterly different from that of the seventeenth century Prince of Orange. The doctrine would assume its most virulent form in the Home Rule crisis of 1912-14 when its malpractice moved the Liberal prime minister H.H. Asquith to denounce it as 'the complete Grammar of Anarchy'.[7]

Many Orangemen really do fail to appreciate the niceties of the 'unwritten' British constitution with its flexible and changing nature, to say nothing of its cardinal principle of constitutional monarchy involving loyalty to the Crown in parliament. They often cannot see that loyalty to the Crown inheres loyalty to democratic parliamentary government and to ongoing democratic change – a subject on which their parliamentary friend the late Enoch Powell MP, a recognised constitutional expert, once felt compelled to lecture them, though sadly without success. This fundamental issue will recur throughout our story, as will become particularly evident when we come to assess those historical episodes in which Orangeism clearly saw itself as above the law and acted accordingly. In fact, this matter was to have the most serious and enduring repercussions for democracy and the rule of law both in Ireland and Britain.

In the context of the ascendancy the word 'Protestant' referred to Ireland's ruling classes – the Anglo-Irish and Church of Ireland landowning minority that excluded even the large numbers of other non-Catholics, the Nonconformists and Dissenters. The large majority Catholic population formed absolutely no part of the Irish polity and had no meaningful legal status in what would now be described as their own country. As Edmund Burke put it, 'No nation in the world has ever been known to exclude so great a body of men (not born slaves) from the civil state'.[8] This was a situation so execrable that he elsewhere likened those responsible for it to rats and Ireland to a ship – but a 'ship that was kept up for the benefit of the rats'.[9] This was the Protestant ascendancy that the Orangemen would covenant to defend – it was oligarchy rather than democracy, the rule of the few over the many, exclusion and not inclusion; and because this was ostensibly based on religious grounds it involved the sectarianising rather than the unifying of the people. It was a narrow and minimalist political philosophy that would have the most tragic and abiding consequences for Ireland, and especially for the North.

Just prior to the founding of the Orange Order, there were signs that Burke's invective against the ascendancy would not go unheeded. The government at Westminster had become embarrassed by the bigotry and corruption of the Castle oligarchy, and concerned by the increasing radicalism and unrest throughout Ireland. In fact, William Pitt now appeared to be moving towards a policy of reform which, by the standards of the time, approximated to Catholic emancipation. Earl Fitzwilliam, the well-meaning disciple of Edmund Burke, was appointed Lord Lieutenant of Ireland early in 1795 and was the repository of much hope for both Catholics and Dissenters. An enthusiastic reformer, he started decisively by expelling some of the hard-liners who formed a powerful junta in the Dublin Castle executive. This was followed by Henry Grattan's parliamentary bill to permit Catholics to sit in the Irish parliament, although given the strictures of the franchise, the emancipation involved would probably have produced no more than four Catholic MPs. Nevertheless, this measure caused consternation to an ascendancy that continually and self-fulfillingly prophesied to England of the dangers of an unstable Jacobin situation in Ireland. The British, who were now preoccupied with the dangers inherent in their own situation *vis-à-vis* France, suddenly lacked the courage to press on with the reforms that were clearly necessary in the different situation obtaining in Ireland.

The Castle junta's complaints did not go unheard. King George III angrily refused to approve the reforms he wrongly believed to be in violation of his coronation oath, and the rapidly retreating William Pitt decided to revert to a hard-line policy. He aborted reform, clamping down on all anti-ascendancy activity, and recalled Fitzwilliam after only a few months in office. This recall caused great disillusionment and fury among the Catholics and the radical Dissenters who for so long had advocated and hoped for relief by means of peaceful parliamentary reform. In fact, this reaction against reform was potentially far more dangerous than the reforms themselves could possibly ever have been. The situation was further inflamed when new Lord Lieutenant Camden immediately brought back the expelled hard-line members of the Castle junta (many of whom were soon to become Orangemen), and embarked upon a policy of 'rallying the Protestants'. This *volte-face* was part of a new programme of strong coercive measures that were designed to contain the Catholics and to suppress the United Irishmen.

Thus the ascendancy junta was reprieved – just a matter of weeks before the creation of the Order that would pledge so strongly to its defence. As we have seen, the Orange Order initially was made up of farm workers and farmer-weavers, William Blacker probably being the only member of the gentry who had joined at the very beginning. However, the role of special agent Captain John Giffard should not be forgotten, and it was not long before the landed and military classes were made aware of the opportunity that Orangeism presented for the underpinning of the ascendancy *status quo*. Thomas Knox MP and his brother General John Knox, the British military commander in mid-Ulster, now agreed that the Order could usefully be put to political and military purposes, and they advised Lord Lieutenant Camden accordingly.

The historian Kevin Whelan writes:

> Faced with a mounting United Irish challenge in this very region, gentry and military leaders jettisoned their qualms about its democratic tinge and its predilection for ugly sectarian violence. The elite Anglican layer in mid-Ulster, socially vulnerable and politically isolated, quickly grafted themselves on as the leadership of the organisation.[10]

This was very much more than token leadership. It was an effective exercise in direction and management by men of political and legal influence, but it was discreetly delegated to those whose finger was on the local pulse, such as the County Armagh magistrates who had been on the fringes of the events at the Diamond. William Blacker of Castle Blacker has already been mentioned. Those who subsequently joined included the Verners of Church Hill (one of whom was soon to become the very first Orange Grand Master of Ireland), the Atkinsons of Crowhill, the Clarkes of Summer Island, the Maunsells of Drumcree, the Warings of Waringstown, and the Brownlows of Lurgan. Other influential figures, including many Church of Ireland clergymen, soon joined the leadership as Orangeism increased and spread from Armagh through Ulster and beyond, even to the heart of the ascendancy itself where the Dublin Grand Lodge was founded in 1797. This was a far cry from the days of the Peep O' Day Boys of the Diamond. Indeed, the new management takeover was such that in just two years the original founders Wilson, Sloan, Winter and their like had, in the words of the Orange historian John Brown, 'retired from notice'.

On 4th June 1797 Thomas Verner founded Orange Lodge No. 176 in Dublin, and within a few months it had become perhaps the most influential club in that city, with over three hundred members. In March 1798 it became the Orange Grand Lodge of Ireland, with Verner its first Grand Master. Verner quickly set out to establish a new system of central authority for control and regulation, and embarked on a programme of reform and 'improvement'. Significantly, this involved the jettisoning of the original neo-Masonic degree system, now known as the 'Old' or 'Diamond System', and its replacement by the 'New System' with a much simpler and ostensibly more Christian orientation. These moves were designed as part of a new beginning, but were not unconnected with the ascendancy government's drive against Freemasonry, which had been strongly linked to the now disbanded Volunteers and which remained associated with the United Irishmen. Thus after less than three years existence the original Orange Order was effectively abolished. All its members had to re-apply and be re-initiated into what on the face of things appeared to be a quite new Orange Order. But in the event, things turned out rather differently. Although the growth of radical and independent Freemasonry was successfully curbed, and Orangeism now provided an effective substitute for it, the ritualised form of Freemasonry that had been adapted and internalised by the Orange Order was a very different matter. Many Orangemen, in reaction to the reforms, began to participate in an illicit internal movement that was designed to preserve and retain the ritualistic 'Higher Orders' of the Old System. This would result in years of conflict with Grand Lodge. However, by dint of much dissembling and manoeuvring the Orange ritualists would eventually succeed in preserving not only the old neo-Masonic degrees but several others, albeit under the aegis of the new and inter-related Orders of the Royal Arch Purple and the Royal Black Preceptory. This matter is covered in greater detail in chapter 13.

Despite the Orangemen's early reputation as Peep O' Day Boy wreckers and sectarian lawbreakers, their new establishment leadership drawn from the magistracy, military, gentry and clergy quickly recognised their capacity for Protestant action and defence. These leaders therefore sought to discipline and control the Orangemen by encouraging tenants' law and order associations, and by their patronage succeeded in giving the Order considerable status, support and sanction. The historian David Miller explains how this worked:

When the Orange gentry framed the rules of the institution, they ensured that the higher orders would mingle with their humbler brethren by requiring that each member of the elite Grand Lodge would also join a local lodge.[11]

The common Orangemen, for their part, could relish that 'special relationship' with the Orange gentry which fellowship in lodge and the sharing of signs and secrets seemed to confer. It was therefore an effective arrangement, which the ascendancy class now hoped to use for physical defence and the protection of political privilege. Indeed, these objectives might be advanced by utilising the Order as a manpower resource for a proposed Yeomanry defence force, an idea which, because of the twin threat of invasion and insurgency, was at that time being widely canvassed within the ascendancy class. However, the new British viceroy Earl Camden, who was of a careful disposition, was unused to such 'democratic' liaisons and was initially both fearful and sceptical of General Knox's proposals as to the 'lawless' Orange Order's potential usefulness. The reinstated Castle junta, which included Orange sympathisers such as Beresford and Cooke, was beginning to favour the idea of using the Orangemen for politico-military purposes, but a Castle official, Pelham, stressed the need for 'infinite prudence and dexterity in the management of such an undertaking'.[12] Camden, in finally agreeing after much soul-searching to permit the use of the Orange Order for political and paramilitary purposes, strongly supported Pelham in urging a 'covert and discreet approach'. He wished to ensure that the government was suitably distanced from the measures likely to be used, and certainly from their inevitable consequences. His fears were well-founded.

Shortly after their victory at the battle of the Diamond, the Orangemen had embarked upon a series of bitter pogroms against Catholics, which came to be known as the Armagh Outrages, although these in fact spread far beyond that county. Homes and looms were wrecked, chapels burned and, in an evocation of Oliver Cromwell, large numbers of Catholics were given the choice of going to 'hell or Connaught'. The respected Irish historian W.E.H. Leckey cites a figure of up to 7,000 driven out of County Armagh alone, many of them to far flung areas of Connaught.[13] This provides a rather different impression of those terrible events from that recently given by the Orange historians of Portadown in their paltry and obfuscatory reference to 'a few Roman Catholic neighbours whose homes had been attacked by the Protestant Peep O'Day Boys'.[14] Dr William Richardson, a local Church of Ireland clergyman and magistrate who was very close to the events in question, expressed the matter rather more plainly and certainly more accurately when he wrote in 1797:

> The Orangemen had no moderation after their victory. They continued harassing the Catholics with great cruelty for many months, with little interruption from the magistrates.[15]

Yet, as we have just seen, the Castle ascendancy was beginning to acquiesce in the encouragement of such Orangemen for its own purposes, apparently agreeing with Thomas Knox MP who wrote that 'on them (the Orangemen) we must rely for the preservation of our lives and properties should critical times occur'. Preparations were now being made to 'arm the Protestants that can be relied upon'. This dangerous strategy was delegated to the ascendancy's agents in the hope that both means and ends would be astutely and discreetly distanced from Dublin Castle's responsibility. But the Castle probably did not foresee that the lower orders of Orangeism would take such advantage of their indemnity as to 'uphold the ascendancy' by sectarian measures of such extremity. Nor did it foresee that the Orangemen's respectable masters in the magistracy would so blatantly turn a blind eye to the Orange excesses. The nervous Camden could therefore lament naively that 'some of the magistrates have been incautious enough not to carry out this measure so secretly as to have escaped the notice of the public'.[16] He had no problem with the policy if only it could have been pursued without adverse publicity. After much private and nervous deliberation a predominantly Protestant armed Yeomanry was established in October 1796, just over a year after the founding of the Orange Order. Initially there was no public policy to link Orangeism ostensibly with the Yeomanry, which would have been quite impolitic. However, the Orangemen through their leaders had received advance knowledge of the proposed force. Strategic discussions were held in the secrecy of Lodge meetings, where it was decided that they should bide their time until the Yeomanry was established, after which the Orangemen would come forward and join in numbers.

Having dipped a timid toe into the swirling waters of the Boyne, Camden therefore had finally been persuaded to take the plunge. He authorised the arming of the Protestants and, whether he liked it or not, this soon amounted to the deployment of militant Orangemen for military and political purposes. The Yeomanry served to create an effective barrier that would contain the United Irishmen within their stronghold of Belfast, Antrim and Down, and prevent their influence from spreading into mid and west-Ulster. The Yeomanry was officered by carefully chosen ascendancy-supporting gentry, and was armed, equipped and centrally controlled from Dublin. Significantly, in County Down the Yeomanry only received substantial numbers of recruits from the Church of Ireland and therefore Orange districts. Its numbers soared from 18,000 within a few months to over 66,000 in the course of the next two years, by which time it had been all but swamped by the flood of incoming Orangemen and had become a veritable 'army with banners'.

The activities of the Orange Yeomanry extended beyond mere defence or containment, their patrolling of Catholic areas often being seen as a deliberate form of repression and coercion. The large Orange marches and demonstrations that commenced that same year were broadly similar in purpose to that of the Yeomanry's patrolling. These were triumphalist shows of ascendancy strength, which were designed, as Orange historian John Brown frankly admits, 'as an assertion of old rights and to keep Papists in their places'.[17] Marching, however, is such an important aspect of Orangeism as to warrant separate treatment in a later chapter. On the subject of this Orange militancy it will suffice here to allude to the words of two noted Protestants of that time. Commenting on the Yeomanry, Henry Grattan likened its Orange militants to an ascendancy army whose 'idea seems to be blood',[18] for in many respects their actions were a re-enactment of the then recent Armagh terror. Indeed, 'terror' was precisely the word used by General

Knox for the policy of coercion that was now being pursued by his Orange Yeomanry. With equal bluntness he privately described these men as 'bigots', as though this were the all-essential qualification for the job in hand. [19]

It is not our purpose to cover the detail of the United Irishmen's rising and defeat of 1798. It will suffice to say that, on the one hand, the United Irishmen were strong on optimism and political ideology, but weak on the logistics of war. Obviously they had been greatly debilitated by the government's policy of attrition and coercion. But even so, their seriously flawed military strategy, together with the fatally riven nature of their organisation and a fundamental lack of cohesive leadership, virtually ensured their defeat from an early stage. On the other hand, the well-armed and influentially led Orange organisation, with its Yeomanry network and military intelligence working in solidarity with the more disciplined and better trained British army, provided the necessary muscle to ensure victory and the defence of the ascendancy. Thus the primary objective of the original Orangemen with that of their subsequent ascendancy leaders seemed, for the time being at least, to have been achieved. But there was to be a twist in the tale, and of a far-reaching kind.

Immediately after the 1798 Rebellion some of the victorious Castle ascendancy politicians sought to reinforce their position by means of a black propaganda campaign against the defeated United Irishmen. In particular, the analysis of the leading Orangeman, Sir Richard Musgrave, amounted to an attempt to depoliticise the Rebellion. He depicted it as just another popish plot – a sectarian crusade to destroy Protestantism in Ireland.[20] But precisely the reverse was true, for it was the Protestant ascendancy that had deliberately fostered Orange sectarianism as a religio-political weapon to be used against an ideology that was inclusive of all denominations or none, and led largely by Presbyterians. Yet this early example of government spin-doctoring caught the prevailing mood among many of those now disillusioned Dissenters who hitherto had rejected Orangeism, with the result that more Presbyterians began to join both the Orange Order and the Yeomanry. The ascendancy propaganda did not go unanswered, however, for it was soon followed by a countervailing liberal analysis of the causes of the rebellion, in which influential British Whig commentators effectively placed the blame where it undoubtedly belonged – on the corrupt ascendancy and Castle system.

The British government was certainly under no illusions. While the Irish rebellion was still proceeding, the strong but liberal-minded Lord Cornwallis was appointed Lord Lieutenant and commander-in-chief, and sent to Dublin with a clear mandate to make an end not only to the rebellion but to the ascendancy government itself. In victory over the United Irishmen, Cornwallis was quite magnanimous. Like Earl Fitzwilliam before him, he quickly outed the Castle's Orange junta of Foster, Fitzgibbon, Beresford and Cooke, and embarked on a policy of wooing Ireland to a new political position. His policy was designed to weaken if not to break the ascendancy's power, and to create a new polity for Ireland under the Act of Union. In the course of this Ireland's hopes were raised once more, but as things turned out Ireland yet again was to be seriously disappointed.

The Orange Order initially opposed Lord Cornwallis's proposal to remove the Irish parliament and to introduce direct rule under an Act of Union. True to Orangeism's original objective to support the Protestant ascendancy, the rank-and-file Orangemen earnestly wished to support a campaign to preserve the 'Protestant constitution'. But their ascendancy leaders were divided on the issue, for despite their Orange principles many of them stood to gain financially and in other ways if they accepted the government's proposals, supported as these were by back-handers and bribery. Thomas Verner, the Orange Grand Master, became a keen supporter of the Union. Albeit with only a very small majority in Grand Lodge, Verner managed to ensure that the Orange Order remained neutral and therefore silent on the issue. Even in-lodge debate on the proposed Act of Union was strictly forbidden, so that the natural and anticipated Orange opposition to it was stifled and such protest as there was proved to be of little or no consequence. In fact, the shock waves of the Irish rebellion had had a powerful impact on all concerned, not least on Prime Minister William Pitt, who had now lost any remaining confidence in the Castle administration. In turn the ascendancy had lost much of its own confidence and was now heavily dependent on the British military, and even more dependent on British money.

In these circumstances, many Protestants and even considerable numbers of Orangemen began to see certain advantages in the Union, and eventually they decided to give it their support. So too did many Catholics, especially when given to believe by means of behind-the-scenes lobbying that the Union would be connected with reforming measures of the highest importance, not least of which would be the long-deferred Emancipation of Catholics. Later, when this was deferred yet again (for almost thirty years), the Irish Catholics would reflect on the whole episode with bitterness and consider themselves cheated. But yet once more the withholding of Irish reform would prove infinitely more disadvantageous to the British than would the granting of it. For the great mass of the Irish people would subsequently come out against the Union, presaging those later generations who, in company with British radicals like Gladstone, would look back on the Act of Union as an unmitigated disaster.

Lord Lieutenant Cornwallis eventually succeeded in buying off a majority of the Dublin parliament to support of the Union and to accept the concomitant weakening of the Protestant ascendancy. However, the process involved was not without difficulty, as Cornwallis himself put it, 'negotiating and jobbing with the most corrupt people under heaven'. Many years later, W.E. Gladstone would describe the entire business as one of 'unredeemed blackguardism'. Edmund Burke's judgment on the ascendancy had once again been vindicated. It is interesting to observe that many generations later Burke and Gladstone's assessment of the corrupt nature of the Protestant ascendancy would find the unlikely approbation of the Ulster Unionist leader and Orangeman David Trimble. Writing in 1996 on the partition of Ireland and the 'necessary abandonment' of Southern unionists that was consequent upon the creation of the Northern Ireland state in 1921, Trimble comments that:

> When it became necessary, it was done without compunction. A close affinity had never existed between the mass of Ulster folk and the southern ascendancy – many of the great-grandfathers of the Ulster Volunteers having rebelled against that ascendancy and the corrupt Dublin establishment.[21]

Apart from under-scoring our point about the corrupt nature of the ascendancy, the comment is irresistible that Trimble's 'two-nations' theory, deployed in justification of partition, is based on the notion that the people of the southern ascendancy were of a different ilk from the mass of Ulster folk. But where was the difference? Prior to 1798 the Ulster Protestants were divided between those who supported the ascendancy and those who opposed it. Many of those who opposed it were on the side of the United Irishmen, whereas the ascendancy's most staunch defenders were the northern Orangemen. It was the ascendancy-supporting Orangemen who prevailed, and eventually won over the large majority of northern Protestants to their cause. There was therefore no lack of affinity, either in terms of political objectives or religion, between the northern Orangemen and the Dublin establishment they had pledged to defend.

We therefore need hardly be surprised that such a flawed hypothesis has to throw out several babies with the bath water. It implies that the southern Protestant people who produced Edward Carson were so different from the northern Protestants as to be expendable. Yet this 'justifiable abandonment' also involved the Ulster Protestants of Monaghan, Cavan and Donegal whose only lack of affinity was that they lived on the other side of a very arbitrary political line, many of them quite literally at the wrong end of a border field. Strangest of all, the Trimble hypothesis implies by extension that Ulster's founding fathers of Orangeism set out with a specific pledge to defend what was admissibly corrupt. They defended the corrupt Protestant ascendancy against the rebellion of the United Irishmen, here generously accredited as the 'great-grandfathers of the Ulster Volunteers'. In fact the Orangemen would continue to defend the corrupt principle of Protestant ascendancy ever after. Thus by logical extension the Trimble hypothesis is demonstrably anti-Orange, implying as it does that the United Irishmen were not so wrong after all and that, as is argued throughout this book, it was the Orangemen who had blundered originally, and have continued to do so ever since.

Conclusions

The Act of Union of 1st January 1801 ostensibly brought about the defeat of Orangeism's first great objective and cause, in that it seemed to have curtailed the Protestant ascendancy which the Orange Order had set itself up to defend. The corruption and coercion, and the withholding of reform for reasons of expediency, which were involved in the ascendancy's political defence, had only served to fuel violence and counter-violence. All these things had drawn even greater attention to the ascendancy's malignancy, and seemed to have hastened its demise. However, in the turn-out things were not quite so simple. Promises and understandings were broken, and the trappings of Protestant supremacy would continue in all parts of Ireland for a long time to come. Orangeism would have a leading role in ensuring this. For despite this setback for the ascendancy, new means would soon be found for the defence of Protestant supremacy, ironically in the very instrument of its apparent defeat – the Act of Union. But the inevitable antithesis of such a utilisation of the Union would be a renaissance of an Irish nationalism seeking Catholic Emancipation, the repeal of the Union, and the return of an Irish parliament – a parliament that this time would be properly representative of the Irish people.

Thus the agenda was set for nearly two hundred years of political conflict, during the course of which the maintenance of Protestant supremacy, the defence of the Union, and support for the British Empire would be perceived by Orangeism as calling for the continued suppression of Catholics. Many would contend that for reason of foreign policy and military considerations at the time there was justification for this Orange-unionist perception, which was widely held despite those influential and far-sighted condemnations of it mentioned earlier. But this state of affairs could not last. Indeed, it is arguable that in the aftermath of the 1798 Rebellion the long and gradual demise of ascendancy politics had in a sense already begun. The democratic and classical republican ideals of the United Irishmen would eventually prove more durable than the sectarian politics of a privileged ascendancy class. In the long run their unifying and egalitarian politics would be seen as more akin to those of the emerging Western democracies than would the divisive policies of the Orangemen.

Protestant ascendancy-supporting Orangeism had been fostered to provide a divisive barrier to that kind of progress in Ireland, a function it would serve until it could do so no longer. Thus the greater part of Orangeism's history is to be located in Ireland's political hiatus – in a 'between-the-times' situation. But the point of our story is that, in Ulster, Orangeism's resistance to change and progress was destined to continue right up to our own time, to that point where it would be universally perceived as being far 'behind the times'. Indeed, long after other Protestant countries had abandoned ascendancy politics, the Irish ascendancy's old sectarian objective of 'keeping the papists in their places' would remain the grand *cause célèbre* of Orangeism in Northern Ireland, and with the dire consequences that sadly are now all too well known.

6.

1801 - 1869
Keeping the papists in their places

Orangeism at grass roots level had initially opposed the Act of Union. This was not just because of its zealous support for the Protestant ascendancy, but because it feared the Catholic Emancipation (the right of elected Catholics to sit in parliament) which British Prime Minister William Pitt had signalled as an early consequence of the Union. Against that background, and as the Orange Order continued to grow, Lord Cornwallis tried to marginalise its influence, but the Order was now sufficiently well entrenched to thwart all his efforts. This attempt to suppress the Order was motivated by the British government's continuing disquiet at Orangeism's unashamedly sectarian objectives and its propensity for civil disorder. It therefore marked the beginning of a recurring cycle of anti-Orange enquiry, proscriptive legislation and censure over the next several decades. Despite this, the Orangemen had reason to feel vindicated when King George III vehemently rejected the Catholic Emancipation Bill because, as was the case with the Irish parliament's earlier proposals, he regarded Emancipation as in violation of his Coronation oath. The King's rejection of the Bill embarrassed William Pitt who had clearly promised the measure. This precipitated his resignation just five weeks after the Act of Union. Orangeism therefore came to see that the Union without Emancipation, far from repudiating Protestant supremacy, might well become the very means of underpinning it. From being a small minority within Ireland they could now see themselves as part of the great majority within the strongly Protestant United Kingdom. Thus the old sectarian lines were redrawn, as the relieved Orangemen increasingly placed their hopes in the Union, while the Catholics once again and not for the last time considered themselves to have been seriously defrauded. This would inevitably produce reaction.

Sectarian violence continued into the new century, with skirmishes between Ribbonmen (successors to the Defenders) and Orangemen, one such being the so-called Battle of Garvagh in 1813. Yet at this juncture violence was much reduced due to the fact that after 1798 there seemed to be greater determination on the part of the British to govern firmly and more fairly, particularly in matters of law and order. Robert Peel was appointed Chief Secretary in 1812 and, despite his nickname 'Orange Peel', immediately set about creating new justice measures, including what was intended to be an impartial and mobile constabulary and an independent stipendiary magistracy, both clearly designed to weaken Orange power. In fact, the British government would subsequently endeavour to suppress Orange parades and demonstrations and even the Order itself, but these measures were to have only limited and transient success in the troubled years that lay ahead.

At this time Daniel O'Connell was emerging as a skilful propagandist and charismatic leader of Irish Catholic nationalism. It was also the time when Orangeism began to spread into Britain, inevitably giving rise to outbreaks of sectarian riots in cities such as Liverpool and Glasgow. These serious developments brought the Irish problem right into Britain's own backyard, and gave poignancy to parliamentary attacks on the Orange Order and on Orange Tories by British radicals such as Joseph Hume. When there was renewed trouble in Ireland between Catholic Ribbonmen and Orangemen, parliament took action by passing the Unlawful Oaths Act in July 1823. This Act was directed against both protagonist organisations, but the Orange oath and its conditional allegiance to the King was the subject of particular parliamentary scrutiny and concern. The effect of this was to force the Orange Grand Lodge to instruct Lodges to stop administering oaths, which in turn meant that it had to carry out yet another major revision of its rules and constitution. Fear of more civil strife and therefore of further anti-Orange legislation caused Grand Lodge to cancel the marches and demonstrations arranged for July 1824.

Meanwhile an important new factor had entered the equation when Daniel O'Connell established the Catholic Association in 1823. This was a non-violent but powerfully organised mass agitation for Catholic Emancipation covering the whole of Ireland. Ireland therefore now had two mass movements with diametrically opposed objectives, both given to regular, massive and potentially dangerous public demonstrations. The government became alarmed, and in 1825 passed the Unlawful Societies Act suppressing both the Catholic Association and the Orange Order. Secret societies are never comfortable with public scrutiny, but this was especially the case with one that had obvious links with the Yeomanry and with that *laissez faire* paramilitarism that now had such a reputation for armed violence. Many of the Orange Order's members, particularly those from the upper echelons of society, were embarrassed and began to dissociate from it. It was now branded as an illegal organisation, and the ruling Grand Lodge of Ireland decided formally to dissolve itself on 18th March 1825. The Orange Order became an underground organisation but, consistent with the doctrine of conditional loyalty, some individual Lodges resolutely refused to recognise both Grand Lodge's dissolution and the government's ban.

To circumvent the law the Catholic Association transformed itself into a new organisation, and in the autumn of 1828 decided to carry its non-violent campaign for Catholic Emancipation into Ulster, that part of Ireland where it had been least successful. The campaign was led by Belfastman Jack Lawless, and was known as the 'invasion of Ulster' because the Orange-loyalists regarded its supporters as outsiders who had no territorial authority to work for Catholic rights in 'Protestant Ulster'. Despite their legal suppression the Orangemen decided to resist the Emancipation campaign. A rally, proposed for 23rd September in Ballybay, was diverted when eight thousand armed Orangemen took over the town. On returning home, supporters of both sides met on the road and some retreating Catholics were killed or wounded when the Orangemen opened fire. Lawless's next rally, which was to have been held the following week in Armagh, also occasioned a large mustering of armed Orangemen who, when they poured into the city, discovered that the Catholics had already called off the rally. The historian Jonathan Bardon, quoting from press reports at the time, tells us that:

> In celebration the Orangemen marched through the city, beating drums, huzzaing, and now and then firing shots. In Scotch Street, upwards of thirty shots were fired... Several of the guns were bright, and were evidently yeomanry arms, and the cavalry swords were of the same description.[1]

These Orange demonstrations and counter-demonstrations, with all their attendant violence, were the work of an Order that allegedly stood for civil and religious liberty, and yet were expressly directed against the very idea of Catholic Emancipation, the chief object of which was to enable democratically elected Catholics to sit in parliament. This was a somewhat warped view of liberty, which will be examined at a later juncture. But these unambiguous challenges to law and order by an already banned organisation were not likely to be treated with impunity by the authorities. In this situation the Orange Order, in conjunction with some hard-line British Tories, decided in October 1828 to take a leaf out of O'Connell's book and to create a new front for itself by founding a number of Brunswick Clubs throughout Britain and Ulster. The name 'Brunswick' was chosen in honour of the Royal House of Brunswick that had long been to the fore in upholding the principle of Protestant ascendancy. It therefore exemplified a form of strong, doctrinaire Orange-Tory opposition to Catholic Emancipation. The meetings of these new clubs were the occasion for great demonstrations, marching on Catholic areas in the usual Orange manner, and accompanied by massive displays of arms. Quoting from the *Newry Telegraph*, Jonathan Bardon writes:

> ... an estimated forty thousand had met at Tandragee, and after the Moy demonstration a group went to a nearby townland, where all but two families were Catholics. Their approach was announced by drums, fifes, bugles and by playing party tunes such as Holy Water, Croppies lie down, and Kick the Pope ... till two in the morning, when they marched back playing the same tunes, huzzaing, and firing shots.[2]

The new front made no attempt to conceal the old sectarian habits, and Orangeism remained unremitting in pursuit of its anti-Catholic agenda. But it did change some aspects of its rules and constitution with a view to keeping within the law. When the 1825 Unlawful Societies Act lapsed, the Duke of Cumberland (brother of King William IV and an implacable opponent of Catholic Emancipation) was appointed Orange Grand Master. Known as the 'damnable Duke', Cumberland would later be described as the wickedest of Queen Victoria's wicked uncles, his name being associated with rape and incest and 'the symbol of the darkest and fiercest passions'.[3] Cumberland was particularly adept at intrigue and at stirring up sectarian politics. Indeed, on becoming Prime Minister in 1827 the Duke of Wellington had good reason to describe Cumberland as the most mischievous fellow he had ever known, and soon had to threaten him with imprisonment in the Tower. Yet despite the Duke of Cumberland's low reputation his high rank and fierce anti-Catholicism made him appear useful to Orangeism, although this later proved to be a serious miscalculation. As of now, however, the Duke and his brother Orangemen had the support of the Presbyterian leader Henry Cooke, who bluntly declared that he regarded the emancipation of Catholics with 'horror, disapprobation and dismay'. Cooke would have accepted the extraordinary idea of a 'limited' emancipation[4] – limited to Catholics outside the north of Ireland. But it was incongruous that a Christian leader should qualify his principles of liberty and citizenship by a sectarian and territorial exclusion, and especially since his Church was Presbyterian – and 'the Presbyterian Church in Ireland' at that.

This was no more than a restatement of the old Orange ascendancy doctrine of 'keeping the papists in their places', a doctrine which if no longer feasible in Ireland as a whole could at least be maintained in the northern part of it. It was the shape of the Ulsterisation that was to come. But even at that time the idea of partitioning or sectoralising justice in such a way as to grant it to Catholics in one part of Ireland yet not in another seemed absurd, as indeed it was. The Catholic threat from Europe was long perceived to have subsided in the aftermath of Wellington's victory at Waterloo in 1815, and generally speaking British public opinion against Catholics was now somewhat relaxed. This is not to say that anti-Catholic sentiment no longer existed. It did, and the Orange Order in Britain and Ireland did its utmost to exploit this. However, there was a growing recognition that the continued repression of Catholics was unjust, and that their contribution to Britain's war effort ought now to be rewarded by granting them civil rights. It therefore seemed providential that Wellington the soldier statesman was now Prime Minister. As an Anglo-Irishman with much personal and political experience in Ireland, the 'Iron Duke' knew that, despite his innate high-Tory prejudices, the claims of the Catholic majority in Ireland, and also of the Catholics in Britain, would have to be satisfied. Wellington felt that he could persuade the King, with the crucial though ambivalent support of Sir Robert Peel who could lead the issue in the Commons, whilst he himself would do so in the House of Lords. There could have been no more effective parliamentary combination for the achievement of that most difficult reform.

When O'Connell convincingly won the Clare by-election in 1828 after openly campaigning for Catholic Emancipation, Wellington with typical pragmatism decided that he would have to act if civil war in Ireland was to be averted. He did so with skill and patience, finally overcoming George IV's inherited Royal opposition to Catholic relief. When passed, the Emancipation Act was not without criticism, but it was nevertheless surprisingly acclaimed and Wellington widely praised as 'the only man living who could have carried the measure'. As is often the case with long-deferred albeit justifiable reform, the main problem with Catholic Emancipation had been the lack of moral courage on the part of would-be reformers in the face of bellicose and often exaggerated criticism. But Wellington was not lacking in that department. And so yet another Orange objective, like its earlier defence of the ascendancy in Dublin Castle and its initial opposition to the Union, ended in defeat, the aftermath of which was marked yet again by outbreaks of serious rioting and murder in the North of Ireland. It seemed that neither its recent proscription nor the latest of its anti-Catholic failures had made for any fundamental change in Orange attitudes. The British could change, the world could change, but Orangeism would still believe in the maintenance of Protestant ascendancy.

The Twelfth of July demonstrations of 1830 were yet again marked by violence. A number of Catholic homes were burned at Gulladuff near Maghera, an atrocity that Orange historian the Rev. John Brown, incredibly for a minister of Christ, impassively dismissed by reiterating Orangeism's own contemporary version of the event – it was simply a case of 'the nest cleared out'.[5] However, the authorities viewed the matter rather differently and the Orange arsonists were transported to Botany Bay. Later that year the small Catholic village of Maghery was burned in reprisal for an attack on an Orange band in which some Protestant drums had been punctured. A village for a drum appeared to be the Orange idea of measured retaliation, but it was often much worse than that. In June 1831 the largely Orange Yeomanry, deputising for regular troops on duty elsewhere, responded to the taunts of a Catholic crowd in the Co. Cavan town of Newtownbarry by firing on them, killing seventeen people and wounding twenty. These violent events incurred the anger of the British government, and once again Orange demonstrations were outlawed, this time by the Party Processions Act of 1832. The Orange Order again sought a way around this proscription by holding the Twelfth celebrations on the mid-Ulster estates of gentry leaders such as Orange magistrates Blacker and Verner, but not with impunity, for these men were subsequently expelled from their positions on the Commission of the Peace.

Meanwhile, O'Connell, who was now in alliance with the Whigs, was unsuccessfully advocating repeal of the Act of Union. This incurred the ire of the Presbyterian leader Dr Henry Cooke who by dint of his earlier opposition to O'Connell's campaign for Emancipation had become a great hero of the Orangemen. Cooke was the principal speaker at the 'monster rally' called by Orangeman Lord Roden at Hillsborough on 30th October 1834 – a gathering of doubtful legality that was variously described as Conservative, Protestant and Orange. It was all three, being designed to unite 'Protestants of all sects in defence of their privileges and supremacy'. Privilege and ascendancy were principles of which Orangeism never felt reason to be ashamed. Though not exclusively Orange, the Hillsborough rally epitomised Orangeism. Dr Cooke, who was never an Orangeman, used the occasion to 'publish the banns of marriage' between Presbyterianism and the Church of Ireland for the purpose of a united stand against nationalism and its campaign for Repeal. Orangemen, who already enjoyed this union now that their ranks included lay Presbyterians, welcomed the 'marriage'. But the Presbyterian historian Finlay Holmes tells us that the Hillsborough proposal earned Cooke 'savage criticism' from within his own Church. Henry Cooke was a great man, who would have acknowledged the biblical truth that 'great men are not always wise'. We can but imagine the furore then or since if a Catholic bishop had made similar forays into politics.

Some apologists for Orangeism would credit Cooke and the Orange Order with creating an early catalyst for ecumenism. This is to ignore the fact that the proposed 'marriage' was essentially a union of sectarian interests, a matter of political expediency that, far from being ecumenical, was directed against Catholics and specifically designed to protect Protestant supremacy and narrow political privilege. It was a supreme irony, however, that this supremacy and privilege were now understood to be protected by the Union, whereas thirty years earlier Orangemen had regarded the Act of Union as detrimental to the Protestant ascendancy. Either way these supremacist attitudes were at the expense of a people whom the radical and egalitarian Presbyterians of 1798 would have been most happy to regard as their fellow citizens. Indeed, for a variety of reasons the whole Hillsborough episode was hugely embarrassing to many Presbyterian clergy. Whatever their views on Catholicism or the Union, these clergy were unhappy about making such close cause with the Church of Ireland and with the militant Orange movement that was so regularly at odds with law and order and with democratically elected government. Their fears were confirmed when other large demonstrations involving many thousands of marching and armed Orangemen took place in the weeks after Hillsborough.

In 1835, rumours were circulating about a serious Orange conspiracy within the British Army, involving the Duke of Cumberland, and which might even affect the succession to the British throne. The situation was serious enough to enable Joseph Hume to persuade the Whig government to set up two parliamentary select committees to investigate the Orange Order in Great Britain and Ireland respectively. The conspiracy theory was that the Orange Grand Master, the Duke of Cumberland, was plotting to depose his brother, King William IV, and thus succeed to the throne himself instead of his young niece Victoria. Germane to the thinking behind the theory was the notion held by some ultra-Protestants that Victoria was sympathetic to Roman Catholicism, and that a strong Protestant was needed to run the country. For the most part the speculation was regarded as lacking in credibility, and Orange apologists were subsequently happy to dismiss it as 'too insane to be true'. Yet too ready a rejection of the theory could screen out the fact that there had been other conspiracies that were true though also insane. It was not unreasonable to think that the mischievous and machinating 'damnable Duke' was neither above nor beyond that kind of crazy activity, as evidenced by his subsequent behaviour on becoming King of Hanover. Kevin Haddick-Flynn, who has painstakingly reviewed the evidence surrounding the conspiracy theory, eventually comes out against it.[6] My own view is that if there was no fire there was certainly a good deal of smoke. Probably the conspiracy was at least an incipient one, and at most ill-managed and abortive, but it had a significant aftermath.

A massive 4,500 page report by the Parliamentary Select Committee in 1836 found that the Irish Yeomanry (to nobody's surprise) was controlled by the Orange Order. It also found that the British Army harboured many Orange lodges that had been established by military warrants signed by a field marshal – none other than the Orange Imperial Grand Master, Ernest the Duke of Cumberland. As this practice was quite illegal and in contravention of War Office instructions the government had no alternative but to act. There was no further reference to any Cumberland conspiracy, but in August that year King William IV, much to the ridicule and discomfort of his brother, condemned secret societies and indicated his intention to 'prevent' them. Replying to an Address from the Commons in February 1836, King William declared that

> he would be pleased to take such measures as may seem to be advisable for the effectual discouragement of Orange lodges and generally of all political societies excluding persons of a different religious faith, using secret signs and symbols, and acting by means of associated branches.

The Orange leaders sought to down play the role of King William in this severe censure of Orangeism. They argued yet again the false constitutional doctrine that in giving expression to the will of parliament in his Reply to an Address, the King's words had 'no power to restrain the subject in the legal exercise of constitutional rights'.[7] But the Crown in parliament certainly did have the power to determine whether any given activity was constitutionally lawful. Indeed, given that the Orange Grand Master Cumberland had so over-reached himself, the Crown in parliament clearly had to take action. In repudiating secret political societies that exclude people of a different religion – to this day still a near perfect definition of the Orange Order – both King and parliament dealt a severe blow to Orangeism's exclusive and sectarian ascendancy principles. In so doing it struck at the very heart of Orangeism's erroneous constitutional doctrine. For although Orangeism was pledged to support the King so long as he remained loyal to what it saw as true Protestant constitutionalism, it had not reckoned on the King's government exercising its sovereign right to repudiate the Orange Order's outmoded and erroneous ideas on that very matter. The sovereign right of the Crown in parliament was and is the true British constitutional power, something that even the modern Orange arbiters of constitutional rectitude still cannot understand or accept.

Parliament's impact was immediate and decisive. The very next day the Duke of Cumberland advised the Home Secretary that he would dissolve the Orange Order in Great Britain, which he immediately did. Soon afterwards and amid great controversy, the Grand Lodge of Ireland also ignominiously decided to dissolve itself. Subsequently the 'damnable Duke' of Cumberland departed for Europe and became King of Hanover in 1837. Here the 'most mischievous fellow' promptly provoked a disastrous rebellion, which was put down with great difficulty and only with the help of several other European kings. Back in Ireland the abolished Orange Order now had a largely under-cover existence, although some Lodges continued to parade 'according to opportunity'. But many of the gentry and certainly all its dignitaries had now deserted the Order. Indeed, such now was Orangeism's notoriety that had been built up over the first forty years of its history – a sad record necessitating much proscriptive legislation, parliamentary enquiry, and finally dissolution on the intervention of King William himself – that it would take the next fifty years for it to recover.

County Armagh has nearly always been the focus for Orange dissidence, and it was the Armagh Grand Lodge that refused to acquiesce with dissolution, deciding to assume the leadership of Orangeism 'until the Grand Lodge of Ireland resumes its function'. This proved to be an uphill struggle. Although in

1837 the Grand Lodge of Ireland was reconstituted in Dublin under Grand Master Lord Roden of Tollymore it was, in the words of John Brown, 'not really able to guide and give cohesion to the remains of the institution'.[8] And so in default of an effective Grand Lodge of Ireland, the Grand Lodge of Ulster was formed on 12th February 1844. Soon thereafter, the expiry of the Party Processions Act led to a resurgence of marching in 1845, but Ireland was now beginning to suffer the horror of the Great Famine and the country entered a period of deathly quietness. Afterwards, and motivated by that disaster as well as by the Jubilee of the 1798 Rebellion, the 'Young Irelanders' planned a revolution for 1848. This turned out to be an abject failure, but it did serve to raise the sectarian temperature once again, as did the activities of some Catholic Ribbonmen (successors to the Defenders), all of which put the Orangemen back on the alert. Events were soon to prove, if proof were needed, that during the intervening years nothing had really changed.

Dolly's Brae, which has been deeply etched in the Ulster folk memory by one of the most sectarian of Orange songs, epitomises much of what constituted Orangeism's chief objective down the years – that of 'keeping the papists in their places'. In 1849 a number of local Orange lodges decided to march on 12th July from Rathfriland to Lord Roden's estate at Tollymore Park, set among the beautiful Mountains of Mourne. The chosen direction of the march was the cause of much local dispute and concern. This would start from the demesne of an Orange magistrate Francis Beers and by a circuitous and obviously provocative route lead through the Catholic townland of Magheramayo. That aspect of the proposed march greatly alarmed the government, and urgent but unsuccessful representations were made to the Orange leaders, who included magistrate Beers, to take the more direct and non-controversial main road that by-passed Catholic Magheramayo. However, as had often been the case previously, the authorities hoped that confrontation between rival sectarian groups could be prevented by a heavy presence of police and troops. These were now positioned at the pass of Dolly's Brae – the scene of earlier trouble.

The outward march of between 1,200 and 1,400 Orangemen, most of them armed and accompanied by carts that were presumed to conceal further supplies of arms and ammunition, drummed its imposing way to Tollymore Park, escorted by police, dragoons and magistrates. The magistrates who walked at the front included Francis Beers who for the disputed and dangerous part of the march carried his Orange badge and ribbon in his pocket. But all passed off peacefully, despite the presence on the Magheramayo hills of several hundred Catholic Ribbonmen, some of whom were armed and whose numbers increased during the course of the day. By late afternoon, when the homeward march of the Orange army with banners was about to begin, army officers were perturbed to learn that the Orangemen, many of whom had taken drink, had not been instructed by their leaders to take the safe and direct route back to Rathfriland. They intended to return the way they had come. One magistrate, Thomas Scott, told the subsequent Inquiry that he had pleaded with Francis Beers and Lord Roden to have the homeward march redirected: 'My Lord, if they wanted a triumph they had got it now; and why go back and run the risk of bloodshed?'[9]

Scott then reported that both his fellow magistrate Beers and Lord Roden washed their hands of any responsibility for the situation. Yet this was in circumstances where it had become quite obvious that the marching Orangemen intended to achieve a 'double triumph' – which, as will be argued in a later chapter, is what such marching is really all about. Meanwhile, as the Orangemen's homeward march proceeded by the same route as they had come, the Ribbonmen distanced themselves from the troops who still held the pass at Dolly's Brae and took their position on a hill overlooking the road. When the Orangemen reached the Brae, a leader of the constabulary spoke to each file as it passed, urging them 'to pass on quietly and not to fire a shot, even for fun'.[10] Suddenly there was a loud bang, like a firework, apparently from the front of the march, which immediately triggered a blazing shoot-out on all sides. Immediately identifying with the Orange marchers, the constabulary took to the hill and opened fire on the Ribbonmen, who quickly broke off the engagement and beat a rapid retreat.

Although the general encounter was quickly over, and despite orders from the police, military and magistrates to forbear, the Orangemen followed in hot pursuit firing what were later described as hundreds of shots. In the process of the running cross-country fracas Catholic homes were attacked and burned, and the subsequent government inquiry estimated that at least thirty Catholics had been killed. One week later, Francis Beers' brother William, also a magistrate and Orange Grand Master of Down, attended a celebration dinner in nearby Downpatrick. With great insensitivity, especially so soon after the killings, Beers made a triumphalist speech in which he coined the phrase that would later resound in sectarian song. That phrase was 'Dolly's Brae no more' – because the Orangemen had renamed the Brae 'King William's Hill' to commemorate the Orange victory. The following is a verse of the song.

> And when we came to Dolly's Brae
> They were lined on every side,
> Praying for the Virgin Mary to be their holy guide.
> We loosed our guns upon them and
> We gave them no time to pray.
> And the tune we prayed was the Protestant Boys
> Right over Dolly's Brae.

One outcome of the tragic episode, which even John Brown recognised as 'the failure of 1849',[11] was that the Orange leaders Lord Roden, William Beers and his brother Francis were summarily dismissed from their positions on the commission of the peace – now a fairly standard punishment for errant Orange leaders. In his detailed report on the Inquiry, Walter Berwick QC wrote:

> … all I do mean to say is this, that the Orange body is an exclusive body, plainly opposed to the Roman Catholic body in that county, and looked upon them as an enemy; and the magistrate of the State is bound to hold the scales of justice impartially, and free from all bias, between the Protestant and Roman Catholic subjects of this country; and those who believe that an administrator of the law should not only act fairly, but guard himself from all cause of suspicion by placing himself in a state of perfect neutrality between

the accuser and the accused, which alone gives confidence and weight to his acts, will readily admit that the magistrate should not voluntarily place himself in the anomalous condition of belonging to a body, many of the members of which are engaged in frequent collision with a large class in the State, between whom he is constantly called on to stand as umpire, and of whose misdeeds towards each other he is sometimes the only judge.

Berwick then made the following recommendation:

> ... there is one matter for sincere congratulation on which all parties who came before me appeared perfectly unanimous; I refer to a strong feeling evinced by all, of the necessity of putting an end for the future to all party processions whatsoever, and thereby terminating the disgraceful occurrences so constantly resulting therefrom ...

The outcome of all this was yet further anti-Orange legislation in the form of the new Party Processions Act of 1850.

For years after Dolly's Brae, rural Ulster was relatively quiet. At this time small farmers came under the influence of the Tenant Right Movement that had been established in 1847 to press for land reform and to protect the interests of tenant farmers against the landowners. Presbyterian and Catholic farmers, supported by their clergy, joined together under the banner of that Movement. In the longer term their work, together with that of the later Land League, would be rewarded by Gladstone's beneficent Land Acts – developments that would be warmly welcomed by Protestant farmers of all denominations, despite the vigorous and self-interested opposition of the Orange landlord leadership. During these intervening years of the land struggle, the land movement served as a counter-weight to Orangeism, which for many Presbyterian farmers, whatever its other attractions might be, was far too strongly associated with landlordism and with the Church of Ireland ascendancy interest.

But this was also a time of retreat from the countryside as thousands, driven by eviction, poverty and hunger, made their hopeful way to the rapidly growing and industrialising Belfast. This process, which has been described by some historians as 'modernisation', gave rise both to geographic mobility and social dislocation. These things brought significant changes to the demographic and political landscape of north-east Ulster. In the late eighteenth century Belfast had been the centre of Presbyterian radicalism and was known as the Athens of the North. But by 1861 due to industrialisation it had become a mixed and very different city, a large Catholic and Church of Ireland influx from mid and west-Ulster reducing the now considerably de-radicalised Presbyterian proportion of the population to only one-third. The problems of mid-Ulster were now about to be visited upon Belfast.

Demographic and politico-religious changes of this magnitude were bound to bring such developments in their train, and the rapidly expanding and now religiously diverse city soon became divided along what has been described as 'seismic' sectarian lines. This led to the growth of an urban Orangeism that hitherto had not been strong. However, according to David Miller membership of the Orange Order in Belfast even now stood at only one-tenth of the male

Protestant population, whereas elsewhere throughout Ireland that proportion was more like one-quarter. A possible explanation for this variance is the social and geographic dislocation that was created by urbanisation. This produced substantially different socio-economic conditions, which provided working men with more diverse and perhaps more interesting social distractions than those of the rural Orange lodge. Another possible explanation is that the 'special relationship' between rural Orangemen and their Tory gentlemen leaders was not so readily replicated in the urban situation. Belfast's civic leadership was still substantially Presbyterian and, although now much de-radicalised after the failure of '98, it was still largely Liberal and as yet not given to Orangeism.

Nevertheless, the Order continued to grow and did its utmost to provide a focus for its people, underpinning the Orange perception as to the importance of Protestantism's covenanted role in Ireland. Orangeism increasingly exemplified the significance of what David Miller has called 'public banding' and the need for solidarity to a wider urban Protestant community now living and working in much closer proximity to Catholics than ever before. In that respect Orangeism was able to exert an influence and leadership far beyond the bounds of its own membership. Indeed, it could now be perceived as a diffuse belief system – an 'ism' that transcended the actual membership of the Order itself. Examples of such an Orangeism include the various loyalist organisations both then and now whose memberships partially overlap with that of the Order. There were also those individual Protestant leaders such as Henry Cooke and erstwhile Ian Paisleys who, though not in membership of the Order, could be regarded as sufficiently 'Orange' or ultra-Protestant to qualify for invitations to speak at important Orange or pan-Orange demonstrations. Later on Edward Carson could also be included in that category, if in fact he was not an Orangeman – an interesting question we shall address in a subsequent chapter.

One sinister outcome of urbanisation was the incidence of the large-scale and prolonged sectarian disturbances that were to become known as the Belfast riots, the first of which with due sense of occasion broke out on 12th July 1857. (There were many riots before 1857, but these were different in scale and intensity.) Such riots would recur often during the years that followed, and have continued on and off right up to our own time, regularly resulting in heavy loss of life and serious damage to property. Jonathan Bardon tells us that the riots of 1864, 1872 and 1886 alone resulted in more deaths than all the nationalist risings of the nineteenth century put together.[12] The British press often described these disturbances as 'Orange riots', something the Order was at great pains to deny. But in 1857 yet another government Committee of Inquiry came out strongly against the Order and found that:

> It was plainly shown that the happening of outrages at the period (July 12) was a matter of usual occurrence ... The celebration of that festival is plainly and unmistakably the originating cause of these riots.[13]

Differing views as to the culpability of Orange marchers are still with us, and the truth often still hinges on the distinction between direct and indirect cause. The Orange Order has argued, sometimes rightly, that its members were not directly involved in a given disturbance. Yet in many such instances the Order chooses to ignore the fact that the very nature and objective of its marching, the bearing and behaviour of its marchers or bandsmen, and the sensitivities of the chosen route were often the indirect cause that led to violent reaction. This could readily lead to riot and mayhem involving Catholics either directly with the marchers themselves or, more often, with the Protestant camp followers who in a general sense could readily identify themselves with the religio-political sentiments and objectives implicit in the wider Orange public band. In time this broad Protestant public sympathy with Orangeism would find fuller expression in an Orange political party, then later in that party's private army, and ultimately in an Orange-unionist government with its own legalised security forces within the ambit of an Orange state.

As already mentioned, one effect of social modernisation was the changing of the political landscape, as people came together in the urban situation. This involved a broadening of political participation, a process that contributed to and was enhanced by the second Reform Act of 1867. The effect of the Representation of the People Act, which introduced household suffrage, was to enfranchise working class artisans and greatly increase the electorate. The impact of all this was not so great in Ireland as in England. Nevertheless it forwarded a process of reform that would eventually polarise Irish politics into two main camps – the Conservatives who would have a small majority in Ulster, and the Nationalists who would be much more predominant in the other three provinces of Ireland. It certainly worked to the immediate advantage of the Conservatives in Belfast where sectarian patterns were already well established, when they triumphed in the general election of 1868 at the expense of the local Liberals who were all but permanently wiped out. But the outcome of the election in Britain was very different, the Liberals acceding to power under the leadership of Gladstone who, although staunchly Protestant, commenced his first administration with a clear 'mission to pacify Ireland'.

In Ulster the combination of social change and political reform was to provide an opportunity for the populist appeal of hard-line Orangeism. A militant Orangeman William Johnston, on failing to achieve a Conservative nomination, stood as an independent and won a Westminster seat with the support of Belfast loyalists and the Orange and Protestant Working Men's Association. On 12th July the previous year, against the wishes of Grand Lodge and in violation of the Party Processions Act, Johnston had led a large Orange march in north Down, supported by other illegal Orange marches throughout Ulster. Johnston was jailed for a short time, but emerged a hero calling for the creation of an Orange political party and, as we have just seen, soon became an MP. People power, of numbers rather than property, and an increasingly sectarian working class, was beginning to assert itself. But so too was a great reforming British Prime Minister, who would embark of a mission that would eventually change the course of Irish history.

Conclusions

On any summation, the period 1801 to 1869 was a time of great infamy for Orangeism. The Order that allegedly stood for civil and religious liberty had ranged itself against the long-overdue justice of Catholic Emancipation and was opposed to any progressive idea that might benefit Catholics – even some, like Tenant Right, that would also benefit ordinary Protestants. On almost every issue it backed the wrong horse and, even where it did not, it eventually found that its favoured horse was running in a very different race from that which it had contemplated. The Act of Union was a case in point, for after initial opposition Orangeism eventually came to accept the Union under the British parliament because it saw this as the best means of maintaining Protestant supremacy – a strategy that was to fail in the long run. But throughout the period its objective of keeping the papists in their places, and the often brutal manner in which it went about this – as exemplified by Dolly's Brae and the recurring Orange riots in Belfast – were regularly to bring it into conflict with that British parliament.

By foolishly courting the patronage of the 'damnable Duke' of Cumberland, Orangeism ironically fell foul of an embarrassed King William. Time and again the Order that took pride in its loyalty to the Crown found itself at odds with the Crown in parliament, on the receiving end of parliamentary enquiry, censorious government report, proscriptive legislation, prohibitions on marching, and a legal requirement to revise its secret oaths and rules. In the end it was even subjected to the ultimate humiliation of dissolution. None of this was due to what, by any reasonable standard, could be described as the legitimate pursuit of politics or religion, but was the result of acts of extremism, scandal and sectarian atrocity. It was a tragic performance by an Order that professed 'the true religion' and gloried in its Williamite heritage of civil and religious liberty. But time brings change. By the end of the period there was such social, economic and political transformation that Orangeism would find itself in a radically new situation – one in which it could recover and find a new role, albeit one that was perfectly suited to its old ascendancy and supremacist ethos.

7.

1869 - 1894: Playing the Orange Card

One of Gladstone's earliest actions as Prime Minister was to disestablish the Church of Ireland, a measure designed to remove what he described as the 'bitter memories of ascendancy',[1] the very principle of which he thoroughly detested. In every respect a minority denomination, the Church of Ireland was nevertheless the established Church, whose upkeep was paid for by the tithes of the Irish people – a tax based on the tenth part of the increase from the lands, stock and personal industry of a poor and disaffected people. Worse than that, as was stated earlier, the established Church was one of the most corrupt parts of the corrupt Protestant ascendancy. This was exemplified by the staggeringly revealing protest of its own Archbishop Stuart against the appointment of Bishop Beresford of Kilmore. The Bishop's appointment gave effect to one of the deals that had been struck between the British government and the leaders of the Protestant ascendancy, in this case to buy off Beresford's father, the famous Dublin Castle Orangeman John Beresford, in return for his support for the Act of Union. The indignant Archbishop felt constrained to write with astonishing frankness, as follows:

> I have six bishops under me. Three are men of tolerable moral character, but inactive and useless, and two are acknowledged bad characters. Fix Mr. Beresford at Kilmore, and we then shall have three very inactive bishops, and, what I trust the world has not yet seen, three bishops in one district reported to be the most profligate men in Europe.[2]

Much more could be written about this travesty, but it will suffice to say that Gladstone was quite right when he described Irish Church establishment as a 'hideous blot' that needed to be expunged. The Orangemen did not see it that way. After Catholic Emancipation, the state Church establishment principle was virtually the last remaining legal element of the old Williamite ascendancy which, as we have seen, the Orange Order had originally pledged to defend. The established position of the Church of Ireland had been underpinned and carried forward by the Act of Union. The Orangemen and their supporters therefore regarded disestablishment as yet another outrage – 'a gross violation of solemn oaths, compacts and engagements'.[3] Indeed, it was also regarded, though rather oddly, as a surrender to popery. A 'church defence' campaign mounted by Orangemen and Church of Ireland clergy was supported by the Presbyterian leader Dr. Henry Cooke and also by a few of his ultra-Protestant colleagues such as the Rev. Hugh ('Roaring') Hanna. Significantly, unlike Dr. Cooke and unusually for a Presbyterian clergyman at that time, the Rev. Hanna took the opportunity to join the Orange Order.

For the most part the Presbyterians, apart from the ultras and Henry Cooke, stood aloof from a campaign that, as might have been expected, was not marked by any reasoned or compelling defence of the establishment principle. Some Presbyterian lay activists such as the public-spirited Liberal, Thomas Sinclair, took a strong and principled stand against the church defence campaign and, despite the influence of Dr Cooke, clearly won the day. The campaign, which soon degenerated into a ridiculous and unsavoury 'no popery' ranting match by the Orange party, was an attempt to defend the indefensible. It was as though disestablishment – the ending of a gross system under which a whole nation, including the Presbyterians, had been forced to support the ineffectual Church of a small minority – were some kind of popish plot to subvert Protestantism. This was utterly wrong, but it was worse than that, for the imaginary plot was alleged to have been planned and executed by the most religiously aware and conservatively Protestant prime minister the United Kingdom ever had. It was all such nonsense that years later the Orange and Church of Ireland historian, the Rev. S.E. Long, was to take a wholly different view when he wrote:

> With hindsight it can be argued that Disestablishment was a measure necessary to the well-being and peace of the country … The Church had no real title to its privileged position. Its membership was only eleven per cent of the population and many more than the politicians were agreed that it had failed so hopelessly in its mission that it could only be seen as the symbol of the supremacy of a privileged minority.[4]

This 'supremacy of a privileged minority' was precisely what the Orange Order had been founded to defend, and had been its very *raison d'être* for over three-quarters of a century. We may well think, therefore, that neither hindsight nor argument are necessary here, for despite all its privileges and alliances, or more likely because of them, the Church of Ireland had become an inwardly decaying Church with no effective mission outreach. What it did have was a privileged political role and a motivation that fitted well with Orangeism's objectives pertaining to Protestant ascendancy – hence the wholly misplaced and misguided Orange outrage at disestablishment. Yet again Orangeism's blind spot for the obvious and the predictable failure of its objective was due to its own fatally flawed fundamental principle. The Order had staked everything on the maintenance of an allegedly immutable constitutional idea, never mind how corrupt or indefensible that idea might be, or how misguided or impossible the principle of its permanence. Yet again the defence of Protestant ascendancy and the cleaving to 'whatever it was King William had established', had caused Orangeism and its supporters to pursue a course that ultimately could have had no other end than bitter defeat and disillusionment. It was the old, old story.

Orange disenchantment after disestablishment of the Church of Ireland ran very deep. Some Orangemen began to entertain serious doubts in regard to their continued loyalty to Queen Victoria, while others even flirted temporarily with the new idea of

Home Rule for Ireland – an incredible thing in the light of subsequent developments on that matter. The Home Rule Movement, which only really came to prominence after Ireland's disappointment with Gladstone's rather tentative first Land Act, would seek the restoration of an Irish parliament on a more democratic basis than hitherto – one that would take control over Ireland's domestic affairs, albeit within the Union. Some of those who were potential parliamentary supporters of Home Rule contributed to Gladstone's downfall in 1874, although the reason for that defeat had nothing to do with Ireland. So far as Gladstone was concerned even the principle of Home Rule was at that stage so lacking in definition that it had not become an issue of urgent importance in his mind. But he was beginning to think about it.

It was already an issue in Ireland. In the ensuing general election Ireland returned fifty-nine Home Rule MPs, providing the Irish Nationalist leader Charles Stewart Parnell with a strong parliamentary hand. Even though Parnell was a Protestant, this was the time the phrase was coined that would sloganise the great central issue for Unionism – 'Home rule is Rome rule'. Like all smart slogans this one was not lacking in simplistic clarity, but it was a grossly sectarian and scare-mongering misrepresentation, which had great potential for success in the Orange heartland of Ulster. Nevertheless, the next few years would be relatively uneventful, with Gladstone out of power until 1880. During this time the Conservative government showed little interest in Ireland – as was generally the case except on those occasions when the Tories sensed that Ireland might provide needed opportunity for the exercise of party interest.

The Irish Home Rule MPs were now pursuing a policy of agitation and obstruction at Westminster, where their leader Parnell[5] was fast emerging as a formidable parliamentarian. In Ireland most political interest focused on the land issue. A succession of wet summers, disastrous harvests and hard winters had given rise to another period of serious distress which, with starvation and evictions, seemed likely to replicate the disaster of the earlier great Famine. But this time the distress was accompanied by civil resistance, to which the government responded with severely repressive measures known as Coercion Acts. The Land League, established in 1879 under the presidency of Parnell, promoted solidarity among the small-holders who were seeking reform and opposing evictions. Parnell's policy quickly became the powerful cause of an oppressed and angry people. Supporters of the Land League pledged themselves to shun evicting landlords or those who co-operated with them, a practice that in 1880 became known as 'boycotting' when famously applied to Captain Boycott of Lough Mask House in County Mayo.

The strategy was to prove highly successful, and in the long run was to lead to land reforms that would be of considerable benefit to all the farmers of Ireland, whether Orange or Green. Yet even here the Orangemen would find themselves on the losing side of the argument. Firmly aligning themselves with Captain Boycott and against the Land League, the Order provided fifty Orange volunteers to travel to Mayo, where they camped out on Boycott's land, entertaining themselves at night by singing Orange songs and living on potatoes for which Boycott meanly charged the full market price. Eventually they succeeded in harvesting his crop, but only under heavy military protection – an uneconomic operation that cost £10,000 and therefore could not be repeated elsewhere. In the context of the land issue this Orange intervention was not an isolated incident, Orangemen having the previous year shot two people dead at a Land League meeting in Dungannon, County Tyrone. Indeed, just a few weeks prior to the Boycott episode hundreds of Orangemen, many of them armed, had attempted to wreck a Land League meeting at Saintfield, near Belfast.

There were exceptions to this Orange opposition, and some individual Orangemen were by now identifying themselves with the work of the League. This saw the beginnings of progress when Gladstone was returned to power in 1880 and introduced his first Land Act in 1881. Gladstone was later to admit that without the work of the Land League the reforms of that Land Act – and it might be added, of the other and more beneficent Land Acts that were to follow – would not have happened. Landlord and ascendancy-supporting Orangemen naturally remained opposed to the Land League, but once again their opposition proved politically futile. The physical distress, legal coercion and political mismanagement that Ireland had endured for so long had now radicalised many of its people, and raised their expectations. But Gladstone's first land reforms of 1881 were disappointing in that they did not abolish landlordism, and therefore neither satisfied the Land League's objectives nor pacified Ireland. So when agrarian agitation was stepped up, the government responded by introducing further coercive measures. These served only to create more unrest, especially in southern Ireland when Parnell was jailed, an episode that climaxed in the infamous Phoenix Park murders.

When released, Parnell once again managed to have Home Rule placed at the top of the political agenda by calling for an Irish parliament to legislate for Ireland. The combined effect of all this was to 'rouse the Orange blood' and to create a resurgence of sectarian feeling in Ulster, a not unusual situation which Parnell suddenly complicated when his party voted with the Conservatives on a rather trivial issue and brought down Gladstone's government. This turned out to be a master stroke, for the incoming Conservative government under Lord Salisbury, working closely with Lord Randolph Churchill who was now liaising with Parnell, abolished coercion in Ireland. Indeed, much to the annoyance of the Orange landlords, Salisbury introduced generous land reforms that were designed to 'kill Home Rule by kindness'. As it happened, there was more to Parnell's political stroke than the winning of those concessions. A few months later, in late 1885, the caretaker Conservative government was forced to call a general election, which Gladstone's Liberals won by a majority of eighty-six. But in Ireland Parnell's Irish Nationalist party had triumphed by winning eighty-six seats, thus holding a precise balance of power. Parnell, besides being the 'uncrowned king of Ireland', could now, by virtue of the parliamentary numbers, wield such power at Westminster as 'to ride in the whirlwind and direct the storm'.

The 1885 general election had placed the Home Rule question firmly centre-stage in Ulster, amid growing fears of Parnellism and of Gladstone's anticipated return to power. That election campaign renewed the Conservative-Orange coalition, as leading Orangemen like Edward J. Saunderson now came to the fore and sought to regenerate the Orange Order for its original paramilitary and political purposes. Colonel Saunderson had been a late convert. Coming from the wealthy landlord class in County Fermanagh, he had at one stage been a Liberal MP for County

Cavan. In those days he was strongly anti-Orange, and in the Commons debate on the Party Processions Act had scornfully described the Orangemen as 'people whose mania it was to beat drums and frighten papists'. However, in time to come he would epitomise those former Ulster Liberals who would change allegiance and become Orange-unionists, often of the most zealous kind. A Church of Ireland evangelical, Edward Saunderson changed direction in 1882 when he joined the Orange Order. He did so because as a landlord he had become greatly disturbed and angered by the success of the land agitation. Eventually he reached the conclusion that the Orange Order was the only organisation capable of resisting, by force of arms if necessary, the 'anarchy and rebellion' of Parnell's Land League. The new Orange convert took an early opportunity to outline his ideas for an Orange army at the 12th July Orange demonstration at Ballykilbeg that same year, declaring that:

> The duty of offering armed resistance to the authority of Mr Parnell and his followers would devolve in the first instance on the Orange Organisation, which occupies in regard to the Irish Loyalists very much the position the Army does to the civilians in England. As the Orange Institution had been organised with a view to confronting such a crisis as that by which we are now confronted, we could concentrate 50,000 men on any given point in Ulster with the very shortest possible notice.[6]

It is important to notice that Saunderson correctly identified the purpose for which the Orange Order had originally been established, and that his views were fully in line with the long established militant tendency and military connections of the Orange 'army with banners' which have been highlighted throughout this book. Following that speech the Colonel rose rapidly through the Orange ranks. He became Deputy Grand Master for Ireland two years later. In July 1885 he was adopted as an Orange-Conservative candidate for North Armagh, in the very heartland of Orangeism. His adoption attracted a few objections, some small farmers making reference to his relatively short Orange pedigree and to the fact that he was a landlord. The great irony, which had escaped the Portadown brethren, was that Edward Saunderson had only recently turned his coat and become an Orangeman precisely because of his landlord interest, and because he saw the Order as the means of protecting that interest. To put it bluntly, his policy was to deploy Orange force of arms to put down the Land League and the small farmers' opposition. One could speculate as to what the Armagh Orangemen might have done had they known the full facts and understood the *real politik* of the Colonel's mind. But such speculation would be futile, for in the end it was sectarian issues rather than class that decided the matter. On that score Saunderson's religio-political Orange credentials would prove more than sufficient, and his candidature therefore duly prevailed.

As to Saunderson's concern about the 'rebellious' actions of the land issue, time would show that he was not at all averse to the most rebellious activities so long as these were deployed to the advantage of his own class or cause. In fact it is difficult to escape the conclusion that his conversion to Orangeism was another case of the gentry using the Order to pursue its interests by militant means. This would become apparent in a very personalised manner when the new MP was variously nicknamed the 'Dancing Dervish' and 'Fighting Saunderson' because of the fiery temperament he could sometimes unleash on a startled House of Commons. In the course of one particularly violent brawl on the floor of the House between Irish nationalists and Tory unionists, the Colonel was observed to be the leading protagonist, laying about him right and left with great abandon, his coat almost torn from his back.

By 1888 Saunderson would be leader of the parliamentary Unionists. In fact, the military Orangeman was beginning to emerge as the first leader of the incipient unionist movement. He virtually created the position for himself by dint of a strong personal authority together with his deep involvement in, and influence over what has since been described as 'the trinity of Unionism' – the parliamentary party, the party network in the country, and the Orange Order.[7] In achieving this he would, by and in himself, establish the structural criteria for the future Unionist Party as well as the required qualifications for its leadership. As leader, Saunderson had come to see that the Orange Order was the essential force by which to resist Home Rule – now the real issue. This would necessitate it undergoing that military training, discipline and leadership which he intended to provide. Although, as we have seen, his primary concern had been the land struggle, this was never likely to become a seismic issue in Ulster. The popular Orangeism of the Protestant small farmers was now very ambivalent towards Orange landlordism, and the religio-political threat of Home Rule had become a much more important matter. Saunderson saw that for economic reasons the ordinary Orangemen were no longer prepared to be the landlords' lackeys, whereas Home Rule was the one great issue on which all Orange-unionists, and even the emerging Liberal-unionists, could share common cause against British liberalism and Irish nationalism. But on a personal level he never neglected to fight for the Irish landlord interest when opportunity presented.

Given the circumstances leading to Saunderson's meteoric rise so soon after his adoption as an Orange parliamentary candidate, it was not surprising that the general election, which in Ireland was fought on the anticipated Home Rule issue, should have produced an entirely sectarian result in Ulster. The Irish Nationalists returned seventeen Catholic MPs and the Conservatives sixteen Protestant MPs of whom twelve, including Saunderson, were Orangemen. The Ulster Liberals were wiped out. Hitherto they had supported Gladstone, but now they naturally associated him with the idea of Home Rule and blamed him for their electoral demise. There began a great defection to Orange-unionism, while other former Liberals would become Liberal-Unionists – a development that was occurring in Britain under the leadership of the great imperialist Joseph Chamberlain. The 1885 election marked the coming out of Orangeism as a major party political force in Ulster – a force that would become all the more potent as circumstances provided opportunity for stronger links with British Toryism. From that point onwards it would mutate into the Ulster Unionist Party, a committed Orange party under Saunderson's leadership and powerfully in league with the British Conservatives. Orangeism would then be on its way to getting its hands on the levers of power in the north east of Ireland, although the day of its ultimate political power there would still be some way off.

After the 1885 general election Parnell was supremely the key player in the larger context of Ireland as a whole. His Irish Nationalist Party had won a massive majority, and held the balance of power in Britain, where the Liberals formed the new government under Gladstone, who became Prime Minister for the third time in January 1886. This was against the background of rumour that he had already decided to introduce a Home Rule bill. Now that Parnell and the nationalists held the whip hand at Westminster they could give great impetus to a Home Rule policy that by a vast majority had been mandated by the people of Ireland. Most striking of all, a majority of MPs returned even by the nine counties of Ulster had supported this policy – seventeen nationalists to sixteen unionists. Ireland had spoken, and spoken clearly. There were, however, still lingering doubts at Westminster as to Gladstone's precise intentions on the matter, although the besieged Orange-unionists, who never ceased to man the watchtowers of Ulster, did not entertain any such doubts. They believed they knew what was coming, and girded their loins in readiness.

Despite the jingoism that was rampant in Britain at that time, Gladstone was far from being a committed imperialist. Indeed, he was far-sighted enough to envision a glimmering of sunset on an already overstrained empire when, writing in 1878, he presaged the future dominance of the USA. The concept of Home Rule for Ireland could therefore come much more readily to a Liberal 'Little Englander' than to a Tory imperialist. William Gladstone's mind was now clearly moving in that direction. According to Roy Jenkins, he saw that

> the maintenance of the liberal state was incompatible with holding within its centralised grip a large disaffected community of settled mind. The result of the 1885 election convinced him that the Irish mind was settled. The turn of the year convinced him that the Tories would do nothing. As in almost all crises after the days of Peel, they preferred party unity to national interest.[8]

But the Protestant mind of Ulster was also disaffected. Before Gladstone could make any public move, the Ulster Conservatives launched a province-wide campaign against Home Rule, which culminated in a 'Monster Meeting of Conservatives and Orangemen' in Belfast's Ulster Hall on 22nd February 1886.

The meeting was addressed by the brilliant, but mercurially erratic thirty-six year old Lord Randolph Churchill (father of Winston), whose short career might have epitomised the biblical Reuben – 'unstable as water, he shall not excel'. On his way to the Belfast meeting Churchill had already made history by uttering the words that were to become a famous Conservative-Orange slogan, 'Ulster will fight, and Ulster will be right'. This, of course, was fully in accord with the seditious thinking of the Orange leader Colonel Saunderson inasmuch as it suggested that, whereas a nationalist who would fight was a rebel, an Orangeman who would fight was right. This was to set the mood of the meeting. Never one to rein in on a dangerous or an outrageous idea, Lord Randolph Churchill whipped up his Ulster Hall loyalist audience in ninety minutes of powerfully emotive oratory. Fervently urging them to fight against Home Rule, he warned them that 'now may be the time to show whether all those ceremonies and forms which are practised in Orange Lodges are really living symbols or idle meaningless ceremonies'. Those ceremonies are very interesting, and we shall consider them at a later juncture.

Some commentators saw the speech as particularly objectionable, not only because of the extremity of its language and the inflammatory nature of its message, but also because its entire thrust represented such an excessive swing in Lord Randolph's own political pendulum. Not all that long before he had been close to Parnell and occasionally had given the impression of having Home Rule sympathies. He had also been contemptuous of the 'foul Ulster Tories'. Yet even allowing for his wildly oscillating and contradictory temperament, there had to be some significant motive behind all this. Perhaps the clue is contained in the even more famous phrase that Churchill also coined at the time, and which he recorded in a letter to a friend. This indicated that he had, in devising a strategic way forward for the out-of-office Tories, reached the conclusion that if Gladstone went for Home Rule 'the Orange card would be the one to play'. That epigram epitomised an approach to politics that was derived from one of his favourite mottos – 'shuffle up the cards and try again'. Lord Randolph Churchill seemed to regard politics as a game of chance in all the opportunistic and even random meanings of that word. As Roy Jenkins has graphically described him: 'Particularly on Ireland, he was like a door banging in the wind'.[9]

Lord Randolph Churchill once actually admitted that the Tory idea of democracy was 'principally opportunism',[10] an approach he probably first admired in one of the greatest of political opportunists Benjamin Disraeli. In this particular instance he was saying in effect that the best way to defeat Home Rule, and thus to ditch the Liberal government, was to exploit the opportunity to use the Orange Order with a view to stirring up the sectarian fears and prejudices of Ulster. That he was fully aware of the inherent dangers of his proposed strategy is clearly indicated by what he also said in the 'Orange card' letter referred to above, when he added his hope that it would 'prove to be the ace of trumps and not the two'.

There is no doubt that this principle (or lack of principle) governed much of Tory policy throughout the course of the Home Rule crisis, as will be demonstrated later. Yet this cannot furnish a complete explanation for all the Tory policy and practice involved. That great Tory patrician, Robert Cecil, the 3rd Marquis of Salisbury, whose administrations alternated with those of Gladstone for much of the period, was a doctrinaire intellectual who objected to Home Rule on grounds that extended far beyond those of mere opportunism. The Tories could therefore object to Home Rule for either opportunist or doctrinal reasons – or both. In fact, Lord Salisbury warmly congratulated Lord Randolph Churchill on his Belfast speech.

The response of the Ulstermen was also immediate and uncompromising. The Orange Order and the wider ranks of Orangeism now saw themselves as free to pursue what turned out to be the most politicised and significant objective in its entire history – a struggle that would last for more than thirty years. The Home Rule question would give Orangeism a major role in what Roy Jenkins, in the greater context of British politics, has described as 'one of the most powerfully fissiparous issues of the politics of the past two centuries'. But the errant Lord Randolph Churchill was destined to play little further part in the drama. He had long been in ill-health, which may have contributed something to his erratic and unstable behaviour, but this would soon be accentuated by the tragic and embarrassingly long process of losing his mind, culminating in his death from syphilis at the early age of forty-five.

The Orange historian, Rev. S. E. Long, who openly acknowledges what he describes as the Order's 'pre-1886 weaknesses', argues that the Home Rule issue transformed it by providing it with a membership that made it 'a highly respectable and exceedingly powerful religious political organisation'.[11] The Rev. Long appears to forget that for long periods during the previous hundred years Orangeism had been controlled, led and used by the ruling classes in Ireland, including his own class, the Church of Ireland clergy. He also fails to see that the allegedly now respectable Orange Order continued to engage in much the same activities as before. Fully in keeping with its paramilitary pedigree, it responded swiftly to Lord Randolph Churchill's call to fight by carrying out military and drilling exercises in the Orange halls of Ulster. And its leader, Colonel Edward Saunderson, who had once declaimed against the 'rebellious' Land League, now announced with breathtaking arrogance that the Orange lodges had been organised 'to offer armed resistance to any scheme to which they objected'.[12]

The now 'highly respectable' Orange Order, though still unreconstructed, continued to see itself as having the arbitrary right to oppose lawful government on any issue to which it objected, and even by force of arms. The Orange-unionist leader who, as we saw earlier, had boasted that the Order 'could concentrate 50,000 men on any given point in Ulster at the very shortest possible notice' was clearly playing with treason – the threat of armed rebellion against the Crown in parliament. Yet had such a statement been made by a nationalist leader, it would have called forth a ferocious storm of constitutional indignation, and a mighty clamour for the most rigorous application of the law. But as in similar subsequent situations Orangeism would justify itself by arguing that it was those who proposed the reform who were the real traitors. Home Rule was presumed to be unconstitutional and a sell-out of Protestant ascendancy interests. Extreme measures to resist it were therefore consistent with the Orange doctrine of conditional loyalty – Orangemen would only be loyal so long as the Crown continued to support the Williamite principle of constitutional Protestant ascendancy and political supremacy in Ireland. It was therefore the old, old story. The Orangemen were at it again, but now they were being egged-on by the British Tories, for reasons both of opportunity and doctrinal right-wing belief.

The Tory leader Lord Salisbury believed that Ireland comprised two mutually antagonistic nations, and that the great representative institutions of government were 'only fitly bestowed upon a homogeneous people' such as the British. In making these statements he seemed to have forgotten his similarly pessimistic remarks on the 'great conflicts' and 'vast controversies' and even the 'state of bloodless civil war' that then threatened England. Like all the Orange-unionists then and since, Salisbury always overstated the case against Home Rule, arguing that the 'tremendous powers that have been granted in the past to the British people' could not be entrusted to the people of Ireland. This, of course, begged the question whether in fact Home Rule had ever intended such 'tremendous powers', a false assumption we shall examine later. It also ignored another question as to whether Ireland's divisions would continue if the ascendancy politics that gave rise to many of those divisions were removed.

Such questions simply could not occur to Lord Salisbury's patrician mind, preoccupied as it was with preserving Britain's ascendancy interests, and with resisting any loosening of her links with an increasingly restless empire. His brilliance of mind, combined with the reactionary nature of his mindset, had rendered him something of a political pessimist. Now and again this could break out in a cynical frustration that was expressed in what his critics have described as 'blazing indiscretions'. Then he would let the cat out of the bag by arguing, for example, that the Irish people, 'like Hottentots', were quite unfit to rule themselves. In the context of Ireland, he could even express regret that his government could not exercise the autocratic power of a Russian Tsar. In fact, in regard to the Home Rule question and its related religio-political issues, Lord Salisbury was firmly on the side of the ascendancy-minded Orangemen. Interestingly, his sympathetic biographer Robert Taylor has commented that 'the Stormont experiment in devolution between 1921 and 1972 demonstrates the harsh truth of Salisbury's analysis'.[13] This is quite wrong. Stormont's failure was not due to any reasons of that analysis, but rather because both the creation and crude conduct of its ultra-Tory governance were an anachronistic perpetuation of Salisburian ascendancy politics in the hands of Orangemen.

Home Rule was objectionable, not because it involved an Irish parliament, for the Orange Order had once pledged to defend the old Irish ascendancy parliament. It was objectionable because it would involve a devolved and democratic parliament which, although still within the Union, was representative of all the Irish people and in which the Protestants would no longer be in the ascendancy. On this basis Orange paranoia concluded that Home Rule was Rome rule. However, the Orange objection was even less well founded than that, for eventually when Home Rule was legislatively defined this amounted only to the very mildest form of devolution. According to historian Robert Kee, it was 'a fairly modest business',[14] while Jonathan Bardon says it was 'little more than control over the police, civil service and judiciary'.[15] However, what Gladstone had in mind is best described in his own words:

> ... the establishment, by Statute, of a legislative body, to sit in Dublin, and to deal with Irish and distinguished from Imperial affairs; in such a manner as would be just to each of the three Kingdoms, equitable with reference to every class of the people of Ireland, conducive to the social order and harmony of that country, and calculated to support and consolidate the unity of the Empire on the combined basis of Imperial authority and mutual attachment.[16]

Home Rule was therefore not the antithesis of 'attachment' within the Union nor, given its nature and limitations, could it properly be construed as any kind of rule at all, never mind Rome Rule. Sovereignty and the whole apparatus of imperial power would clearly continue to reside at Westminster. Years later, when a form of Home Rule actually did come into being, its scene of operation was Northern Ireland, where it was administered by unionists. Its legal basis was an Act of Parliament that contained a textual reproduction of the main provisions of the abortive Irish Home Rule Bill of 1912. Thus the Orange-card opposition to Home Rule involved a massive sectarian and scare-mongering distortion, which was repudiated by some Ulster Protestants and even by a few independent-minded

Orangemen at the time.[17] However, the old Orange-Conservative distortion still survives as a widely-held historical interpretation that continues to enjoy credibility in Ulster today, as we shall see later.

Home Rule as proposed could have been good for Ireland. An agreement along the modest lines proposed by Gladstone and eventually supported by the House of Commons could have changed the course of Irish history, especially given Parnell's statement that he would accept the terms of the Home Rule Bill as a final settlement. That statement was all the more powerful when taken with his argument that the best guarantee British ministers could have against separation would be 'the knowledge of the Irish people that it is in their power by constitutional means to make the laws which they are called upon to obey just and equitable'.[18] It is a great irony that at that time, and on the basis of those principles, Charles Stewart Parnell was not an all-or-nothing separatist, but technically a 'small u' unionist who would have accepted a limited form of devolved Home Rule government for Ireland under the aegis of Westminster.

It may be argued that the nationalist Parnell subsequently said other things – about separation and about Ireland's right to independence for example – but there is nothing necessarily contradictory in a politician having to consider other options for different contingencies. If the demands of a political party, supported by an elected parliament, are thwarted by extra-parliamentary means, then that party's position and policy must inevitably change. The circumstances and terms of the ultimately acceptable settlement must also change, and harden – a lesson that Orange-unionists have never learned. In such a situation blame must rest on those who in the first place stood in the way of the initially modest proposals for reform. Not that Parnell's political position ever changed very much, for he was no revolutionary, but a great parliamentarian who strove for reform. To the bitter end his more extreme Irish enemies, with ill-disguised reference to his adulterous relationship with Kitty O'Shea, could disdain him as soft and compromising, cruelly lampooning him as 'the featherbed Fenian'. However, the essential point is that in the day of his power Parnell would have accepted and could have delivered Home Rule, had it not been for Orange-Tory intransigence driven by sectarianism and party political opportunism. There is therefore a much greater irony than that of Parnell's politics, for in the end it was the much-vaunted unionism of the Orange-card, with its cynical party interest, which stood in the way of reconciliation with and within Ireland. It was the undemocratic and illegal unionist resistance to Home Rule that paved the way for partition and finally broke the Union, as we shall see later.

At the end of 1885 the Grand Orange Lodge convened a meeting of all the Conservative MPs in Ulster to organise resistance to Home Rule. A committee was soon established for that purpose called the Ulster Loyalist Anti-Repeal Committee, a development that underpinned the beginnings of 'Ulsterisation'. However, as matters turned out, the first Home Rule Bill was defeated due to a schism within the Liberals that resulted in Gladstone's fall from power. That schism of Liberal-Unionists was orchestrated by Joseph Chamberlain who, though a radical, was an anti-Home Ruler and a staunch imperialist who would later defect and become Colonial Secretary in a Tory-led government. The loyalists of Belfast celebrated

Gladstone's defeat by the bloodiest sectarian riots the city had ever seen. Such was their ferocity that it required some 5,000 extra police and soldiers to bring the killing and looting to an end. But Gladstone remained resolute. Instead of allowing his political fate to be determined by the vote of a recalled parliament he decided to resign quickly, because 'if there is to be an anti-Irish government the sooner it begins the sooner it will end'. It would be six years before he would again become Prime Minister, for the fourth and last time in 1892, but those intervening years saw the demise of Parnell and a debilitating division within Irish nationalism. In one sense, therefore, the threat of Home Rule appeared to have diminished. However, as the 1892 general election approached the Orange party, now beginning to call themselves unionists, became uneasy at the prospect of Gladstone making a further move.

A massive pre-emptive strike against Home Rule, in the form of what was called the Ulster Unionist Convention, was held on 17th June 1892 in a large purpose-built pavilion that had been erected with amazing speed near the Botanic Gardens in Belfast. Twelve thousand unionist delegates 'from all walks of life' attended, which ensured a strong Orange presence, although it is often claimed that the Convention's liberal and conservative delegates together showed 'the breadth of opposition to Home Rule'. Yet it is arguable that this 'breadth' should be understood in quantitative rather than qualitative terms, for Ulster liberalism had virtually been wiped out at the previous general election, and many Liberals, following in the footsteps of Saunderson, had now defected to Orange-unionism. These lapsed Liberals were now often far from liberal, and not for the last time in Ulster's sad history of 'I-used-to-be-moderate-but' politics, some had become overtly sectarian. A leading example of this was Major Fred Crawford. Of well-known Liberal stock, he was now a zealous Orangeman and soon to become one of Ulster's leading 'Home Rule is Rome Rule' rebels – in fact a gunrunner of Olympian prowess.

Thomas Sinclair, the chief organiser of the Convention, had once been a paragon of Irish liberalism. A successful Belfast businessman, he was a highly capable and committed Christian – the foremost Presbyterian layman of his generation. He was very politically aware, active and involved, having for years been a staunch supporter of Gladstonian liberalism, sharing the great man's zeal for social evangelicalism. He had strenuously opposed Irish landlordism, Irish Church establishment, and the Orange doctrine of Protestant ascendancy. In fact, he appeared to be the very model of the non-sectarian Presbyterian radical, and stood like a tower against the political conservatism of fellow churchmen such as Henry Cooke and 'Roaring' Hanna. But Thomas Sinclair was appalled and disillusioned when it appeared that Gladstone was moving towards a policy of Home Rule for Ireland – especially when as a result, and usually depending upon sectarian choice, many Irish Liberals began to defect either to Saunderson unionism or to Parnell nationalism. Sinclair responded to these developments by creating the Ulster Liberal Unionist Association in 1886, his supporters taking the view that they could still claim to be socially liberal though now constitutionally unionist in the context of their opposition to Home Rule. However, in the new circumstances the nature of their liberalism inevitably became a moot point. This is still an interesting and instructive matter, and important questions about Sinclair's liberalism may be usefully explored by reference to his statements and responses made during the course of the long-running Home Rule issue.

From that point onwards there can be little doubt that Sinclair's liberalism was slowly but steadily diluted by his unionism. He often had to challenge, and sometimes had to rebut, charges of sectarian and supremacist politics, for as the Liberal-Unionist leader he had now chosen to work might and main alongside the greatest zealots of 'Home Rule is Rome Rule' politics. In the course of this he could scarcely avoid being touched by sectarianism, and occasionally it showed. In his campaigning, for example, he could advert to arguments about the inferiority and illiteracy of the Catholic supporters of Home Rule. Once, in addressing a meeting in Glasgow, he likened a Home Rule parliament in Dublin to a transfer of Glasgow business interests to a Scottish legislature swamped by Highland crofters. His logic suggested that, like the illiterate and feckless Irish, the Scottish crofters were Catholic, inferior and entirely unfit to rule. In this regard Sinclair's politics were wrong not only in principle, but also in fact – although he was not to know that the Highlands and Islands, like the bogs of Ireland, would soon produce statesmen of the very highest class. But be that as it may, the above statements were clearly consistent with Thomas Sinclair's general position on Catholicism *vis-à-vis* the Home Rule question.

If these responses to Home Rule did not reflect the sectarian politics of Protestant ascendancy they came very close to it, suggesting the politics of a superior and separate Protestant hegemony. Sinclair was an early adherent to the idea of a separate Ulster-Scots identity – an idea that would later mutate tortuously into an 'Ulsterisation' based on the divisive 'two nations' theory. This assumed ethnic, national and, of course, religious differences that would eventuate in a sectarian partitioning of Ireland. Yet in many ways Thomas Sinclair epitomised the very best in the Ulster Presbyterian character – that of the upright and generous Christian man who would have abhorred the very idea that he could be regarded as sectarian. After all, he was utterly without ill-will towards his Catholic neighbour, to whom he often showed great kindness, and was known to work closely with individual Catholics on civic and business committees. This did not tell the whole story, however, for politically speaking and because of an Orange-like detestation of the Roman Church, he could not regard the broad Catholic community as trustworthy. Considered collectively, or in the context of shared government responsibility, he could not accept Catholics as full and equal fellow-citizens. It is therefore difficult to escape the conclusion that he bore a paternalistic and patronising attitude towards them – a far cry from the radical Presbyterian egalitarianism of a hundred years before.

Sectarianism comes in various and subtle guises, and often stops short of hatred or violence. Apparently benign cultural or religio-moral 'truth claims' can extend legitimate difference to the point of dangerous division – to superior ideas of an exclusive separateness that will do sectarianism's work much more effectively than the crude efforts of the mob. Whatever we may think about Sinclair, there were things in his psyche that prevented him from regarding Catholics as fellow citizens after the manner of the United Irishmen – hence his refusal to work with them in a limited Home Rule parliament within the Union. This led the former Gladstonian Liberal to throw in his lot with the Orange-unionist rebels and the former-Liberal gunrunners. He would soon become the leading intellect in the anti-Home Rule movement, organising the Ulster Convention and years afterwards drafting the Ulster Covenant. It therefore ought not to be concluded, as some modern commentators have done, that Thomas Sinclair's brand of Liberal Unionism somehow gave liberal respectability or democratic validation to Ulster's great anti-Home Rule Movement. In one cosmetic sense it did, inasmuch as it provided it with links into British Liberal-Unionism led by Joseph Chamberlain, but in the turbulent Ulster context that liberalism would quickly be diluted by, and absorbed into Ulster unionism. In the end, to adapt John Milton's famous hyperbole, the new Liberal-unionism seemed to be the old Orange-unionism writ large.

While the massive Ulster Unionist Convention organised by Sinclair was taking place, supporters estimated at three hundred thousand gathered outside in the Botanic Gardens where several after-meetings were held later in the day. There were no bands, party songs, or the other normal features of an Orange demonstration. The Convention Hall's carefully orchestrated religio-political proceedings, suitably restrained by the religious element, were summed up by the clarion call of the Orange chairman, which was repeated three times by the audience – 'We will not have Home Rule!' Thomas Sinclair made the speech of the day, but although at pains to deny sectarianism – always a sore point with a Liberal-Unionist – he indulged in some heavy Protestant rhetoric, and his allusions to William's revolution had the Orangemen cheering wildly. Clergy from the main Protestant denominations also spoke, scripture was read, prayers said and a psalm was sung. God was therefore presumed to be on the side of Protestant Ulster, which appeared to regard itself as the exception to Christ's teaching that his kingdom was apolitical and not of this world. However, the Convention did succeed, for a time, in providing the anti-Home Rule campaign with a respectable image, and showed that Edward Saunderson's Orange 'army with banners' could behave itself when it was expedient to do so.

Gladstone remained unmoved. He knew too much Christian theology to be influenced by Orange and Liberal-unionist declarations of a narrow theocratic doctrine that was as ill-founded as it was sectarian. No doubt he was impressed by the Convention's display of respectability and restraint, but he remained unconvinced of its case. His mind was as made up on the necessity for Home Rule as was Ireland's own 'settled mind' on the issue. He was not one to be easily moved by demonstrations however large, because as a man with a moral mission he relied on the moral argument. He knew that on the numerical criteria the nationalists could virtually match the unionists in nine-county Ulster and out-number them by far in greater Ireland. In the wider United Kingdom the unionists were also in the minority, as the forthcoming general election would show. At almost eighty-three Gladstone became Prime Minister for the last time in 1892, and placed his second Home Rule Bill before the Commons.

The 'powerfully fissiparous' issue was once again at the very forefront of British politics. A long and acrimonious parliamentary debate rolled on, and Orange-unionist demonstrations continued throughout Ulster, often supported by the presence of leading British Conservatives and establishment figures still playing the Orange card. However, the second Home Rule Bill eventually passed the Commons by a majority of thirty-four on 1st September 1893. One week later and after only four short days of debate the Lords rejected the Home Rule Bill, even though this was the main plank of the government's programme and despite the fact that the Commons had spent no fewer than eighty-two working days on it. The Lords rejected it by a vote of 419 to 41. This was unprecedented both in the strength of the vote and the size of the majority, even though the issue harboured what Roy Jenkins describes as 'no incentive of uncertainty' such as would necessitate so many Tory backwoodsmen rallying to the standard in distant London.[19] The response of the Lords was seen by many as a political outrage – a travesty of constitutional democracy even by the lesser standards of those days – in consequence of which William Gladstone finally retired from office 'all passion spent' in March 1894.

In perpetrating that travesty the British establishment had unwittingly communicated a sharp message to the Irish protagonists on either side of the Home Rule issue, a message which as communicated was the same in both cases, but which as received lay couched in very different responses and contradictory attitudes. In short, the message was 'distrust the British'. That distrust would eventually push elements of nationalism into a much stronger political philosophy, leading to extra-parliamentary action. And it would further alert unionism, which was already more than half-way there, to prepare for a final stand against the probability that the House of Lords would not get away with such a veto the next time a Home Rule Bill came around.

Conclusions

During the Gladstone era Orangeism's misguided ascendancy principles were to lead it astray on issues that, had it possessed a modicum of political judgement let alone vision, it should never have fought. It suffered great disillusionment and defeat on both Church and land questions, in regard to which there is now agreement, even by Orangeism's own historians, that it misjudged those issues very badly. Worse than that, it allowed itself to be misled both by self-confessed opportunism and by patrician Tory doctrinaire politics, both of which fitted well with Orangeism's ascendancy agenda. Thus the Orangemen were encouraged to misunderstand and misrepresent the nature and extent of Gladstone's Home Rule policy, to the extent that 'Ulster would fight and Ulster would be right'. The effects of this were not confined to the Orangemen, for many Ulster liberals became unionists and, in effect, subtle and respectable sectarians, arguing that 'Home Rule is Rome Rule'. Thus the modest concept of Home Rule was exaggerated into a scare-mongering and fractious issue that would have far-reaching and dangerous consequences for all the people of these islands.

This destroyed any chance of a settlement that might conceivably have preserved the Union and won the support of Parnell, thereby changing the course of Irish history. Instead, Orangeism allowed itself to become a mere 'card', to be exploited as need arose by unprincipled political poker players for electoral ends, which years later an embittered and disillusioned Edward Carson would come to realise, and be man enough to acknowledge in a most public and unqualified manner. At this point, however, the Orangemen would continue to follow the fighting Colonel Edward Saunderson who, in his earlier days as a Liberal MP had scorned the Orangemen's 'mania to beat drums and frighten papists'. Now as their leader he would do his utmost to out-rebel the rebels he condemned, training and drilling his Orange army to a much more manic and frightening end, as time would show.

8.

1894 - 1914: Irish unionism versus 'little Ulster' unionism

As the Home Rule issue receded there was a sense in which Irish politics entered the political doldrums, the post-Parnell nationalists remaining seriously divided and the Orange-unionists continuing to be led by Fighting Saunderson until his death in 1906. Saunderson was succeeded by the gentle and genial Walter Long MP, an English Tory squire whose political career had included several ministerial offices, one of which had been Chief Secretary to Ireland, and of whom it was said that his most notable legislative achievement was the compulsory muzzlement of dogs. Walter Long, who was invited to become leader whilst on a golfing visit to Royal Portrush, was to lead the Unionist Parliamentary Party until 1910, the year of the next Home Rule crisis. During this hiatus in the Home Rule issue nothing happened that could compare with the momentous events of the Gladstone era, but nevertheless there were two quite interesting developments. One, to which we have already alluded, was that Orangeism was increasingly given political expression by an emerging Ulster unionism, as Irish conservatives, former liberals and the Orange Party gradually evolved into the Unionist Party. Obviously there was a powerful affinity between the political objectives of Orangeism and those of unionism, although it should be noted that, despite their links, the Orange Order and the Unionist Party were, and are, separate though over-lapping organisations. There always have been unionists, probably more in number now than was formerly the case, who have sought to distance themselves from what they saw as Orangeism's inherent sectarianism, and who believe that unionism would be better served if it were to dislodge the Orange element from its public persona.

The other development was the tremendous progress made on the Irish land question. During the years 1896 to 1909 the British parliament passed a series of Land Purchase Acts under which Irish tenant farmers could become owners of the land they farmed by means of long-term mortgages at low rates of interest. In fact these measures were so successful that by 1920 over eleven million acres, most of the land in Ireland, had changed hands, which obviously was greatly to the benefit of its people and not least the Orange farmers of Ulster. However, we have already seen that the Grand Orange Lodge had previously set its face against land reform and against the work of the Land League, preferring landlordism to the needs of the people, in which respect it generally acted contrary to the best interests of its own rural members.

Once again Orangeism failed to learn from its mistake. Always true to their class, the Orange-unionist leaders in parliament had opposed the land purchase measures, and during one stormy debate Colonel Saunderson had expressed the view that there seemed to be

> a common agreement between the bitterest enemies of England and ministers of the Crown that the proper thing to secure the peace, happiness and prosperity of Ireland was to sweep away the very class who had been the strongest supporters of Great Britain in Ireland.[1]

Nowadays few would doubt that it was the proper thing to do. But one who did was the young Sir Edward Carson, Unionist MP for Dublin University. A brilliant and highly motivated lawyer, Carson had been appointed Solicitor-General of Ireland in 1892 following his unpopular, but in a sense courageous work as a Crown prosecutor. In this role he was perceived as doing the British government's dirty agrarian work for it, and for which the Irish nicknamed him 'Coercion Carson'. He subsequently practised at the English bar, and was appointed Solicitor-General of England in 1900, being knighted that same year. Sir Edward Carson the parliamentarian was now highly regarded in British Conservative circles and, given his earlier work, had also become the darling of the Irish Tory landlords. He had therefore supported Colonel Saunderson in opposing the land measures. In speaking to the issue, Carson supposed that

> the government were revolutionists verging on socialism. I ask myself whether they are mad or I am mad. I am quite sure one of us is mad.[2]

The ordinary farmers of Ulster certainly did not believe the government was mad, nor that they themselves were mad for refusing to ignore their own economic interest. But even if they had considered Carson to be mad this was soon forgotten once the land issue had been settled to their advantage. To the discriminating rural mind of the Protestant Ulsterman the great Carson would be useful on other issues, but on the land issue their verdict and that of history would be that, though far from mad, his judgement here was seriously flawed. And so Orange-unionism, as represented both by Saunderson its first leader and Carson who was to become its greatest hero, had again pursued a bad policy that ultimately was inimical to the interests of their own people and destined to fail. Thus another Orange objective was added to its catalogue of failed policy objectives, although like the rest of those failed policies this would quickly and conveniently be forgotten.

The Orange-unionists of Ulster used this period of hiatus in constitutional politics to take stock and to strengthen their organisation. A communications network was established throughout Ulster, which was based essentially on the local Orange lodges and Orange halls. In 1904 there occurred perhaps the most significant development yet in the embryonic 'Ulsterisation' process. This was the creation of a new governing body for unionism named the Ulster Unionist Council, whose main focus and emphasis was clearly on Ulster and not on Ireland as a whole. At that time the Council comprised not more than 200 members, of whom 50 were directly nominated by the Orange Order, but many of the other 150 members also happened to be Orangemen. This 'Ulster' emphasis was to some extent an outcome of the socio-economic modernisation process referred to earlier. Unionism throughout the rest of Ireland continued to be dominated by Church of Ireland landlordism, whereas the industrialisation of Ulster had strengthened an already significant Presbyterian mercantile and manufacturing class, whose interests and concerns were mainly those of the businessman and the industrial employer. To these modern entrepreneurs the enemies most to be feared were interfering government and organised labour – and the socialism they believed to motivate both. The unacceptability of an interfering Roman Catholic Church was, of course, taken as read.

Ulster's industrialists and entrepreneurs were therefore concerned about current political issues such as the uncertainties surrounding the Home Rule question and its possible future impact on business. They also had reason to be concerned about the activities of the new breakaway Independent Orange Order with its trades union sympathies, at a time of great industrial unrest occasioned by the Belfast labour disputes of 1907. The Orange schism had occurred in 1902 when Tom Sloan, a shipyard worker and ultra-Protestant preacher, was suspended by the Order. This was both for publicly heckling Colonel Edward Saunderson, whom he regarded as weak, compromising and insufficiently Protestant, and for standing soon afterwards as an Independent and defeating the official Orange-unionist candidate in a by-election following the death of the famous William Johnston MP. (Ironically, Johnston himself had initially been a rebel who had successfully stood as a dissident Independent.) Sloan and his evangelical friend, the strongly anti-Catholic Lindsay Crawford, thereupon rebelled against what they regarded as the crass weakness and class injustice of Orange-unionist officialdom, and in 1903 established the Independent Orange Order. In that independent capacity they considered themselves to represent the loyalist working-class interest – a kind of sectarian would-be socialism that now exists under many guises in Northern Ireland today. It is interesting to observe the changes that the 'I Double O' has undergone since its origins. After a few years Lindsay Crawford developed pronounced Liberal tendencies and began to flirt with Home Rule, for which he was expelled from the Independent Orange Order, whereupon he emigrated to Canada and became an Irish republican. Tom Sloan's position was also inconsistent and uncertain – a representative working-man whose politics were sectarian and more Tory than they were working-class, but whose individualist-based Protestant fundamentalism made him distrustful and independent of the ruling ascendancy class. His politics therefore presaged the rise of Paisleyism and the disputes that would rend 'big house' unionism in the 1960s. When Sloan lost his seat in 1910, the IOO went into steep decline, although it has now staged something of a recovery due to the unionist schisms of more recent times. Nowadays, the one thousand strong IOO is in most respects conservative. Like the Rev. Ian Paisley MP who if not a member certainly gives it his patronage, it is slightly leftist on social policy, strongly rightist on the constitution, and stolidly fundamentalist in religion.

At the beginning of the twentieth century socialism, real or imaginary, was utterly unpalatable to the Ulster business class who naturally identified with the Conservative leadership both of official Ulster unionism and of the official and main-stream Orange Order. Together they perceived a common class interest, and an urgent need to organise, combine and stand together. This task was skilfully co-ordinated and achieved by an up-and-coming Orange politician and wealthy businessman, Captain James Craig. Craig later would also seek to give the impression of encouraging working-class organisation, but shrewdly only under an Orange-unionist rather than a Labour Party aegis. And so the Ulster Unionist Labour Association (UULA) was established, a loyalist working-class organisation that Craig would later profess to hold in higher esteem than even the Orange Order itself. However, given their common ground and largely overlapping memberships, there was little to choose between them in terms of what Orange-unionism deemed desirable. James Craig had therefore no need for preference, and no need to choose – he had them both. In achieving this he had spiked the guns of the Independent Orange Order and weakened Labour.

The entrepreneurial modernisers of Ulster regarded themselves as having very little in common with the rest of Ireland, in which they had no substantial business or political interest. Given their roots in industry and commerce, they had no real empathy with rural Irish landlordism either. Increasingly, therefore, they saw themselves not so much as Irishmen who believed in unionism but more as Orangemen and unionists who believed primarily in Ulster. This sat easily with that sense of elective advantage, if not superiority, that was inherent both in their Calvinism and in their concept of Ulster as the 'Imperial Province' with its important trade links into the proud and mighty British Empire. On such ground Thomas Sinclair's Liberal-unionism and Orange-Toryism could readily coalesce. It was therefore unthinkable to these men that they should ever submit to a Home Rule parliament that would be controlled by a Catholic majority and rule them from Dublin. They simply would not have this 'Rome rule', and believed fervently that Protestant Ulstermen should look after their own interests. However, the fact that the Province of Ulster contained nine counties, and was almost evenly divided between Catholics and Protestants, was another matter, and a problem that would have to be addressed later.

There was therefore a growing view that if Home Rule were to become inevitable, as well it might, then Ulster should strive to obtain its own kind of Home Rule. This should be of a kind that would enable Ulstermen to be masters in their own 'little Ulster' and which would fit with their stoutly dissenting and independent philosophy. However, this was just another version of the old Orange principle of Protestant ascendancy which, if now in retreat in the greater part of Ireland, could still be defended in Ulster, or at least in a part of Ulster. And so the ranks of the Orange Order were swelled by Dissenters – men whose forefathers would not have touched Orangeism with a barge pole. This new generation would be greatly taken with the economic conservatism, the anti-socialism, loyalist imperialism and anti-Home Rule rhetoric of the man who was to become their new leader, the great Sir Edward Carson. They would therefore soon sign up with him on the Home Rule issue, which they saw as an anti-Irish issue, even though, whether or not they knew it, Carson was an all-Ireland unionist and of a rather different political mind.

Meanwhile the post-Gladstone hiatus was coming to an end. In power since 1906, the Liberals had largely avoided the Home Rule issue, but when H.H.

Asquith became Prime Minister this seemed likely to change. For three years the House of Lords had regularly opposed the government's legislative programme, and very few measures other than money bills had been passed in their intended form. In these circumstances Asquith had to consider maximising the use of the Finance Bill in order to push measures through, or else find a way to remove the absolute veto of the Lords. Matters finally came to a head when the House of Lords took the unprecedented step of rejecting a money bill, by throwing out Chancellor Lloyd George's 'People's Budget' of 1909. Asquith now decided that he had no alternative but to confront them.

He did so by taking the matter to the country. In the second general election of 1910 the issue was a constitutional one – whether the Lords should continue to have the right to reject the will of an elected House of Commons. The answer to that question, and the outcome of the election, would have big implications for all other elements in the government's legislative programme, not excluding Home Rule. Therefore the early likelihood of a Home Rule Bill would turn on the Liberals' parliamentary strength arising from the detail of the election result. As things turned out this proved to be highly significant in that Asquith's return to power only became possible with the support of Labour and the Irish Nationalists. In these circumstances a new Home Rule Bill was on the cards. Not that the issue was just a matter of political expediency so far as Asquith was concerned. It should not be forgotten that he had been a convinced Home Ruler since Gladstone's time. Indeed, he already had far-seeing, albeit tentative plans for regional Home Rule parliaments in England, Scotland and Wales. During that general election campaign Asquith had, contrary to subsequent unionist assertions, claimed the right of a new Liberal government to proceed with such a measure for Ireland. After the election the new Liberal government therefore had an entirely legitimate mandate for Home Rule.

The inevitable consequence of all these things was that the new government pushed through the Parliament Act of 1911, legislating against the Lords to the effect that any veto against a House of Commons Bill would expire after just three parliamentary sessions, or two years. The Lords accepted the legislation with great reluctance, and only because of its threatened alternative – the creation of several hundred non-hereditary Peers. Thus with the Lords' veto now seriously curbed, and the Irish Nationalist Party holding the balance of power, the way was suddenly paved for a potentially successful introduction of Home Rule. In fact, the third Home Rule Bill, drafted along much the same modest lines as before, was placed before parliament in April 1912. Much in accord with the previously quoted views of historians Robert Kee and Jonathan Bardon, the Ulster historian David W. Miller observes that the kind of Irish 'rule' proposed by the Bill was

> very similar to an American state government. Ireland would have continued
> to be represented in the Westminster parliament, though in reduced numbers,
> which in fact would have more closely reflected her actual proportion of the
> total U.K. population than the swollen representation she still enjoyed in
> deference to a now anachronistic provision of the Act of Union. The
> Westminster parliament would retain power over defence, foreign affairs, new
> customs duties, and to a large extent the level of internal taxation. Even police

would be reserved to Westminster control for six years. There was an appeal in law to the Privy Council, and the Westminster parliament retained supreme power and authority over all persons, matters and things in Ireland.[3]

As in Gladstone's time, the measures proposed hardly amounted to any significant degree of Home Rule never mind Rome Rule. In fact, besides their limitations on the extent of that rule, they included copper-fastened protection for religious minorities. But such was the Orange mind's distrust of the Liberal government, to say nothing of its detestation of Catholic Ireland, there was now no possibility of the unionists being convinced. They had long been making far-reaching preparations to resist. Back in November 1910 a secret committee of the Ulster Unionist Council had been given the task of procuring guns and ammunition, a task that under the leadership of the Orange veteran Major Fred Crawford would be audaciously executed some three years later. By the end of 1910 the Orangemen had been enrolling and drilling, sometimes with dummy weapons, in the many Orange halls throughout Ulster.

Walter Long, whose name would later be canvassed as a possible future leader of the Conservative Party in succession to Arthur Balfour, resigned the Unionist leadership in 1910. Significantly, this was at the very time when Asquith was taking on the Lords – the Unionists' last constitutional line of defence against Home Rule. The Ulster Unionists therefore decided that the need of the hour was for an outstanding leader – a man of real political prestige, strong parliamentary personality and convincing oratorical power. Sir Edward Carson, Conservative MP for Dublin University and one of the foremost lawyers in the Kingdom, seemed to be that man. In truth, however, Carson's unionism held only a limited amount in common with that of the men of Ulster, a people of whom hitherto he knew very little and a place he had visited probably only once before. Nor was he a religious man. He had no genuine affinity with the Ulster Protestant's religio-political and sectarian disposition, in which sense he was poles apart from the aggressively evangelical Saunderson. But although by nature not a religious bigot, Carson was undoubtedly given to extremism and to strong melodramatic tendencies, being once described by Lady Violet Bonham Carter as 'pathetically sincere in his delusions'. He was therefore something of a zealot who could be carried away by his own fervour, especially when playing the negative role of the destroyer. And negative destroyer par excellence he certainly was. One of the major elements in his brilliant success as a jurist was that he was a dedicated and driven man who could give his whole heart and soul to whatever case or cause he prosecuted. Orange-unionism would provide him with a very suitable and stimulating brief.

Fighting Home Rule was a cause with which Carson could readily identify, albeit for different reasons than those of the 'Rome rule' kind. He believed, as also did the Tory and Liberal-unionist imperialists, that the devolution involved in Home Rule was the thin end of a dangerous wedge that would be inimical to the integrity of both the United Kingdom and the British Empire. The trouble was that, like many in the Conservative Party in those days, his belief in British imperialism was very much stronger than his belief in British parliamentary democracy. Carson was also a leader among the 'die-hards', a ginger group of Tory extremists who, following the Lords' rejection of the 'People's Budget', orchestrated an almost fanatical opposition to the subsequent Parliament Bill. The die-hards believed, in the words of the apparently more moderate Arthur Balfour, that 'whether in power or in opposition the Unionist Party should control the destinies of this Empire'. Clearly the die-hards were not democrats, but in common with the Orangemen believed in ascendancy, albeit of a rather different kind and for other reasons. Even to this day there is a tendency within right-wing Toryism to give ultimate loyalty only to the Crown, with a selective and conditional loyalty to parliament. This is the kind of loyalty that often epitomizes the securocrat – what Paul Routldege in his recent biography of Airey Neave describes as loyalty to 'the secret state'. The Tory die-hards were opposed to reform of the Lords because of an imperative to maintain control, even when they could not exercise parliamentary power. They would oppose the Home Rule of British liberalism and of Irish nationalism, not just for the sectarian reasons of Orangeism, nor only for the empire loyalism they shared with the Liberal-unionists, but also because their opposition provided a chance of returning to government. These beliefs and attitudes therefore represented a constellation of power ideas ranging from Lord Randolph Churchill's 'Orange card' opportunism, through Lord Salisbury's right-wing principles, to Edward Carson's armed Ulster resistance in the form of a private army. The corollary of all this was that the opposition's eventual failure to prevent the introduction of Home Rule or its derivative would, together with other events, compel a massive U-turn in Tory politics regarding Ireland, with changes in its philosophy of power.

Die-hard Tory attitudes fitted neatly within a strategy for party advantage in the context of the Home Rule issue. However, the zealous Carson was a conviction politician who saw these matters as much more than means to party political ends. He believed in them, fervently. So when the unionists invited him to become their parliamentary leader in 1910 he decided to take up the challenge. In July the following year he accepted James Craig's invitation to become leader of the Ulster Unionist Council, which effectively made him the champion of Ulster unionism's anti-Home Rule cause. Carson's letter of acceptance declared with typical bluntness that his leadership would be on condition that 'the people over there really mean to resist,' as he was 'not for a mere game of bluff.' He believed that words should be matched by actions.

Captain James Craig, a craggy Boer War veteran and shrewd business millionaire of the new Presbyterian mercantile class, soon dispelled any notion of bluff. He invited Carson to 'Craigavon' his spacious mansion near Belfast on 23rd September 1911, where he laid on a massive reception presided over by the Grand Master of the Orange Order and attended by 50,000 Orangemen, Orangewomen and other unionist organisations, many of whom marched to the party. In a stirring address Carson urged the multitude, to be

> prepared … with such measures as we will carry on for ourselves *the government of those districts of which we have control* … the morning Home Rule passes, ourselves to become responsible for the government of the Protestant province of Ulster (*emphasis mine*).

The revealing reference to 'those districts of which we have control' was perhaps an indication that 'Ulster' might have to be re-tailored to make unionist government possible, which in fact is precisely what happened.

The speech had a powerful impact on political opinion in Britain. Coming as it did from a former Solicitor-General of both Ireland and England and one of the country's top legal authorities, it had clearly threatened the possibility of rebellion against the Crown. In taking that line Carson, like Saunderson before him, was parading the old Orange war-horse of conditional loyalty to the British Crown in parliament. The speech evoked an immediate response from the young Winston Churchill who was a member of Asquith's Liberal government. Winston's politics, supremely those of a parliamentary democrat, were of a rather different order from those of his late father, Lord Randolph Churchill of the 'Orange card' fame. Sternly rebuking Carson in a speech to his Dundee constituency, Winston pointed out that the population of nine-county Ulster was equally divided between Catholics and Protestants, and that Carson had been elected 'Commander-in-Chief of only one-half of Ulster'. This was a simple point, but one that needed to be made to the latter-day advocates of Protestant ascendancy. Their minds seemed caught in a time warp and appeared still to think in the context of the penal laws under which it had been ruled that 'the law does not presume the existence of such a person as a Catholic Irishman'.[4]

It has been shown that although Carson was not a religious bigot he was certainly an arch-Tory who in his legal capacity had worked unremittingly for the Irish landlord interest – an interest that had long and well-established strategic links into the higher levels of Orangeism. Now he was leader of hard-line Orange-unionism, and it was therefore not surprising that in the zealous pursuit of his new cause he more and more found himself having to pose and perform like an Orangeman. The religio-sectarian role did not really become him, but as a fervent Tory die-hard engaged in an imperialist-inspired fight with Irish nationalism and British liberalism he was unencumbered by democratic considerations and, in one sense more surprisingly, by legal constraints either. He was not the quintessential Orangeman, but it was as though the political circumstances of his life had conspired together to cause him to imbibe deeply of the Orange spirit of conditional loyalty to the Crown – a loyalty that was subject to the interests of his class. This would transfigure him into a spiritual if not a substantive Orangeman, with scant respect for parliamentary democracy or any law that seemed inimical of Tory power and ascendancy. And it was this, above all, that the great parliamentarian Winston Churchill could not stomach.

To this day there is disagreement within Orange circles as to whether Sir Edward Carson was ever actually an Orangeman, although this is more a matter of interest than consequence. Sometimes the Orange Order appears to claim that he was, while at other times prominent Orangemen deny it, but by-and-large the Orange leadership seems remarkably ambivalent on the subject. At a recent exhibition held by the Orange Order in Belfast's Waterfront Hall as part of a desperately needed PR exercise Carson's portrait was featured on a large mural entitled 'Faces of Orangeism'. When asked about Carson's membership, an Orange spokesman was obviously much embarrassed and spoke of the Order's lack of records.[5] However, he said he was personally of the view that Carson probably never had been an Orangeman. Despite that widely shared opinion there is some anecdotal evidence to the contrary. This suggests that shortly after he became leader he was persuaded by senior unionists that, in the best interests of the cause, he should became an

Orangeman. By this account he was officially 'made' an Orangeman, a Royal Arch-Purpleman and a Blackman on the morning of 12th July circa 1912. The ceremony is reported to have taken place in Belfast's Ballymacarrett Orange Hall, where by means of a special dispensation he was put through all three initiatory degrees in one session.[6] However, in the context of the mysterious inner workings of a secret society the outsider is obviously in no position to adjudicate on the feasibility of this account. But given its source, one feels that the story has an authentic ring to it and that, like all good stories, it really ought to be true.

The months that followed Carson's accession to the leadership were to be among the most momentous in Ulster's history. Another massive demonstration was held, this time at Belfast's Balmoral Show Grounds, on Easter Tuesday 1912, almost coinciding with Asquith presenting his Home Rule Bill to the Commons. Bonar Law, the new Conservative leader who had just succeeded Arthur Balfour, attended the rally, as did the leading Tory lawyer F.E. Smith who reviewed the 'troops' on horseback, for which he was subsequently nick-named 'Galloper'. Andrew Bonar Law was the son of an Ulster Presbyterian clergyman who had emigrated to Canada, and was regarded as having 'all the political passions and theological prejudices of Ulster in his blood'. It was also said of him, perhaps unkindly, that he rarely understood an opponent's case and only the most salient points of his own. However, he was a very effective and waspish debater. In addition to these Tory notables, seventy English, Scottish and Welsh MPs also attended the Balmoral demonstration, so that together with Bonar Law, Carson and the Ulster MPs their united presence symbolised the Union and the special political relationship between British conservatives and Ulster unionists. The formidable platform party took the salute from no less than a hundred thousand Orangemen and loyalists.

Balmoral was therefore a mutually encouraging experience, giving the Ulster loyalists good reason to believe that a substantial part of the British establishment was behind them. It also gave the Tories hope of a good hand from which once more to play the Orange card in order to defeat Home Rule, thereby facilitating their return to power after seven long years in opposition. But this playing of the Orange card was probably indicative of more than that. Taken as a whole, Tory behaviour in Ireland seems to have been the consistent and natural reaction of an imperious and imperial class that found it difficult to come to terms with the modern democratic process. As Asquith's daughter Lady Violet Bonham Carter once put it, 'Reading the evidence it is hard to avoid the conclusion that in those days the Conservative Party did not believe in ballot boxes.'[7] Certainly any extent to which it did believe in democracy seems to have been strongly subservient to Lord Randolph Churchill's maxim of Tory 'opportunism' – its unprincipled instinct for political power. This, however, was rooted in its more fundamental belief that the Conservative Party and the class it represented were the only people really fit to govern.

When in the course of its progress through parliament the Home Rule Bill reached the committee stage in June 1912, an amendment was moved by Agar-Robartes MP to exclude four Ulster counties of Antrim, Down, Armagh and Londonderry from the provisions of the Bill. This was the first time the idea of such exclusion had been publicly mooted. Carson supported the amendment for tactical reasons, despite a personal ambivalence that would recur in the context of subsequent developments. But although defeated, the amendment's principle would prove to have far-reaching repercussions. The next major move was in September when, after much consultation, a Solemn League and Covenant drafted by Liberal-unionist Thomas Sinclair was agreed for the purpose of placing it before the Protestant people of Ulster. This was a binding oath by which its signatories would pledge themselves 'to defeat the present conspiracy to set up a Home Rule Parliament in Ireland'. Covenant demonstrations were held across the province climaxing in the specially designated 'Ulster Day' of Saturday 18th September 1912. This was an amazing occasion, especially in Belfast, where Carson was received as a conquering hero and where the mood of the multitudes veered between reverential seriousness and crazy tumult. In all 237,368 men who had been born in Ulster signed the Covenant and 234,046 women signed a separate declaration. The doughty Major Crawford signed in his own blood. It was also signed by dignitaries who had not been born in Ulster, notably Carson himself and that great opportunist F.E. Smith, the 'Galloper' of Balmoral who later became Lord Birkenhead, the famous Lord Chancellor. The male version of Ulster's Solemn League and Covenant was typically Orange in that, on the one hand, it pledged fulsome loyalty to 'His Gracious Majesty King George V', and yet, on the other hand, vowed to use 'all means which may be found necessary to defeat the present conspiracy.' This implied the possible use of arms to resist the Crown in parliament – a clause that was excluded from the Covenant's female version.

The Ulster Covenant was a religious concept that invoked the name of God and, contrary to the teaching of the New Testament, postulated a local sectarian theocracy that was political and very much 'of this world'. Protestant Ulster had again become what Conor Cruise O' Brien has described as 'Godland', for the Covenant clearly postulated that the kingdom of God was on the side of the Orange-unionists, even if this meant that God was ignoring the wishes of the other half of Ulster that also professed to be Christian. Nor did it matter that the terms of the Covenant legitimised the taking up of arms in rebellion against the 'powers that be' – the lawful government that Christian citizens were duty bound to obey, in accordance with the very specific teachings of Christ and his apostles. All this made for bad politics and for even worse religion, as will be argued in a later section of the book. The Covenant would be a watershed in Ireland's history, sealing that 'Ulsterisation' process previously embarked upon, in that it excluded the unionists of the rest of Ireland. Encouraged by this unparalleled display of Orange-unionist solidarity, the Ulster Unionist Council announced in January 1913 that those loyalists (who already had been drilling) who had signed the male version of the Ulster Covenant would be organised through the Orange lodges to form a 100,000 strong Ulster Volunteer Force.

Early in 1914 Tory leaders were privately scheming the possibility of the House of Lords amending of the Army Act. Staggeringly, this was designed to cripple the authority of the civil power over military matters and thus to prevent the Liberal government from deploying, if needs be, the armed forces in Ulster. Obviously some kind of military intervention had to be a possibility, given the threat of UVF raids on army barracks for the purpose of procuring guns, to say nothing of the much greater threat of rebellion posed by the terms of the Ulster Covenant. Yet not content with what was clearly constitutionally outrageous political scheming to hamstring the civil government, some Tory army leaders were now plotting to dissuade officers from serving in Ulster in the event of the civil war that was presumed would follow any introduction of Home Rule. A leading figure in this military intrigue was the Ulster Orangeman, General Sir Henry Wilson, a well-known anti-nationalist who was Director of Military Operations at the War Office. As such he was very well placed to influence events and to pass on high level intelligence to Sir Edward Carson and to the Orange-dominated UVF command in Ulster.

In March 1914, Wilson was party to a War Office meeting on arrangements for troop movements into Ulster, arrangements that could involve an excluding dispensation for officers of Ulster domicile. Soon afterwards Sir Arthur Paget, commander-in-chief of the British Army in Ireland, personally communicated a highly confused version of this meeting to his officers stationed at the Curragh. Arising from his bungling mismanagement of the issue, which already had been adversely influenced by Sir Henry Wilson's mischief making, sixty British Army officers of the Cavalry Brigade found themselves in a situation where they felt constrained to resign rather than 'coerce Ulster'. This became known as the 'Curragh Mutiny' and was denounced by Asquith as the 'Complete Grammar of Anarchy'. The Tory Opposition tried to achieve political advantage from the affair, but as was usually the case throughout the Home Rule crisis, Asquith batted confidently on a good constitutional wicket. On this particular occasion he handled a mischievous but badly misdirected attack with coolness, dexterity and skill. He took over the War Office himself, which in those days necessitated his resignation and re-election, but he was returned unopposed with the Tories refusing the democratic challenge. Asquith re-entered parliament in triumph, and on the back of a simple but sharp summation of the situation: 'The army will hear nothing of politics from me, and in return I expect to hear nothing of politics from the army'. The soldiers showed sound common sense and trusted 'Old Squithy' even if some of their Tory officers did not, with the result that the so-called 'mutiny' soon fizzled out. Nevertheless the affair was not without damage to the internal morale of the army in Ireland, although the damage was self-inflicted by the army's own leaders and its professed political friends. The whole matter also had a political effect. If the government ever had considered military intervention in Ulster, this would be much more difficult now. The Orange-unionists sensed this and became more bullish than ever. They could get it wrong, but they could see victory even in defeat and would never stop.

Back in Ireland the Orange army with banners was still largely without guns. However, the task which the Ulster Unionist Council had given Major Crawford in 1910 was about to be completed, with the full knowledge and support of Carson, and probably also of some leading figures in the British establishment. The story is told by A.T.Q. Stewart in *The Ulster Crisis*, a history that reads like a thriller. It will suffice to recount here that during the night of 25th April 1914 Crawford and his men landed 24,000 rifles and 3,000,000 rounds of ammunition at Bangor and Larne harbours, which were successfully distributed to the UVF command throughout Ulster. This brought the total number of rifles available to the UVF to over 40,000. To some it was a strange thing, given the reputation of British military intelligence, that despite the quite explicit public statements of Carson and others, and the clear threat contained in the recent Ulster Covenant, the entire gun-running operation was carried out with no serious hitch and without a single arrest. As a result, Sir Edward Carson had his provisional government ready and in waiting, and backed by its provisional Orange army now armed and in training. This was something to which Orangeism's paramilitary origins, its historic links with the Irish Yeomanry, and its longstanding tradition of British military leadership, naturally and enthusiastically lent itself.

It was therefore hardly surprising that all these developments should have had a profound impact upon the rest of Ireland. Republican opinion, which had been dormant and all but dead at the turn of the century, was greatly enervated by an Ulster at arms. Indeed, it concluded that what Ulster could do in arming to resist Britain the republicans and nationalists could now do also. One republican writer spoke lyrically of 'the thrill of chastened pride that shivered gently through Ireland when the quiet places of Ulster echoed to the march of the Ulster Volunteers'.[8] Eoin MacNeill 'gladly acknowledged the evident truth that they have opened the way for a National Volunteer movement'.[9] And so Irish nationalism took steps to organise its own gun-running and to establish its own army known as the Irish Volunteers, thousands of whom were from Ulster, and out of which eventually would evolve the Irish Republican Army. It is therefore indisputable that Orangeism was a mid-wife, albeit an unwitting one, at the birth of the IRA.

All this was very much to the approval of Patrick Pearse, who could now suggest that the Orangeman with a rifle was a much less ridiculous figure than the nationalist without one.[10] The nationalists therefore made arrangements to run in the guns. A consignment of 1,500 rifles was landed in daylight at Howth on 26th July 1914, despite some violence and the presence of the British Army (which had been conspicuous by its absence during the Ulster gunrunning). Another noticeable difference was that for his part in organising the latter gunrunning the leading nationalist Sir Roger Casement, unlike the Orange gunrunning hero Fred Crawford, would later be executed. Once again such dual-standards brought to the surface the serious disaffection that was growing within Irish nationalism. This was now particularly strong within the new Volunteer movement, its smaller hard-line republican element breaking away, taking with it the name of the Irish Volunteers. Although the majority grouping remained loyal to the nationalist leader John Redmond and became known as the National Volunteers, Orange militancy had made a significant contribution to the resurgence of an armed and disaffected republicanism in Ireland.

If Gladstone's philosophy of political action was to 'take a leap in the dark, and then another', Asquith's policy of 'wait and see' was precisely the opposite. In all the turmoil of the Home Rule issue, he had for two years been waiting hopefully for something to turn up, but whereas nothing had emerged of a positive nature there had been a veritable avalanche of things to the contrary. Perhaps he saw a glimmer of hope when Winston Churchill, adverting at least in principle to the Agar-Robartes proposal, suggested to Carson the idea of excluding Ulster from the provisions of Home Rule. This was something to which, with hindsight, Carson the all-Ireland unionist was personally averse, but towards which, as we have already seen, the Ulster unionists were moving with some alacrity. It was therefore becoming evident that there just might be scope for negotiation, although the negative Carson continued to resist all efforts to have him proffer proposals of his own. The Irish nationalists, and especially the nationalists of Ulster led by Joe Devlin, wanted the full Home Rule Bill for all of Ireland and were passionately opposed to anything that smacked of a partitionist solution. The principle of exclusion, or how much of Ulster should be excluded from Home Rule, therefore only served to heighten the already strong confusion and tension. That tension was by no means confined to Ireland. Home Rule, the 'most fissiparous issue for two hundred years', had split British politics asunder.

Following the bitterness engendered by Lloyd George's contentious 1909 'Peoples' Budget' and the tempestuous Parliament Bill that ensued, it was the next (and third) Home Rule Bill that finally filled the Tory cup of wrath to the full. The political temperature was feverish, and the conventionally cordial inter-party social relations between British politicians were shattered as never before or since. Lunching on one occasion at that time with his high-Tory colleague Arthur Balfour, a nephew of Lord Salisbury, the mercurial Edward Carson was in danger of shattering other things when, in emphasising a point against having social relations with Home Rulers, he was observed 'banging the table till the glasses rang'. This was despite the probability that the urbane and languid Balfour would have gone along with the sentiments of Carson's diatribe, even though embarrassed by the dramatic manner in which these were expressed. The Liberals, though long the party in power, were ostracised by the great and the grand of British society during those fissiparous and stirring times. Writing about this strength of feeling, the Ulster historian A.T.Q. Stewart has made the significant observation that:

> In retrospect, it seems strange that a measure as limited as the Home Rule Bill should engender such political passion, for it merely granted Ireland local government powers under the Crown, and its federal basis was an attempt to win over those members of the Conservative Party who had all along advocated such a solution.[11]

But perhaps this 'political passion' was not so strange given A.T.Q. Stewart's subsequent statement just a few pages on when he tells us that

> ... political leaders were made aware of an effective means of resistance to Home Rule, for the Orange Order provided a framework for a citizen army totally opposed to *Ulster's exclusion from the United Kingdom* (*emphasis mine*).

Taken in juxtaposition these two statements seem quite incongruous. If the introduction of Home Rule meant in effect 'Ulster's exclusion from the United Kingdom' then surely there would have been many powerful reasons for what Stewart had just described as 'such political passion'. That such passion should seem 'strange in retrospect' can only mean that exclusion from the United

Kingdom had neither been intended nor implied by the government's 'limited measure'. If this were so, then there was absolutely no valid reason for the political passion of the anti-Home Rulers, which was in fact plainly the case. Where then did all that bluster come from, and what gave rise to the wholly erroneous, yet still extant notion that Home Rule meant the exclusion of Ulster from the United Kingdom? The political chicanery of those playing the Orange card is an obvious source, but one has to be intrigued as to why some professional Ulster historians still allow themselves to get into a muddle over it.

King George V, who was torn apart by this division of his country, was in favour of Home Rule, but because of pressure from the Tory grandees he had become obsessed with the need to reach an accommodation with Ulster. At the King's request and reluctantly agreed by Asquith, an all-party conference was held in Buckingham Palace on 21 July 1914, to discuss the question of Ulster's exclusion from Home Rule, the amount of territory to be excluded and for how long. The nationalist leader John Redmond was naturally opposed to exclusion, but argued reluctantly that any exclusion must not involve any predominantly nationalist areas. Carson, in contradiction of previous and subsequent Orange-unionist positions, called for the 'clean cut' of the whole nine counties of Ulster, on which generous basis Ulster might later, within reasonable time, be willing to re-join an integrated Ireland.[12] Politically, a temporary exclusion of nine county Ulster would not have been 'clean cut' as the unionists were well aware, but coming from Carson this was an extraordinary proposition – one that might lead eventually to an all-Ireland within the Union and under precisely the kind of Home Rule that Asquith's Bill now proposed. It has been argued that his approach may have been tactical, demanding too much of the nationalists in order to kill off the whole principle of Home Rule, and in any case he soon reneged on the temporary aspect of exclusion. But if tactical then the tactic was a dangerous one that nodded at the principle of separation within Ireland, a principle that might lead anywhere. It certainly did not kill off Home Rule, and in the end probably contributed to the kind of partitionist settlement that Carson abhorred and which would leave him an angry and disillusioned man.

In any event the Buckingham Palace conference failed to resolve the crisis, but not before Asquith had clearly indicated the principle of exclusion for the six counties that now constitute Northern Ireland. When war broke out in Europe a few weeks later, Asquith announced that the Home Rule Bill would now become law but that its implementation would be held in abeyance until the end of the War, at which time there would be amending legislation to make special provision for Ulster. So the problem was shelved, but not without a firm indication of the government's intentions as to the shape of things to come.

Conclusions

In the context of Irish politics, the years 1898 to 1914 were substantially dominated by Sir Edward Carson, who with James Craig took up paramilitary Orangeism and linked it powerfully to Conservative-unionism. In their anxiety to oust the Liberals and return to power the Tories played the Orange card as never before, transforming the Home Rule issue into Britain's most divisive political issue for two hundred years. By thus misrepresenting and resisting the measure, Carson and the Tory die-hards found themselves in the paradoxical situation of loyalists of the Crown becoming rebels against that Crown. This sat more easily with Orangeism's principle of conditional loyalty than with a Tory approach to politics that at least had to take some account of democracy. However, the difference between them was a relative one, given the Tories' behaviour in respect of the Orange gunrunning and the Curragh Mutiny – issues that outraged parliamentary democrats like Asquith and Winston Churchill. In fact, the Tories' Irish agenda was of such a dissembling and opportunist nature as to amply justify Lady Violet Bonham-Carter's remark that 'in those days the Conservative Party did not believe in ballot boxes'. But the rebels who truly believed the 'Home Rule is Rome Rule' doctrine were the Orange-unionists, with Carson now to some extent their prisoner. In keeping with their long tradition, the Orange 'covenanters' would only be loyal to the Crown in parliament so long as the sovereign authority remained loyal to their notion of whatever it was King William had established. This was the fundamentalist unionism of Protestant ascendancy that, contrary to Carson's best instincts, was becoming more overtly sectarian and Ulsterised. The Orange-unionism of that time was disastrous both for Ulster and for Ireland. It paved the way for other rebels who with no loyalty whatsoever to the Crown would thereafter pursue their own cause with a far stronger logic and much readier justification.

And so a confused and confusing episode was suspended rather than concluded, with the great Irish Unionist leader, having first compromised his legal principles now jeopardising his political principles also by participating in negotiations for the exclusion of Ulster, or a part of Ulster, from the provisions of Home Rule. This would involve potential political separation from the greater part of Ireland, which had been his birthplace. The 'Ulster' territory would be tailored to become sufficiently Protestant to ensure the essential Orange objective of ascendancy over 'those districts they could control',[13] and in the end would be the only part of Ireland to have Home Rule. Separation would become far more radical and significant than Carson had envisaged, for now the 'thrill of chastened pride was shivering gently through Ireland' as other rebels who had taken a leaf from the Orangemen's book prepared to fight a different cause and with an even more dramatic outcome. But suddenly the great issue had to be temporarily shelved, and a crisis with all the potential for a fierce civil war would only be averted by the most serious of all crises – that of a most terrible World War.

9.

1914 - 1921
Home Rule for the anti-Home Rulers

Shortly after war was declared both Carson and Redmond pledged their armies to fight the Allies' cause in France. Redmond believed that participation in the war would eventually earn Ireland the right to Home Rule in the form originally intended. Yet Carson's men could be equally confident of their own earning power in regard to Ulster's right of exclusion from any Home Rule arrangements under the deferred legislation – given that this in fact had already been promised. Substantial contingents of both Volunteer forces went to war and in almost equal numbers. However, whereas Carson's UVF was allowed to retain its homogeneity and Orange identity within the 36th (Ulster) Division, and fought under its own badge and banners, war secretary Lord Kitchener ensured that Redmond's National Volunteers were dispersed through some British regiments and served under British officers. This was the latest example of British partiality towards the Orange-unionist interest in Ireland. Given such historical baggage, we need not wonder why nationalists today are so insistent on the principles of parity of esteem and equality across the Northern Irish political spectrum.

Meanwhile the breakaway Irish Volunteers in the South, led by determined republicans who had long-since been disillusioned by the many deferments of Home Rule, were now totally cynical about British intentions, especially in regard to what had already been flagged up in the way of a likely settlement for Ulster. Thus at the very time when Redmond's National Volunteers were winning VC's for gallantry in Europe, the Irish Volunteers were planning the Easter Rising of 1916, following the principle that England's difficulty is Ireland's opportunity. The republicans arose in Dublin with a view to establishing a separatist republic of the whole island of Ireland, but at that stage the Rising was lacking in popular support and was promptly put down. However, although in every sense a minority at the start, the republicans had set in motion a chain of events which, in the prophetic words of the poet William Butler Yeats, would ensure that nothing would ever be the same again:

All changed, changed utterly:
A terrible beauty is born.[1]

The next few cataclysmic years would see the partitioning of the country, the war of independence, the Anglo-Irish Treaty, the establishment of the twenty-six county Irish Free State and the subsequent civil war, to say nothing of the equally seismic events in the North.

The consequences of 1916 and other events of that year were to have serious implications for the Orangemen and unionists of Ulster. Edward Carson became a minister in Asquith's government, and his Ulster Volunteers, now in France, were moved up to the battle-front on the Somme. On 1st July, the old anniversary of the Battle of the Boyne, the Ulster Division marched on enemy lines, some of them wearing orange lilies and sashes, and with the Ulster cry of 'No Surrender' on their lips. The Ulster Volunteers made some rapid gains in the course of heroic fighting, but the advance was soon repelled when their exposed ranks were cut to pieces by the German machine-gun fire. In just two days over 5,000 men were killed or wounded, and every one of their hard-won territorial gains was quickly wiped out. The terrible news soon filtered back home to a stunned community, and the impending Twelfth of July Orange marches and celebrations were immediately cancelled. Protestant Ulster was plunged into deep mourning. Calling a halt to the Twelfth proceedings in circumstances of such tragedy and communal mourning was obviously the right thing to do. But leaving that aside, the propriety of thousands of able-bodied men marching military-style at a time when the country was engaged in the most terrible war the world has ever seen was a question that as yet did not seem to have occurred to the loyal Orange mind.

The Ulster Volunteers would not be alone in their sacrifice. In the full course of that calamitous war in which millions fell it has been estimated that up to fifty thousand Irishmen gave their lives, half of whom were Roman Catholics.[2] Nevertheless, in terms of recruitment and numbers of enlisted servicemen, Orange Ulster's war effort was not outstanding – a point which, in the absence of conscription, was not lost on the British press at the time. This was given added poignancy when set in contrast with Ulster's much vaunted super-loyalty to King and Empire. An even worse situation would obtain in the Second World War when Ulster's war effort, and the leadership of Northern Ireland's unionist government, would be severely criticised both at home and in Britain. This time the government of Northern Ireland at least took steps to ensure that the Twelfth of July processions were discontinued at the outset. That decision was taken not because of some particularly great tragedy like the Somme. It was designed to avoid the embarrassing criticism of a now more prurient and aggressive press – criticism that obviously would have been occasioned by the public spectacle of the large and able-bodied Orange army with banners marching away from the war.

We have touched upon some of the political developments during the course of the Great War. In 1916, H.H. Asquith and Lloyd George persuaded a reluctant Carson to accept the exclusion of the six counties of north-east Ulster from the provisions of Home Rule, and in turn Carson with no great enthusiasm persuaded the Ulster Unionist Council to agree to this. In the aftermath of the failed 1916 Rising in the South there began a gradual but significant movement towards republicanism, which at the turn of the century had been all but dead. Now there was agitation for a stronger version of Home Rule for the whole of Ireland than was on the statute book, albeit deferred. But such an aspiration appeared ill-founded if the understandings already reached in the North were anything to go by. However, the Irish nationalists were now placing high hopes on the principle of 'the right to self-determination of small nations' for which the war was ostensibly being fought. They therefore seemed quite confident that this right would soon be granted to Ireland as a whole.

That hope received a tremendous fillip almost as soon as the war ended when, as a result of the 'khaki election' in December 1918, Sinn Féin won a massive victory in Ireland, taking 73 out of the 102 seats. The Unionist Party, which won 26 seats, had a majority of only 4 seats in the province of Ulster as a whole, but significantly were in a much stronger position in terms of the already agreed six-county configuration. David Lloyd George, who was returned as Prime Minister of a largely Conservative coalition, offered Carson a position in the cabinet, which he refused, but Sir James Craig, who had been knighted in 1917, was appointed financial secretary to the Admiralty. The new British government's attitude towards those politicians, who just a few years before had been perceived as gunrunners and rebels, now appeared to be conferring legitimacy on Ulster's position. This did not go unnoticed in the South. Ireland was about to enter a time of considerable political turbulence.

The newly elected Sinn Féin MPs refused to take the oath of allegiance to the Crown, adopting an abstentionist policy toward the Westminster parliament, a policy that in effect isolated them from political influence. This was later to prove greatly to the advantage of the unionists when legislative arrangements for the new Northern Ireland were being made. Instead, the Sinn Féin MPs met in Dublin in January 1919 as Dáil Éireann, the Irish parliament. Some regarded this as an act of bravado, or a mere gesture, but in *real politik* it would soon be seen as an effective declaration of intent by a 'shadow' government that was now determined upon a very different course of action. Amid growing violence British Prime Minister Lloyd George declared the Dáil illegal and in September 1919 proscribed Sinn Féin. Any semblance of democratic control was lost as the Irish Volunteers, now known as the Irish Republican Army, unleashed a ferocious guerrilla war. This war became known variously as the Irish war of independence, or the Tan war, named after the specially drafted-in force of British ex-servicemen, nicknamed the Black and Tans because of the colour of their black-belted uniform.

For the most part the actual guerrilla war was confined to the South, but it did have some spin-off effect in the North when a few IRA incursions, local republican activity, or the perceived threat of either, were considered by Ulster loyalists to call for retaliatory action. As sectarian violence in the North increased, Sir Basil Brooke, a prominent Orangeman and Captain in the British Army, gave the lead by mobilising a group of rural vigilantes, whom he armed with UVF weapons that had previously been hidden away on his Fermanagh estate. On foot of this Captain Brooke was later able to claim that he was the originator of the Ulster Special Constabulary.[3] Brooke's illegal initiative was swiftly emulated elsewhere when in June 1920 the Ulster Unionist Council decided to revive and reorganise the illegal UVF. The Orangemen and their Orange halls were once again called into service for the task.

In such a heavily charged atmosphere it seemed more than likely that the Orange marching season in the summer of 1920 would be the occasion of further serious sectarian conflict. That likelihood became an absolute certainty when on 12th July Sir Edward Carson, in his most mercurial and melodramatic mood, delivered himself of an inflammatory speech to a mass demonstration of Orangemen at Finaghy, on the outskirts of Belfast. Consciously using the most powerful rhetoric, Carson postulated a situation in which

> we will take the matter into our own hands. We will reorganise … in our own defence, throughout the Province, the Ulster Volunteers… and those are not mere words. I hate words without action.[4]

In its editorial comment on the speech the following day, the London *Times* was of the opinion that 'upon Sir Edward Carson lies largely the blame for having sown the dragon's teeth in Ireland.' Yet Carson's words from Orangeism's most important public platform were absolutely typical in that, beyond the rhetoric, they were clearly a self-fulfilling prophecy in the best Orange-unionist tradition. We have seen that the Orange army with banners had already begun to gather quietly at the behest of the Ulster Unionist Council in June. However, the matter became public on 23rd July when adverts were placed in newspapers announcing the reorganisation of the UVF and requesting all members and former members to report for duty.

Immediately after the industrial holiday period of that July the predicted storm of sectarian violence broke out and rapidly escalated, taking on the new and far-reaching dimension of pre-planned and supervised expulsions of Catholics and socialists from their jobs in the Belfast shipyards and other large engineering establishments. It has been reckoned that some eleven thousand Catholics were thus expelled, of whom about two thousand had served the cause of freedom in the recent World War. In most cases these sectarian expulsions were to prove of permanent effect, not only for the individuals concerned but, by extension, for subsequent generations of their co-religionists. This was an act of calculated deliberation. Incredible as it may seem, the Orange-unionist leader and soon to become Prime Minister of the incipient state of Northern Ireland, Sir James Craig, addressed a mass meeting of shipyard workmen just two months after these violent expulsions, specifically approving, even applauding the shipyard men's actions.[5] In saying 'well done' to the workmen Craig had not fallen prey to some mad, heat-of-the-moment aberration, but was firmly laying down the basis for what would soon become the official Orange-unionist employment policy in Northern Ireland.

Orange lodges were established in places of work to encourage the protection of Protestant employment, which would be a recurring topic at the massive Orange demonstrations of each and every marching season. These demonstrations would regularly become the platforms for clarion calls from Orange-unionist leaders to Ulster's businessmen either not to employ Catholics, or to give preferential treatment to fellow Protestants. In large industrial establishments such as the shipyards this was easily managed in that the mostly Orange-unionist foremen were in control of the weekly labour 'markets'. Here the unemployed stood in line every Monday morning, hoping desperately to receive the nod or sign from the foreman that would indicate a job. As to the question of promotion, usually from manual to staff positions, there was a perception that Freemasonry could be a rather more influential ladder than Orangeism. There is no doubt both these Orders had influence and exercised it when and where they could. However, there was such a high proportion of workers in membership of the various Orders that in the end such membership probably offered little advantage. Indeed, it was sometimes argued that it was probably more distinguishing and therefore more beneficial to belong to none of them! Long before the introduction of modern employment legislation, both the crude labour markets and the ostensible influence of the Lodge in employment matters had diminished, due to the growth of bureaucracy, trade unionism and other factors. However, more often than not the real question remained as to whether the candidate for a given job was Protestant or Catholic. That question, more important than any pertaining to membership of an Order, could be determined by other means. In that sense Orange *ism* was more important than the actual Orange Order.

In the early aftermath of the war the reorganised UVF took on its pre-war character and in effect became a private Orange army which, in the words of Sir Basil Brooke, was 'to all intents and purposes an illegal organisation'.[6] In the disturbances of 1920, small UVF groups acted locally as unofficial constables, but from time to time some of these were apprehended and found guilty of riot, looting and even the burning of Catholic homes. During the next two years – in the course of which the state of Northern Ireland was established – Belfast and other parts of the North experienced outbreaks of sectarian violence that have been described as more vicious and lethal than all the Northern riots of the previous century put together. Street rioting, gun and incendiary attacks directed in the main against Catholic people, their homes and businesses were of common occurrence during this period of extended trouble. Sinn Féin was certainly involved in the situation, and the IRA sporadically engaged in guerrilla attacks on the security forces and on businesses. But these served only to elicit massive reprisals by loyalists against uninvolved Catholics, who were made to pay the price for the sins of the IRA many times over.

For much of the time the IRA in the North was on the back foot. It saw itself as being 'in no position to challenge loyalist military ascendancy' and for long periods claimed to be preoccupied with what it regarded primarily as the defence of the Catholic community. In a recent book Jim McDermott writes:

> In essence, republican violence in Belfast was largely reactive and defensive. Frankly, the organisation was not strong enough for the actions to be anything else'.[7]

This assessment is borne out by the published facts. The statistics alone suggest that republicanism was often the excuse for, rather than the cause of the lethal loyalist violence that was directed against the ordinary Catholic people. It was tragic that the Orange-unionist leaders appeared content to allow loyalists who were later in league with, or in the guise of the new Specials to continue their terror with virtual impunity. Some commentators believed that the Orange-unionist leadership's greatest concern was with the management of adverse publicity and with the need to dampen down any 'bad news' that those terrible actions might attract. In this regard the unionists received some support and co-operation from the local loyalist press. However, they were not always so successful with the British national press, powerful elements of which were beginning to take a critical interest in their so-called 'security' activities.

The Catholics, who were heavily out-numbered and relatively poorly armed, were largely on the receiving end of the violence, an estimated twenty-three thousand of them having been being driven out of their homes. During a two-year period nearly five hundred people were killed with over two thousand wounded, but Catholics were killed on a ratio of two to one, even though they constituted only one-third of the population. In fact, the situation is thrown into even sharper relief when we bear in mind that, in terms of the areas where most of the troubles took place, the Catholics constituted a mere one-sixth of the population. Indeed, nearly half the Protestants who died were killed by British military fire in riot situations.[8] There can therefore be no doubt as to the real nature and general drift of these outrages. Many sectors of the British press clearly understood the situation and were becoming quite hostile to Orange-unionism, sometimes likening the murder and mayhem, the expulsions from home and workplace, the burnings and reprisals to the infamous Russian and Polish pogroms.[9] It was at this time that the term 'Belfast pogroms' found its way into the political lexicon.

The unionist leader James Craig had a great capacity for selective amnesia, blandly ignoring the leading role of loyalists in the terror, and often blaming the Catholics for riots that clearly had been started by Protestants. In fact, halfway through the Belfast pogroms he used the general level of the violence to justify his call for a strengthening and legalising of the then illegal loyalist forces. What he really wanted was the legalising of the UVF, which he hoped to achieve by creating a new special constabulary based on the structure and personnel of that organisation. He soon submitted detailed plans for this to the British government. The proposal quite literally terrified some British government ministers, who could see the obvious dangers of recognising and arming the very people who were playing such a large and indeed leading part in the continuing violence. However, the wily Craig's plan held certain pragmatic and political attractions for some British ministers.

Winston Churchill, always creative but dangerous when he gave his lively imagination to military stratagems, saw the plan as an opportunity for releasing several battalions of British troops to fight Sinn Féin in the South. This could be achieved by, as Churchill put it, 'handing over Ulster to the Ulstermen'. This conception of Ulster and its citizenry was rather different from that of the inclusive Ulster, equally embracing both Catholics and Protestants, he had brilliantly highlighted in his Dundee speech of 1911. Then he had rebuked the Carsonite sectarianism that was ignoring the other half of the Ulster people – the almost equal number of nationalists who also lived there. However, once again expediency got the better of principle, and soon afterwards Craig and the militarists had their way. In October 1920 the British government authorised the creation of the Ulster Special Constabulary, a paramilitary police force of three sections – the 'A', 'B' and 'C' Specials. The part-time armed and uniformed 'B' section was eventually to become the largest section, its planned number being almost 20,000. Later on, following the disbanding of the 'A' and 'C' sections for financial reasons at the end of 1925, the 'B' section would exclusively become the Ulster Special Constabulary and for the next fifty years be eponymously known as the B-Specials.

Operating locally, the Special Constabulary was recruited in the main from contingents of the recently revived but still illegal Ulster Volunteer Force, many of whom now joined the new force en bloc. As a general principle, the British government, which was footing the bill for the new force, never intended that it should be exclusively Protestant. It therefore made provision for Catholic involvement that would reflect their one-third proportion of the population. However, contrary to the impression given in a recent Orange Order apologia[10] there is powerful evidence to show that it was never the intention of the Ulster unionists to facilitate Catholic participation. Indeed, the very fact that the Grand Orange Lodge of Ireland has gone into print in defence of the Specials is of itself evidence enough of the Orange and Protestant pedigree of that force.

From the beginning, the very possibility of Catholic participation was bitterly resented in Orange-unionist circles, even though it was acknowledged that this was unlikely to happen to any substantial degree, given the deeply sectarian situation in the country as well as the essential nature of the new force itself. The truth is that when the force finally became operational, leading Orange-unionists like James Craig and Sir Henry Wilson could note with satisfaction that, like the Orange Order itself, the Ulster Special Constabulary was entirely Protestant. As things turned out, the Ulster Special Constabulary was virtually a legalised UVF and like that organisation rooted in Orangeism, as the Order's own current literature fully verifies. All these things were most disturbing to the minority community in the North, whose fears were soon to be matched only by their loathing for the new force. This was graphically articulated by the nationalist leader Joe Devlin MP in a memorable speech to the House of Commons at Westminster:

> The Chief Secretary is going to arm pogromists to murder the Catholics...
> Their pogrom is to be made less difficult. Instead of paving stones and sticks they are to be given rifles.[11]

There can be no argument but that the new USC turned out exactly as its Orange-unionist leaders intended. It was an aggressive Protestant paramilitary force bearing the same relationship to the Orange Order as had the Yeomanry from the 1790s, and it was similarly determined upon maintaining Protestant supremacy and keeping the papists in their places. It was therefore but a new regiment of the old Orange 'army with banners', as Craig freely acknowledged in his 12th July 1922 speech to the faithful when he said:

> It is also from the ranks of the Loyal Orange Institution that our splendid Specials have come.[12]

From the beginning the Specials were confined to the six counties of north-east Ulster, and were expected to police events on the ground in the turbulent situation leading up to the creation of Northern Ireland in 1921. All this was regarded as an unmitigated disaster by the nationalist people in the North who, after all the years of patient waiting for the fruits of Gladstone, Parnell and Asquith, now seemed further away than ever from enjoying the benefits of a democratically representative Home Rule. In fact they were now in a much more parlous state than at any time since the Act of Union inasmuch as, to an extent of which they were yet unaware, they were once again to be ruled by Orangemen. Such fears seemed to be confirmed when in the very early days after the formation of the USC a platoon marched around Enniskillen singing Orange songs and firing shots at the local Catholic Church, an event that compelled Sir Basil Brooke to issue a public apology.[13] Far from being an isolated incident, this was the shape of things to come, for the Specials were soon to be involved in other shootings, burnings, robberies, looting of Catholic-owned public houses, and sometimes very much worse.

This was an inauspicious start for a force that for the next fifty years would be perceived by the nationalist community, and not without good reason, as an instrument of repression. After all, it was the offspring of that illegal army which under Carson and Craig had been the chief instrument in thwarting the democratic aspirations of the Catholic nationalists. As Joe Devlin MP had anticipated, those anti-Catholic militants who joined the Specials when the force was established mid-way through the Belfast pogroms continued to participate in what some had come to describe as the 'Orange Terror'. Now officially authorised and armed, the Specials could act with relative impunity, apart from the occasional shoot-outs with the British Army, which of course tells its own story. Their activities were commonly reported to involve the regular raiding of Catholic homes in the middle of the night, evicting householders under any pretext or none, and even sometimes summarily executing suspects.

It is therefore simply not good enough for Orange apologists to suggest, as in a recent pamphlet on the subject, that the main thrust of the Specials' activity at that time was directed against the IRA and that press references to pogroms were just so much anti-Orange propaganda.[14] As already pointed out, the IRA was sporadically involved in terrorist attacks in the North, but for the most part its activities there were heavily circumscribed by circumstances in which the Catholic population was virtually under siege. This was at a time when its organisation was largely tied down by the Tan war, which was followed by the Civil War in the South. But it was also at a time when the security forces in the North included more than 50,000 regular and part-time paramilitary police, plus 9,000 British troops – one armed member of the security forces for every twenty-five people, or more than one armed policeman for every two Catholic families.[15] Whatever the Specials' main preoccupation or problem was, it was certainly not the over-stretched IRA. Rather, it appeared that the Specials, whom Prime Minister Lloyd George once compared with the Fascisti of Italy, had come to regard their Catholic neighbours either as Sinn Féiners, or as their fellow travellers, and treated them accordingly. As a result of the situation where the Specials regarded ordinary Catholics as the enemy, and sometimes took random reprisals against them, the British Army often had to hold the ring.

Meanwhile, during the course of 1920 Lloyd George had been pressing on with the Government of Ireland Bill. The Bill provided for two Home Rule parliaments in Ireland, one in Belfast for the six counties to be known as Northern Ireland and the other in Dublin for the twenty-six counties of Southern Ireland. Both parliaments would have very limited devolved powers, and both parts of Ireland would continue to send elected representatives to the sovereign parliament at Westminster. There would also be provision for a Council of Ireland with a view to the later establishment of a Home Rule parliament for the whole of Ireland, an idea that had originally been proposed by Carson. Lloyd George had secured Carson's agreement to the six county principle, but none of this was in accord with Carson's deeper Tory and imperialist instincts, which were opposed to any form of Home Rule for Ireland, North or South. Carson therefore viewed with distaste what seemed at the time to be the worst of all possible options, that of Home Rule separately for both. However, from his point of view there was worse to follow, for the Home Rule provisions for the South would soon be jettisoned in favour of a much more radical arrangement.

The die was now well and truly cast so far as the North was concerned. Carson, on foot of his agreement with Lloyd George, advised a troubled Ulster Unionist Council to work the proposed new arrangements, even though he was shortly afterwards to make it clear that the partition of Ireland and a Home Rule parliament in the North were as bitter ashes in his mouth. He subsequently declined the offer to be Prime Minister designate of the new Northern Ireland established by the Government of Ireland Act in 1921, and dejectedly turned aside, handing the premiership and party leadership to Sir James Craig. Soon afterwards, as Lord Carson of Duncairn, he entered the House of Lords as one of the Lords of Appeal, and eventually left politics altogether. Enoch Powell once opined that 'all political careers end in failure', but perhaps this applied to Sir Edward Carson more than most. Measured against his defining anti-Home Rule campaign, his political career certainly ended in failure, in consequence of which he suffered deep personal disillusionment and despair.

But the great majority of unionists were well satisfied that the Union with Britain had been secured, even though that Union had never been threatened by the terms of any of the Home Rule Bills going back to Gladstone's time. In fact, much more had been lost than was preserved, for the Union's writ in Ireland now ran only to six out of thirty-two counties, and even that amount of territory was to remain in doubt for some considerable time. The unionists could certainly be happy, however misplaced that happiness, that Home Rule on an all-Ireland basis had been avoided, even though this was the only basis on which the Union could have been saved. Their concept of what had been avoided was almost entirely a figment of an imagination created by party political misrepresentation that was shamelessly exploited by the Tories, fostered by reactive exaggeration, and inspired by the atavistic distrust of Catholicism that was inherent in Orangeism. Whatever had been achieved was at the cost of sundering not only Ireland but Ulster as well. The creation of Northern Ireland involved the cutting off of the Orange-unionists of the three Ulster counties of Cavan, Monaghan and Donegal. It severed over 400,000 northern nationalists from those they regarded as their fellow citizens in what would become the Irish Free State. This created a festering sore, particularly in the border areas, with adverse socio-economic and political implications that continue very poignantly to this day.

This was one of the worst of all possible outcomes, and it is a supreme irony that it was the Orange-unionists, the only party in Ireland to resist Home Rule, who in the end were the one party who had to implement it. The Anglo-Irish Treaty of December 1921 excluded the twenty-six county Irish Free State from the provisions of the recent Government of Ireland Act and therefore entirely from Home Rule, which now applied only in the six counties of north-east Ulster. The new Irish Free State received dominion status instead. Thus Home Rule, which was never in danger of creating the kind of united Ireland the Orangemen feared, became through their intransigence the means of dividing Ireland on a most unsatisfactory basis and of breaking the greater part of the Union.

Conclusions

It has often been argued that the events after 1914 proved the rightness of playing the Orange card and of unionist resistance to Home Rule. The 1916 rebellion and the eventual triumph of republicanism in the South is seen as vindicating the unionists' stand, showing them to have been right all along. It is as though in resisting Home Rule the unionists were all along resisting an Irish Free State, or even a united Ireland outside the Union as one Ulster historian has recently inferred.[16] Home Rule was none of those things, yet this kind of logic has been deployed to argue that de Valera's 1937 'Catholic' Constitution confirmed that Home Rule was equivalent to Rome rule. This is quite wrong. It was the Orange-unionist agitation that forced a change in the whole political situation and compelled a completely new policy and approach from that envisioned under Irish Home Rule. In that new situation the unionists accepted Home Rule for themselves, while the greater part of a divided Ireland became the Free State that years later could regard itself as free to legislate a constitution of a kind that would have been impossible under Home Rule as originally proposed.

Hindsight reasoning from a political or historic outcome is seriously flawed if it ignores the process that produced such an outcome. This kind of ignoring refuses to see that a different process, with an alternative political approach, might well have produced another outcome – an outcome with very different consequences. It has certainly screened out the major unionist contribution to the development of that political situation which in the end made partition inevitable. It forgets the deployment of the old Orange strategy of the self-fulfilling prophecy that had been used so successfully in the 1790s – that of misrepresenting the enemy's position and then by every frustrating and illegal action driving him into the very situation prophesied. From the 1880s the Orange party had similarly pursued paramilitary and sectarian policies that were as illegal as they were undemocratic, and which eventually provoked a revival of republicanism. Many who had come to despair of any possibility of peaceful reform sensed that armed Orange-unionism had 'opened the way' for the emulation of republicans. The result of all this was a growth in extremism leading to a rapid break-down, to a hopeless polarising of the situation, and ultimately a settlement that settled nothing and was anything but an enduring solution to the problems of Ireland.

This could be regarded as a harsh or even hostile view, but it is arguably the verdict of history. In fact, it is a judgement that to a considerable extent was eventually accepted by Sir Edward Carson himself, who at the end of his career was a most disappointed and disillusioned man. In a fine biography, *Edward Carson*, A.T.Q. Stewart sums up the matter as follows:

> The Union was his lodestar, and when it set he plumbed depths of bitterness and defeat… It was no part of his intention to dismember Ireland, or to see Unionism survive in the form of a Home Rule parliament – rather the contrary was true – but having used the resistance of the Ulster loyalists as the trump card to defeat Home Rule, he became to some degree their prisoner. Paradoxically, the very success of the Ulster cause ensured the ruin of his own.[17]

It was typical of Carson to express the matter rather more bluntly himself, when in a scathingly seething speech to the House of Lords early in 1922 on the subject of the recent Anglo-Irish Treaty he exclaimed:

> At that time I did not know, as I know now, that I was a mere puppet in a political game. I was in earnest. I was not playing with politics. I believed all this… What a fool I was! I was only a puppet, and so was Ulster, and so was Ireland, in the political game that was to get the Conservative Party into power.[18]

Here Carson amply confirmed the point made earlier in the book when we quoted Lord Randolph Churchill on the subject of Tory 'opportunism'. The general thrust of his startling outburst bears a striking resemblance to Roy Jenkins' rather calmer indictment of the Tories when, writing in the context of Gladstone's first Home Rule Bill, he drew attention to their party-political preference for unity in the interest of power rather than the national interest. But be that as it may, the northern Orange-unionists would for their own religio-political reasons have had certain reservations about some aspects of Carson's attack on the Treaty. Deep down the 'little Ulster' Orangemen were quite happy with this Home Rule settlement that provided them with the only viable means of perpetuating their Protestant ascendancy, albeit like little Jack Horner in their own small six county corner.

10.

1921 - 1972
The rise and fall of the Orange State

Having secured under the Government of Ireland Act what Prime Minister Sir James Craig was later, when glorying in his Orangeism, to describe as a 'Protestant state', the unionists now determined to hold on to it. However, there was one fly in the ointment. Article XII of the Anglo-Irish Treaty of late 1921 was giving rise to deep unionist uncertainty and grim foreboding. That Article provided for a Boundary Commission that would review the territorial composition and boundary of Northern Ireland, in the context of those areas bordering on the Free State that were predominantly nationalist. Article XII had been cleverly crafted by the Welsh wizard, Lloyd George, to sweeten the Treaty for the Irish nationalists, many of whom believed that this would be the means of alleviating partition, if not ultimately ending it altogether. These were of the view that this could be brought about by the Boundary Commission ceding large areas from Northern Ireland, perhaps even the entire counties of Fermanagh and Tyrone – which could eventually render the residual Northern statelet non-viable both in political and economic terms.

It is hard to believe that Lloyd George saw the Boundary Commission as much more than window-dressing to secure Irish nationalist acceptance of the Treaty. But the Orange-unionists were appalled and, choosing to believe the worst, immediately determined to yield 'not an inch' of territory, vowing that 'this we will maintain'. These policy slogans clearly implied resistance to the work of the Boundary Commission by every means at the unionists' disposal which, given their past record, would include the threat of armed force against the Crown should this be deemed necessary. It is interesting to note that the idea of such a commission had originally been put forward in 1919 by James Craig himself. However, now that Northern Ireland was established, he as its first Prime Minister clearly believed that the territorial issue had already been immutably fixed and settled. Thus any attempt to tamper with the border at this late stage would constitute a serious breach of faith. On receiving details of Article XII in late 1921, the angry Craig stormed back to Belfast and wrote a bitter letter to the Austen Chamberlain, now leader of the Conservative Party. Austen, the devoted son of Joseph Chamberlain the great imperialist and anti-Home Ruler, might for many reasons have been expected to be sympathetic to Craig's cause. He was not; the times had changed. Craig wrote as follows:

What attitude will the British Government adopt if the government of Northern Ireland finds it necessary to call upon their friends and supporters – *more especially the members of the Loyal Orange Institution – to come to their assistance by means of arms* …? … Many already believe that violence is the only language understood by Mr Lloyd George and his Ministers (*emphasis mine*).[1]

The violent and treasonable nature of this language from a relatively insignificant regional premier to one of the most senior statesman in the sovereign British parliament was quite staggering. Yet it was consistent with Craig's previously well-documented gunrunning record. Furthermore, it was just another variation on a very old syndrome – that of the Orangeman, whose ascendancy was being marginally called into question, invoking the doctrine of conditional loyalty to the Crown and threatening to summon up the illegal assistance of the Orange army with banners. Austen Chamberlain and most Conservatives were not impressed. After 1916 they knew at last that things in Ireland had changed – in the words of the poet W.B. Yeats, 'changed utterly'. Indeed, given even a modicum of political perception they must also now have realised that the seed causes of that change had in no small measure been sown by themselves, and by the Orangeism they had sponsored. At the annual (1921) conference of the Conservative Party, Chamberlain made the speech of his life in favour of the Anglo-Irish Treaty, thereby crushing a threatened unionist revolt by a massive majority. Like Carson, it is obvious that Craig and the Orange-unionists had failed to discern the signs of the times. They seemed like a pack of lumbering, mauling rugby forwards rolling on in their imagined progress, quite unaware that the ball had already been turned over and was in the hands of a fleet-footed opposition, which was now running rapidly in the opposite direction. Once again Orange-unionism had got it wrong.

The perceived threat of the Boundary Commission receded with the outbreak of the Irish Civil War combined with Lloyd George's departure from office in the autumn of 1922. This led to the brief accession to power of the new Conservative leader and former die-hard, Andrew Bonar Law. The new Prime Minister, as we saw earlier, was a Canadian-Ulsterman, a convinced anti-Home Ruler and more than just a good friend of the unionists. Bonar Law was a unionist through and through and, as Roy Jenkins wryly puts it, 'an Ulsterman to his fingertips'. It was therefore probably inevitable that the whole idea of the Boundary Commission would be allowed to atrophy. In fact, little more was heard of it until 1924 when it was revived under a very new administration – that of James Ramsay MacDonald's first Labour government.

Unlike Bonar Law, James Ramsay MacDonald was no friend of the Ulster unionists. Twelve years earlier, when justifiably making adverse comparisons between Belfast's socio-labour conditions and those of the rest of the United Kingdom, MacDonald stated in the British House of Commons with some accuracy that 'whenever there is an attempt to root out sweating in Belfast the Orange big drum is beaten'. He now appeared to mean business, and just a few weeks after taking office he called a conference on the subject of the Boundary Commission. At this conference he made clear his intention that the Commission should be set up quickly and get on with its work. The Orange-unionist government of Northern Ireland bluntly refused to participate. Instead, its response was to organise highly visible, large-scale mobilisation drills of the Ulster Special Constabulary, particularly in the border areas. As though that signal were insufficiently clear, Craig's government commissioned further substantial consignments of weapons, including Vickers and Lewis machine guns and fourteen million rounds of ammunition, 'enough for a small war' as one writer put it.[2] This clearly re-echoed the warning Craig had issued to Austen Chamberlain two years previously, and was tantamount to threatening a further Orange-unionist armed rebellion against the British Crown in parliament.

The Boundary Commission was set up, although there is some evidence to suggest that Ramsay MacDonald hoped to steer it in the direction of making only minor alterations to Northern Ireland's border. A leaked report of the Boundary Commission's first draft in November 1925 suggested no more than small two-way transfers of territory, none of which fired much enthusiasm on either side of the Irish border. In fact, all three governments eventually agreed that the Report should be suppressed and binned, on the basis of a deal that would ensure the agreed integrity of Northern Ireland, and which would release the Free State from its Treaty obligation to make contributions to the United Kingdom's national debt. It was entirely predictable that border nationalists and republicans would vehemently oppose the deal, for the existing border delineating partition was a very rough cut business that satisfied very few who were affected by it. In fact, it was the alienation of these nationalists that contributed much to Eamon De Valera's return to constitutional politics as leader of the new republican Fianna Fáil party. However, most people were now war weary. The year therefore ended with all three governments in agreement and, for the first time, both parts of partitioned Ireland at peace.

Sir James Craig's unionist government now had opportunity and scope to show its true mettle, especially given the British government's policy from then onwards to play little part in Northern Ireland's internal affairs. Craig, who as Lord Craigavon would remain in power until his death in 1940, personified the Orange-unionist ethos. This ethos that went far beyond constitutional politics in that it impacted on virtually all departments of life in Northern Ireland – all aspects of government, local politics, religion, marriage, business, employment, etc. As Craigavon famously put it in a speech to the Stormont parliament in 1934 when well into the second half of his long tenure of office:

> I have always said that I am an Orangeman first and a politician and a member of this parliament afterwards … All I boast is that we have a Protestant parliament and a Protestant state. Therefore, it is undoubtedly our duty and our privilege, and always will be, to see that those appointed by us possess the most unimpeachable loyalty to the King and Constitution. This is my whole object in carrying on a Protestant Government for a Protestant people.

It was not the first time he had openly boasted his government's Orange credentials, nor would it be the last. At an Orange demonstration on 12th July 1936 he said that 'Orangeism, Protestantism, and the Loyalist cause are more strongly entrenched than ever and equally so is the government at Stormont'. Nor was

Craigavon alone in this matter-of-fact sectarian ascendancy, for many other Orange-unionist leaders such as Sir Basil Brooke would time and again reiterate similar sentiments for the encouragement of the faithful, who seemed ever fearful of their leaders becoming soft. Yet such statements and restatements of the Orange ethos were no more than the obvious truth. Without exception every Prime Minister of Northern Ireland would be an Orangeman, as would 95 per cent of all unionist MPs, and the Orange Order would continue to be officially and powerfully represented in unionism's ruling body, the Ulster Unionist Council. Thus the incipient 'Ulsterisation' of Orange-unionism that began to be apparent in the days of Henry Cooke, and which took on the formal shape of the Ulster Unionist Council in 1905 when a burgeoning Northern unionism began to front Orangeism's political interests, had now reached its consummation. The unionist government of Northern Ireland was now the supreme representative and guarantor of Orangeism's chief political objective – that of maintaining the Williamite revolution by the constitutional link with Britain under a Protestant Crown, and the defence of an all-pervasive Protestant ascendancy in Ireland, albeit now only in the Northern part of it.

The Rev. Martin Smyth MP, who for over twenty years and until recently was Worshipful Grand Master of the Grand Lodge of Ireland, once said that the Orange Order was a pressure group to ensure that the Ulster Unionist Party remained firm on the constitution. He argued that its right to do so was based on the fact that the party was born out of that institution. He added that this influence would be achieved either through the selection of parliamentary candidates, or by withholding support from the government in and through the Ulster Unionist Council on which it was powerfully represented.[3] Given that down the years the eponymously named unionist government saw this great constitutional issue as its very *raison d'être* there seemed to be precious little likelihood of any clash with Orangeism on that matter, nor was there any such clash for over forty years. Indeed, during the long tenure of the Ulster Unionist Party's power there were so few instances of any other kind of clash between successive unionist governments and the Orange Order that Michael Farrell's then description of Northern Ireland as 'the Orange State' seems singularly apt.

With successive British governments adopting a hands-off policy, Orangeism was free to become the most powerful force in the Protestant ascendancy government of Northern Ireland. To all intents and purposes the Orange Order appeared both to have achieved, and to be well in control of, its major political objective. However, because of its inherently flawed philosophy of a covenanted loyalty to the Crown conditional upon the maintenance of Protestant supremacy, Orangeism contained within itself the seeds of its own ruin. In the long run this was also to prove true of Orange-unionist government. The final bitter harvest came after many years during which unionist ministers pursued this philosophy to such extreme lengths – something that will be examined in the next chapter – that things suddenly came to a crunch when this kind of political ascendancy was no longer practicable, and certainly not with impunity. The situation finally erupted, first in political protest and violence, then in terror and counter-terror that was to last for nearly thirty years, during which it claimed well over three thousand lives.

There were preliminary eruptions in the course of the Northern Ireland civil rights protests and demonstrations of the 1960s. These arose out of years of pent-up nationalist frustration and anger, and developed into a massive and co-ordinated reaction to Orange-unionist political discrimination that suddenly seemed particularly grotesque in the United Kingdom of the 'swinging 60s'. The election of Harold Wilson's professedly modernising Labour government after 'thirteen years of Tory mis-rule' provided a great fillip to nationalist expectations. Nationalism had been radicalised under a new kind of leadership, pre-eminent among whom was the young John Hume, and a real possibility of change seemed to be in the air. But the civil rights marches and demonstrations were regularly confronted by equally determined Orange loyalist counter-demonstrations, whose zero sum mentality refused to concede anything to the nationalist case. Although ever insistent on their own right to march, the Orange loyalists did their utmost to prevent or disrupt the civil rights marches, and often succeeded in doing so. The resultant street politics therefore involved a clash of the irreconcilable aspirations of equality and ascendancy, and the inevitable crowd confrontations often necessitated the intervention of the RUC and 'B' Specials. Such situations regularly ended in serious riot and bloodshed, the most notable example of this being the Derry Civil Rights march of 5th October 1968, when several nationalist MPs and countless demonstrators were unceremoniously batoned by the police, in full view of the world's TV cameras. These incredible events created the most vicious sectarian crisis thus far in Northern Ireland's history, but there was much worse to follow. And yet it is a supreme irony that while these things were unfolding on the streets the unionist government was being led by its most liberal and probably most able prime minister, Captain Terence O'Neill – yet another former military man. As we shall see later, O'Neill would eventually be crushed between the upper and nether millstones of a desperate need for reform and ascendancy reaction to such reform, when he was eventually forced to resign in the spring of 1969.

Given the disturbed political circumstances of the time, it was hardly surprising that the next loyalist and Orange marching season would again become the catalyst for sectarian violence. John Hume had anticipated trouble and asked an Orangeman, whom he knew as 'kind and decent', why it was necessary to perpetuate these annual provocations. The reply was brutally honest: 'We have to show them who's master'. On 12th August 1969 some 15,000 Apprentice Boys poured into Londonderry for their annual parade through the city and along the ancient walls that tower above the nationalist Bogside. The Apprentice Boys of Derry is a distinctive loyalist organisation that places some emphasis on historical pageantry. However, in common with Orangeism it is a religio-political Williamite organisation that participates in Orange celebrations and shares Orange facilities. Indeed, an estimated 75 per cent of its members are also members of the Orange Order – a good example of the overlapping nature and membership of the Loyal Orders. The demonstration of August 1969 would lead to a politically explosive situation. In the course of the march the Apprentice Boys threw pennies from the walls and down to the Catholic people below – an ascendancy insult calculated to signify the inferior status of the nationalists. The march soon came under attack by stone-throwing Catholic youths, which led to severely violent clashes between nationalists, loyalists and police – clashes that turned into a massive and extended riot involving the throwing of petrol bombs by the rioters and the use of CS gas by the police. After hours of fighting, the situation took on the proportions of a virtual insurrection of the nationalist community against the Orange-unionist government. The Apprentice Boys' parade, designed 'to show them who's master', and its concomitant events would in many respects mark the beginning of the Troubles. As a near-revolutionary situation seemed to teeter on the brink of civil war, the Labour government took the momentous decision, despite many misgivings, to send the British Army into Northern Ireland.

On 14th August the Army replaced the beleaguered RUC on the streets of Derry, as a result of which there was an uneasy peace. But the disturbance and destruction were soon to be visited on Belfast. Factories and hundreds of homes were burned or seriously damaged in two days of fierce sectarian rioting, arson attacks and gun fighting in which some armed B-Specials actually aligned themselves with loyalist rioters. Several people were killed. It was therefore no surprise when further British troops arrived in Belfast on 15th August 1969 in an effort to take control of the situation. The British government was well aware that the Army would have only a limited 'honeymoon period', and hoped that it might be possible to withdraw the troops after perhaps a few months. But things were very much worse than had been imagined, and the Army remains in Northern Ireland to this day – more than thirty years later.

Like the army, the government found that once it engaged directly with Northern Ireland it became very difficult to disengage. As each day passed it became ever more clear that the years of Orange-unionist ascendancy politics had created a monster. As never before an awakened nationalist community was now challenging unionist supremacy. A perplexed British government had no alternative but to deal with the situation as best it could. Following Lord Hunt's Report on the police, the RUC was reformed under a new British chief constable and the B-Specials were disbanded, much to the fury of loyalists and the delight of nationalists. Loyalist protests and further riots ensued, in the course of which a policeman was shot dead by loyalists – the first police fatality of the Troubles. Things were now out of hand and before the end of the year a split in the IRA led to the creation of the Provisional IRA. For a time, however, the Provisionals kept a fairly low profile.

Despite the Troubles, Orange marching continued. On Easter Tuesday 1970 an Orange parade through nationalist areas in west Belfast was once again the trigger for serious rioting. British troops, followed by Protestant rioters, entered nationalist housing estates and used CS gas against rioting Catholic youths. An Orange march on 27th June in the Ardoyne area of Belfast sparked a further outbreak of sectarian rioting, which soon developed into gun fighting involving several fatalities. This was now typical of Ulster's annual declension from marching, through mayhem, and on to murder. Amid increasing violence the Orange marching season of that summer constituted a major problem for the uncomprehending and over-stretched security forces. Observing one parade, the British military GOC General Freeland became so frustrated by the entire spectacle as to exclaim, 'Grown men! Pathetic! Ridiculous!' [4] His outburst was not caused merely by his view that Orange religio-political pageantry was anachronistic, but because it stirred up atavistic reactions and sectarian hatreds. It was dangerous. That summer the gloom and despair of all concerned further deepened when the Provisional IRA began its terrible bombing campaign.

In the very nature of things, British military intervention greatly diminished the power of the unionist government now under new prime minister, Major Chichester-Clark. For obvious reasons he could not exercise command over the British Army, and therefore had no direct control the security situation, which meant that some of Northern Ireland's most vital ascendancy powers had in effect been removed. This greatly irked the unionists, who wanted to obtain more rather than less power. Jonathan Bardon quotes the observation of one senior British Army officer on this matter: 'Just as well they didn't! My God! They had no broad political ideas. They just wanted to smash the Catholics'.[5] The army officer's judgement was deadly accurate, and certainly in line with the opinion of this book. As ever, the Orange-unionist idea of security and strong government was simply a matter of 'keeping the papists in their places' and 'showing them who's master'. The antidote was the cause of the disease.

In an attempt to achieve stronger security measures Major Chichester-Clark resigned in March 1971, and was succeeded by Brian Faulkner. This seemed to make a difference, for by August that year Faulkner had persuaded the reluctant British prime minister Edward Heath to give him a more control of security and to introduce internment without trial. This policy, which was contrary to the opinion of the British military, was disastrous both in execution and result. As to execution, it was entirely one-sided in that it did not include a single loyalist, and in any event all the top IRA men escaped the net. As to result, there was quite massive alienation among the nationalist community, which led to a storm of protest, to the withdrawal of the Opposition SDLP from the Stormont parliament, and to greatly increased recruitment to the IRA. A nationalist campaign of protest reached a crescendo with the massive anti-internment march in Derry on 30th January 1972, a day that became known as Bloody Sunday. This was the infamous day when the British Paratroops, in the subsequent words of the coroner, 'ran amok' killing fourteen and wounding a further thirteen unarmed marchers, some of them shot in the back. Faulkner's internment policy proved to be a tragic misjudgement. Nationalist alienation was complete, and three days later thirty thousand people marched on the British Embassy in Dublin and burned it down. As a direct consequence of internment, the Troubles and the IRA's 'armed struggle' – together with loyalist counter-terror – were institutionalised, and what almost amounted to a civil war, albeit waged on the fringes of 'normal' life, continued almost unabated for the next twenty-five years.

A few weeks later, Brian Faulkner and his senior ministers were called to London and advised by Prime Minister Heath that total control of security matters, including the RUC, would be taken over by Westminster, and that a Secretary of State for Northern Ireland would be appointed. This was widely regarded as the most severe censure of the unionist government's whole policy and ethos. It was so unacceptable to Faulkner and his government that they resigned en bloc the next day. Edward Heath, who obviously had anticipated Faulkner's response, immediately prorogued the Stormont parliament for a year, but effectively Heath's prorogation proved to be the final end of unionist government in Northern Ireland as then understood and exercised. This marked the end of Orange-unionist ascendancy power through a Protestant parliament for a Protestant people, and from that time onwards it has seemed increasingly unlikely that such an ascendancy government could ever return. Sadly, the unionist people would be painfully slow to learn from this, and many of them have yet to do so, but Brian Faulkner was certainly one who did.

Conclusions

The rise of the Orange state of Northern Ireland occurred when Orange-unionism rebelled against the Crown in parliament and refused to accept a limited form of devolved and democratic Home Rule government for Ireland. It did so because this was entirely incompatible with its doctrine of Protestant ascendancy. Instead, it accepted Home Rule for a cut-down 'Ulster' re-named Northern Ireland, where it could exercise majoritarian ascendancy by means of a Protestant parliament for a Protestant people. The manner in which it did so eventually led to a virtual rebellion of the nationalist people and to the fall of the Orange-unionist state after fifty years of one-party government. Orange-unionism's intransigent opposition to demands for modest civil rights, its final rejection of the potentially reforming leader O'Neill, and its determination despite everything to continue with the old ascendancy Orange attitudes as reflected by its sectarian marching through nationalist areas, brought things to a head. Ascendancy politics had become intolerable to a growing and determined minority, as was the coat-trailing Orange marching through sensitive areas that seemed to symbolise that very ascendancy. Such policies and practices were now impracticable and unacceptable in a changing society that was now almost half-nationalist and striving for equality, and all the more so in what, under the aegis of the United Kingdom, purported to be a modern pluralist democracy. A more detailed analytical account of the spectacular failure of Orange-unionism's politics is contained in the next chapter.

11.

Aftermath: Summation and Sequel

In concluding this section on the objectives of Orangeism, the outcomes of those objectives are summarised by reference to three salient aspects of unionist government political strategy – first security policy; second socio-economics; and third the management of politics. Particular attention is paid to the Orange influence behind that political strategy, which caused the almost total alienation of the nationalist community and led to the eventual collapse of the Orange-unionist state. Finally, there follows a brief survey of the sequel to that failure, and of Orangeism's position on some of the political issues that have arisen during the past thirty years leading up to our own time.

Security Policy

It has often been said that the first responsibility of government is to ensure the security of all its citizens, and doubtless a certain kind of security or defence was the primary preoccupation of the first unionist government of Northern Ireland. This was not entirely due to the prevailing political situation, but owed much to the military-minded frontier spirit of its Orange pedigree, which since Colonel Saunderson's time had always ensured a unionist leadership that would include an impressive array of commanders, colonels and captains. Not that this military emphasis was motivated by the security needs of the country's citizens *per se*, for a substantial proportion of the ordinary Northern Irish people were regarded as virtual or potential enemies. Thus the Orange-unionist government's preoccupation with security was to ensure the defence of the Protestant ascendancy that had been institutionalised in the Orange state of Northern Ireland.

We have seen that the early priority of the incipient unionist government in 1920 was to establish a paramilitary reserve police force based on the Orange UVF, and known as the Ulster Special Constabulary. This did not augur well for the security of Northern Ireland's minority citizenship. Indeed, precisely the opposite was the case. The militant Specials soon came to be regarded with terror and hatred, largely because they were seen as the sectarian strong-arm of a virtually one-party state, and also because of the arson, looting, reprisal and pogrom in which some of their members had been implicated from the beginning. Any subsequent change either in their attitude or in their perceived standing in the community was insufficient to make them acceptable to nationalists – a situation that obtained until the outbreak of the Troubles when they were finally disbanded in 1969, much to the chagrin of the Orange Order.

Northern Ireland's police force, the Royal Ulster Constabulary (RUC), which was established in June 1922, was initially of a quite different pedigree inasmuch as it had its origins in the former all-Ireland police force, the Royal Irish Constabulary (RIC). The original idea was that the RUC would be 3,000 strong, one-third of which would comprise Catholic transferees from the RIC, together with not more than 1,000 Protestant RIC transferees, and the balance made up from the new Specials. This proportional arrangement was largely due to British government pressure to ensure that the new Northern Ireland security forces would be acceptable to the whole community. But such an even-handed approach did not sit well with a policy of Protestant ascendancy, and Orange-unionists were therefore vehemently opposed to it.

The proposed arrangement provoked a storm of protest from the Orange Order, one example of which was the threat sent to Prime Minister Craig by County Armagh Orangemen to the effect that they would 'not guarantee the safety of any Roman Catholic retained in the force' in that area.[1] James Craig sought to mollify these sectarian protesters with the sage remark that in all the circumstances of Northern Ireland it was most unlikely that the Catholics would take up all their places in the RUC. Sadly, the only merit in Craig's observation was that it was true. In fact, Catholic involvement peaked quite quickly at 21 per cent because of the transfer mechanism – a figure that dropped to 17 per cent in 1936, to 11 per cent in the 1960's and to a mere 8 per cent by 1991.

By not taking up their full quota for reasons that Craig had anticipated, and which he had also done much to create, the Catholics effectively handed over their places in the RUC to the Orange Specials, with whom in any event the new police force would have to work closely. This and other things therefore conspired to give the new RUC an Orange and anti-Catholic image. This regrettable situation was not improved by the unionist government's draconian security policy. Of that policy the South African prime minister Henrik Vorster later declared that he would willingly exchange all the coercive apartheid legislation of his country for one clause of Northern Ireland's Special Powers Act of 1922. Those 'special powers', which in practice were mainly directed against Catholic nationalists and renewable every five years, were made permanent in 1933 – at a time when there was no longer any serious threat from the IRA. It seemed that whatever the circumstances, the original Orange objective always had to be pursued. Protestant ascendancy had to be maintained. The papists, like Henrik Vorster's natives of South Africa, always had to be kept in their places.

The Orange ethos of the RUC received poignant acknowledgement when an RUC Orange Lodge – the Sir Robert Peel – was established with government approval in 1923. (The appellation was doubly clever, for in the previous century Sir Robert Peel had founded the British police – the 'peelers' – and had been nicknamed 'Orange Peel' by Daniel O'Connell.) Sir Dawson Bates, the Minister of Home

Affairs in charge of the policing of the whole community, was guest-speaker at the first meeting of the Peel Lodge. Evidently he saw no conflict of interest either in his own or the RUC's membership of a secret and sectarian order. Shortly afterwards the Peel Lodge's office of Worshipful Master was filled by the notorious District Inspector John W. Nixon, who was widely believed to have led a group of RUC and B-Specials in the reprisal killing of Catholics during the then recent pogroms. Nixon was so extreme that the unionist government became embarrassed to the point of trying to get rid of him, by finding him a job in the Canadian police. Nixon refused to co-operate and rejected the offer, eventually being dismissed for making violent and subversive speeches from Orange platforms. The Orange ethos was to plague the RUC for many years. The plague was exacerbated by the particular nature of the RUC's politico-policing responsibilities. There was, for example, their requirement to police the Special Powers Act, as well as their presumed duty to force Orange marches through Catholic areas, and conversely, because of the Flags and Emblems Act, their duty to prevent the process of nationalist marches almost anywhere in Northern Ireland. Because of the biased nature of their 'job description', it followed that the paramilitary RUC could not have been fully acceptable to the nationalist community in almost any circumstances.

The RUC and the associated B-Specials came to be regarded by most of the minority Catholic community as the strong-arm of Orange ascendancy in Northern Ireland. However, there were occasions when anti-establishment loyalists could also feel the weight of that strong-arm, as did the young Ian Paisley in the 1950s when he was moved to attack the Special Powers Act and to describe Northern Ireland as a police state. Trade unionists, socialists and civil rights activists were also sometimes on its receiving end. But in the essential nature of things it was largely the minority community that suffered what was inevitably perceived as sectarian police repression. As a result, Catholic-nationalist resentment and alienation smouldered on until the volcano finally erupted in the late 1960s, in the extended violence that produced an even greater polarisation of society and with it an image of the RUC that seemed more partisan than ever.

It is only fair to point out that, in the context of fifty years of Orange-unionist government, it was probably inevitable that Northern Ireland's police force should reflect the attitudes and values of the political polity in which it had to operate. Conversely, the abolition of the old Stormont parliament and the introduction of direct British rule undoubtedly made for subsequent reform that compelled the RUC to cast off some of the old Orange ethos. This provided it with the opportunity to project an improved and more impartial image. But given the predominantly Protestant makeup of the force, it is hardly surprising that there were occasions when the new image slipped. One example was the situation surrounding the Orange march at Drumcree in July 1996, which brought Northern Ireland close to anarchy and in circumstances where the role of the police was subsequently severely criticised.[2] There were reports of police complicity in the Orange protests which, when combined with the substantially increased absenteeism from duty at that time, gave rise to parliamentary questions about the numbers of policemen in membership of the Orange Order. The question could not be answered, because of the absorption of the RUC's Peel Lodge into other Orange Lodges, but it was estimated that in the mid-1990s Orange membership of the RUC stood at around 2,000.

To many nationalists, including liberal nationalists, those events, together with the RUC's earlier sectarian baggage and paramilitary role in the Troubles, seemed to confirm its casting in a perceivably partisan role. That enduring perception, and the fact that the RUC was so under-representative of the minority community, militated against its cross-community acceptance in Northern Ireland – a fatal flaw in any police service. This was recognised by the Good Friday Agreement (1998) which, among other things, provides for major police restructuring and reform – all of which justified the quite radical findings of Chris Patten's subsequent report on policing in Northern Ireland. Membership of the Patten Committee combined sound local knowledge, broad experience and not a little wisdom, and it produced a report that was generally welcomed by nationalists and republicans, as well as by Protestant liberals. But some of its findings, particularly that calling for the removal of the title 'Royal Ulster Constabulary' (RUC), were opposed by unionists, and vehemently so by the Orange Order – all of which tended to confirm the widely-held view that the Orange-unionists have always regarded the RUC as *their* police force. That, of course, was precisely the point at issue. A completely new title, the 'Police Service of Northern Ireland' was introduced, together with a new recruitment policy designed to achieve 50/50 Protestant/Catholic participation.

Given that a completely new beginning on policing was imperative, a change in title became the essential symbol for the change involved. This was especially so inasmuch as the title 'Royal Ulster Constabulary' involved terms that were historically and politically inaccurate and pejorative. The term 'Royal', which for obvious political reasons could never command cross-community loyalty in Northern Ireland, is an appellation that is not applied to any other police service in Britain. This poses the obvious question: if not for reasons of coat-trailing ascendancy, why of all places in the entire Kingdom should use of the term 'Royal' in the name of a police force have been confined to Ireland? As to the term 'Ulster', it has been shown at several junctures throughout the book that this was a deliberately misused term involving many politically sensitive issues. In fact, as used by Orange-unionism it was almost always geographically and politically inaccurate. The question of name or title therefore had to be very important in the context of the reforming principles necessarily involved in establishing genuine community-wide policing. When all is said and done, the achievement of full cross-community support and respect are the vital essentials for the successful functioning of a modern police service, and Chris Patten's proposed reform package therefore continues to be of tremendous importance in that respect.

Socio-economic policy

In pre-Keynesian times devolved regional government provided no great advantages for the administration of social and economic policy. In fact, probably the reverse was true. It can be argued that in the case of the new state of Northern Ireland devolution not only increased its political isolation, but also exacerbated the natural economic weaknesses that were inherent both in regionalism and remoteness from the real centre of power at that time. Thus viewed, the Unionist government would in any circumstances have found it difficult to achieve substantial improvements in the economic situation, although it might be argued that none of Northern Ireland's adverse circumstances precluded the possibility of government mal-administration making that situation considerably worse than it otherwise might have been. In the event, the Orange-unionist government was not a good economic manager, and devolution was not to the benefit of Northern Ireland as a whole.

For much of the fifty years of unionist rule Northern Ireland was the most deprived region of the entire United Kingdom whatever yardstick was used – poverty, housing, public health, infant mortality, or unemployment – as Jonathan Bardon shows in his detailed and graphic account of that most squalid time.[3] Bardon is not lacking in powerful support from other eminent historians here, for Robert Kee draws from what he describes as F.S.L. Lyons's 'terrifying summary' when pointing out that:

> Although in the mid-1920s it had been found that eighteen per cent of the population ... was living at a density of more than two to a room very little was done to remedy this until after the war. After eighteen years of the state's existence eighty-seven per cent of the houses in the countryside were without running water. Public health was worse than in any other comparable area of the British Isles: forty-six per cent of those who died between the ages of fifteen and twenty-five died of tuberculosis. After nearly twenty years of the state a quarter of all the children who died under the age of one died in a workhouse.[4]

Terrifying summary, indeed. Wretched and unsanitary ghetto housing, often involving one house being shared by up to four families, lay at the root of an abysmal public health problem. This was a situation so bad that only the worst imaginable disturbance and damage such as that inflicted by the German air raids of 1941 could exacerbate it. The renowned British journalist Robert Fisk has recently written that:

> When Northern Ireland suffered its 1941 Calvary, the morale of its bombed survivors collapsed while the Northern Ireland home affairs minister, the mean-spirited and alcoholic Dawson Bates, urged the opening of camps for thousands of refugees whose 'personal habits. . . are sub-human'. No wonder the Moderator of the Presbyterian Church was to warn that 'if something is not done now to remedy this rank inequality, there will be a revolution after the war'. Brooke intended to avoid any such civil unrest, whatever the cost to Britain's wartime allies. Secret communications ... show that Brooke was fearful of British plans to farm out thousands of Polish troops to the North after the war. The Poles had fought alongside Northern Irish regiments at Monte Cassino, but could not return to their now-communist homeland. Brooke refused to have them. The Poles were Catholics.[5]

Long after the war Northern Ireland's socio-economic situation remained so bad that even as late as 1974 the housing authorities, covering both public and private interests, together constituted what was described as 'the largest slum landlord in Europe'.[6] At that time 20 per cent of Northern Ireland's total occupied housing stock was classified as statutorily unfit, a figure which rose to 24 per cent in Belfast, and to 50 per cent in some of the inner city areas. No government could absolve itself from blame for such an appalling situation. Indeed, it has to be contended that this failure of social policy was of such a nature and extent that it had to be deliberate, and rooted in a belief-system – the minimalist and sectarian politics of Orangeism.

Severe unemployment was of course an underlying cause of the overall problem of poverty and deprivation, although it should be acknowledged that there was nothing unusual about unemployment in the context of the depression in the 'hungry thirties'. But the distinctive feature of Northern Ireland's unemployment was in its nature as well as its scale. At that time things had become so bad that for once, in October 1932, Belfast's Protestant and Catholic workers united in a trade union protest, only for this to be suppressed first by the batons and then by the guns of the RUC. But the guns were turned only on the Catholic workers.[7] By 1938 unemployment had reached a level of 30 per cent of the insured population compared with 24 per cent in Wales, then the worst affected region in Britain. Yet the important fact is that these figures do not tell the whole story, for Northern Ireland's terrible deprivation had not been confined to the depression. Many people had been out of work for so long that they were not included among the insured population and therefore formed no part of the statistics of the depression. It is significant that, unlike the people of Britain after 1928, these people had no entitlement to benefit.

The majority of the permanently impoverished lived in Belfast and, for reasons that will be explained later, most of them were Catholic and had to rely on the Poor Law for subsistence. The Belfast Guardians, a *petit bourgeoisie* of careful shopkeepers who knew the value of money if not of their fellow human beings, were responsible for administering this. The Guardians seemed less concerned about providing relief for those they regarded as enemies of the country than about minimising the burden on their own rate-paying class. Relief was therefore discretionary, selective and given in kind – such as a chit for groceries. Some of the beneficiaries received the added bonus of having their names posted on the gable-end of the street in which they lived.

In a harrowing account of this practice, the Belfast socialist Paddy Devlin has pointed out that those Protestants who did not qualify for social benefits at least had the safety net of Poor Law relief. But the large number of long-term unemployed Catholics were rarely found worthy of the Guardians' discretionary favour. This explained the disparity at that time between the Poor Law statistics of Belfast and Glasgow, where eighty people per thousand received relief as compared with only seven per thousand in Belfast. Devlin maintained that the essential objective of the whole system in Northern Ireland was one of socio-political control, designed to keep the papists in their places. This, of course, clearly suggests that the policy was not unconnected with the minimalist ascendancy politics of Orange-unionism:

> The Government had a vested interest in ignoring the calls for a change of the system. They believed it affected only their political enemies whom they were

already excluding from employment and from unemployment insurance. And they believed that if the enemies were further excluded from relief, they would be forced to face the grim choice of starving or emigrating.[8]

What was unusual about Northern Ireland was not just the sheer scale of its deprivation, but the structure of its often politically located unemployment, together with the sectarian administration of its welfare system. This gave rise to the widely held belief that the unionists were manipulating deprivation as a weapon by which to control the Catholics. Of course it can be rightly argued that thousands of Protestants also suffered from unemployment at that time. Paddy Devlin's thesis does not deny that. But he suggests that the unionist government – to the extent it could and by whatever means at its disposal – sought to manage unemployment and the benefits system to the detriment of Catholics and to the advantage of its own Protestant supporters. There is no doubt that many working class Protestants also suffered, but the system was such that for sectarian reasons the Catholics suffered very much more.

This analysis fits with the previously quoted words of Prime Minister Craig, who said it was an Orange-unionist duty 'to see that those appointed by us possess the most unimpeachable loyalty to the King and Constitution' – a doctrine that was tantamount to Catholic exclusion. There is much evidence of this. Dawson Bates, the Minister of Home Affairs, made it clear that he 'did not want his most juvenile clerk or typist, if a papist, assigned for duty to his Ministry'.[9] John Andrews, the Minister of Labour who succeeded Craig as Prime Minister in 1941, learned on return from holiday that two Free Staters were employed by his Ministry and immediately sacked them, even though the men in question had excellent British Army records. He then proceeded to tighten the regulations to disqualify automatically any future such candidates.[10] There were relatively few Catholics employed in the Northern Ireland Civil Service, but that paucity did not prevent the Orange Order from carrying out surveillance of such Catholic civil servants as there were, and even of those Protestants who were married to Catholics.[11] But the doctrine of Catholic exclusion was of much wider application. Captain Basil Brooke, the land-owning Minister of Agriculture who was to become Northern Ireland's third Prime Minister in 1943, had a reputation for being its most blunt proponent. At an Orange demonstration on 12th July 1933 he was reported as saying:

> He felt he could speak freely on this subject as he had not a Roman Catholic about his place... There was a definite plot to overpower the vote of Unionists in the North. He would appeal to Loyalists, therefore, wherever possible, to employ Protestant lads and lassies (cheers).[12]

Similar messages were regularly proclaimed by leading Orange-unionists from Orange platforms, with the result that many employers either deliberately or by default increasingly practised discriminatory recruitment policies – a situation which became almost endemic in Northern Ireland until outlawed by the relatively recent imposition of British fair employment legislation. Despite the repeated denials and selective amnesia of some current unionist politicians, it is beyond argument that successive unionist governments deployed socio-economic policy as a weapon of control, and openly encouraged employment discrimination against Catholics. This was another means of enacting the old Orange policy of keeping the papists in their places. Such discrimination is much more difficult to practice nowadays thanks to prohibiting legislation, but the controlling sectarian mindset that gave rise to it in the first place is still very much alive. A current example is that of the Orange organisation in mid-Ulster that strategically buys and sells land and property 'in order to prevent it from falling into the wrong hands' – new words, but the same old message.

Politics

In the classical sense of the word, politics concerns the governance both of the constitutional state and all its citizens. Strong on the former, the Orange-unionist government was notoriously weak on the latter. The manner and extent to which unionism concentrated on the narrow ground of constitutional politics proved greatly to the detriment of a holistic politics that would have addressed the general good of all Northern Ireland's citizens. Thus unionism was singularly ill-equipped to handle the wide range of political matters necessary to the good government of the people – a short-coming that had nothing to do with political efficiency, but everything to do with political philosophy and priority. As ever, unionism's problem lay in the minimalist and single-issue credo that came with its Orangeism – the maintenance of a Protestant ascendancy under the Union – which by its very nature was the antithesis of good government for a whole citizenry that was at least one-third Catholic. John Arlott, the much loved cricket commentator and a noted British Liberal, speaking as a panellist on the BBC Radio discussion programme 'Any Questions' (circa 1960), said of Northern Ireland's Orange-unionist ministers, 'They are so far to the right that they almost frighten me'. Their politics were indeed frightening, so much so that for years British governments shrank back from political involvement in Northern Ireland. These were the ascendancy politics of an extreme credo that inhered repression, discrimination and inequality, which alienated the minority and ultimately led to the collapse of the very state itself.

Given its minimalist political philosophy and the absolutism of its power complex, it was inevitable that the first unionist government should endeavour to control the whole apparatus of politics. In 1922 it abolished proportional representation for local elections, which the British government had specifically written into the Government of Ireland Act (1921) in the interest of those non-sectarian minority parties who might benefit from the second preference vote. The new policy, which had the effect of sectarianising the political situation yet further, was combined with a quite arbitrary redrawing of the local government ward boundaries to ensure unionist majorities. The nationalists were already disadvantaged by a restricted franchise, but the new gerrymander involved a calculated herding of their numbers in the newly drawn wards. This ensured that nationalist seats were won with massive majorities, whereas the unionist wards were drawn in such a way that unionist seats could be won comfortably and without significant vote wastage. As a result, the unionists could now win a majority of seats even in council areas where they were much in the minority.

Whereas in 1920, proportional to their numbers, nationalists were in control of about one-third of local councils, by 1924 their control of councils was reduced to one-fortieth. This was as a direct consequence of the gerrymander. Derry City was to become the classic example of this when, to take the statistics of the 1960s as a yardstick, the unionists who represented only 37 per cent of the enfranchised population controlled the Derry Council by 12 seats to 8. By holding the vast majority of local councils throughout Northern Ireland, even in districts were they were in the minority, the unionists were able to control local authority employment as well as the allocation of council housing. However, unionist discrimination in these matters, though quite brazen, was never really considered wrong. Rather it was regarded as a majoritarian right and in the best interest of the state. The bullish nature of the unionist approach to local politics is best illustrated by the fact that in 1945, when the British government extended the democracy of local government by introducing universal adult suffrage in Britain, the response of the Stormont government was to do precisely the opposite by legislating for an even more restricted franchise.

In the ensuing parliamentary debate the Stormont Chief Whip, L.E. Curran, tried to defend the unionist position. With a frankness that was naïve in the extreme he said: 'The best way to prevent the overthrow of the government by people who had no stake in the country and had not the welfare of the people of Ulster at heart was to disenfranchise them'.[13] The statement appeared in the press the next day, but was edited out of the Stormont Hansard, even though the Opposition's outrage against it was fully reported. But when all was said and done this was no more than the latest example of political Orangeism on the hoof, snorting its conditional loyalty to the Crown while defiantly trampling on British political and democratic standards – all in the interest of defending Protestant ascendancy. Once again the Orange-unionists were prepared to go to almost any lengths in order to maintain control.

Not content with this, the unionists subsequently decided to abolish proportional representation for Northern Ireland's parliamentary elections as well. Prime Minister James Craig, showing scant regard even for his own parliament, unashamedly indicated the nature and objective of his new policy by choosing to announce it from an Orange platform on 12th July 1927. Following the same principles as for local government elections described above, this policy led to a further sectarianising of the political situation in that it ensured that subsequent elections would now involve simple and direct confrontational contests on the narrow issue of the Union. There can be no doubt that this minimalist politics deliberately polarised the working people, destroying the political middle ground and with it any reasonable opportunity for normal socio-economic party politics. In fact, it was widely believed that the new electoral strategy was specifically aimed against socialists, whom unionists regarded as particularly sinister, and whom they sometimes seemed to fear more than they feared the nationalists. However, even at the ordinary work-a-day parliamentary level, insult was added to injury when palpable personal arrogance and rudeness were seen to accompany this minimalist politics, as this 1932 newspaper commentary shows:

Whenever they (the nationalists) rose to address the House the Prime Minister and other Ministers and many of their followers retired ostentatiously and deliberately to the smoke-room. This wilful rudeness to the minority's representatives was repeated in their dealings with the people who comprised that minority ... the stamp of scorned inferiority was stamped on the brows of one-third of the area's population.[14]

In all the politics of the western world it would be difficult to find a more poignant example of crude political minimalism. A nasty, sectarian and zero-sum politics had been institutionalised, and was to be perpetuated by successive unionist prime ministers until the 1960s when, as some people believed and hoped, Captain Terence O'Neill purported to introduce reforms to Northern Ireland. A mild mannered man, O'Neill would certainly have eschewed the crudity and rudeness described above, and he did try to improve interpersonal political relationships at various levels within Northern Ireland.

It should be acknowledged that O'Neill did make a number of courageous cross-community gestures in an endeavour, as he put it himself, 'to change the political climate in Ulster'. But any suggestion that he made substantive policy efforts to change the sectarian face of Northern Ireland's politics would be an exaggeration. O'Neill was something of an enigma, and history will to some extent always be unkind to him because of the almost impossible situation in which he found himself. He sometimes appeared to be anti-sectarian, and yet he remained an aristocratic Orangeman, albeit one who gave the impression of studied condescension when marching with his Orange Lodge. It is significant, however, that after becoming Prime Minister in 1963 he actually strengthened his association with the Loyal Orders by joining the Royal Black Preceptory and the Apprentice Boys of Derry. His policy and approach in regard to reform vis-à-vis traditional loyalism was therefore marked not so much by compromise as by ambivalence. His tendency to face both ways and then to remain transfixed indicated his acute awareness of the serious threat that 'not an inch' unionism posed to any would-be liberal or liberalising leader. He was right.

The truth is that O'Neill did nothing in the way of substantive reform to deal with Orange ascendancy politics until the very end, when he suddenly announced his intention to concede the Civil Rights Movement's claim for 'one man one vote' in local elections. But by then it was too little, far too late. In the opinion of some political commentators of liberal mind O'Neill 'had no such reforming zeal', his modernisation being aimed 'not at dismantling sectarian structures but at denying the legitimacy of a reformist strategy in this area'.[15] He remained attached to the ethos of Orange-unionist power, and felt he should not turn his back on what was a 'very honourable tradition'.[16] Instead, he built his hopes on a form of socio-economic planning, believing that

> if you give Roman Catholics a good job and a good house they will live like Protestants, because they will see their neighbours with cars and television sets. They will refuse to have eighteen children... If you treat

Roman Catholics with due consideration and kindness, they will live like
Protestants, in spite of the authoritative nature of their Church.[17]

Social and economic planning is a two-edged sword. Maurice Hayes has observed
that 'inequality could be fudged or ignored ... so long as it was not quantified. When
the masses start to read the establishment is in trouble – when they start to count the
game is up'.[18] O'Neill's statement acknowledged that hitherto the Catholics had not
been treated with due consideration, but that if this were now changed, and if their
economic position sufficiently improved, then Catholics would behave like
Protestant and unionists, and acquiesce with the Northern Ireland state. But the
game now was up. Nationalists reckoned that this was just another form of political
minimalism that, *inter alia*, took no notice of those emotive cultural and citizenship
issues of full equality and involvement. They saw O'Neill's statement as
patronising. In fact, there was good reason to believe that his economic policies were
primarily designed for a quite different purpose – to deal with the threat which the
then Northern Ireland Labour Party increasingly posed to the working-class unionist
vote. Unionism always was, and is, out there on the right wing with 'die-hard' Tory
politics. It was therefore arguable that 'O'Neill's economic policies bore no relation
to the problem of inter-communal relations. Their *raison d'être* lay only in political
conflicts within the Protestant bloc'.[19] This was probably true, but even if we could
ascribe higher motives to O'Neill it is certain that his economic policies alone could
not have redressed the problems of a sectarian Northern Ireland.

In that sense Terence O'Neill was little more than an unusually liberal
Orangeman who conducted himself like a benign colonial secretary, and largely
confined himself to some rather tentative 'politics of gesture'. This, however,
caused him to fall fatally between two stools. The good things he did – such as
receiving visitations from successive Irish taoisigh Lemass and Lynch, and
visiting Catholic schools and hospitals – were certainly enough to alienate the
frontier-style Orange-unionists who refused to yield an inch on anything and
wanted nothing more than the old 'no surrender' politics. But his policies were not
enough to impress the now impatient nationalists who wanted real reforms rather
than empty gestures or promises. O'Neill therefore epitomised the tragic
inadequacy of the Orange-unionist approach to politics even when, in his case,
this was sweetened by decency and well-meaning attitudes.

O'Neill's premiership was deliberately and fatally wounded in 1968 by a
sinister bombing campaign that subsequently proved to be the work of loyalist
extremists. This targeted several vital public installations and falsely purported to
be the work of the IRA. The bombing campaign, which coincided with a rowdy
and virulent 'O'Neill must go' propaganda campaign mounted by loyalist hard-
liner Ian Paisley and synchronised with a rebellion of Orange-unionist
parliamentary dissidents, eventually forced his resignation in April 1969. Later in
his autobiography O'Neill acknowledged that:

> If Ulster does not survive, then historians may well show that it was the
> *Protestant extremists yearning for the days of the Protestant Ascendancy*

who lit the flames which blew us up. This, of course, was coupled with the fact that for far too long no effort had been made to make the minority feel that they were wanted or even appreciated (*emphasis mine*).

Protestant ascendancy attitudes had always been the problem. O'Neill's enforced resignation solved nothing for the Orange-unionists, but quickly led on to other things that eventually precipitated the final end of unionist government in 1972. In all the circumstances the ending of such government was inevitable, but the timing and manner of its going might have been different if unionism had only listened to Carson's final piece of advice in his farewell speech to the Ulster Unionist Council on 4th February 1921, when he said:

> From the outset let us see that the Catholic minority have nothing to fear from Protestant majority. Let us take care to win all that is best among those who have been opposed to us in the past. While maintaining intact our own religion let us give the same rights to the religion of our neighbours.[20]

Carson's prescient call for equal respect and equal rights for Catholics had quite deliberately touched the weak spot, for this was precisely what Orange-unionism had always refused to do. It could not do so because such an attitude was entirely incompatible with the old Orange precept of Protestant ascendancy and its irreducible policy of keeping the papists in their places. Catholics could not be trusted with the liberty and rights that were primarily for Protestants. Thus unlike Carson, the Ulster unionists had no foresight that Orangeism's Protestant ascendancy attitudes would eventually become what would now be described as 'politically incorrect'. In the end they would be dysfunctional in the context of a democratic United Kingdom, to say nothing of the new post-war Europe that would include a modernising Ireland in which non-sectarian citizen rights would eventually become mandatory. So unionism's minimalist ascendancy politics was eventually doomed to failure, even as Orangeism's earlier political objectives had failed in the old Ireland after 1798.

As has been demonstrated time and again, this was all because those policies were the product of the flawed philosophy of loyalty to whatever it was King William had established, involving a conditional loyalty that was subject to the British Crown maintaining a religio-political Protestant ascendancy. That concept, so fundamental to Orange-unionism, was now increasingly incompatible with the development of an egalitarian social democracy in the post-war United Kingdom. This development was now also happening throughout Europe and the post-colonial world – a world in which even the Tories under Harold Macmillan had to acknowledge the irresistible strength of the 'winds of change' that were blowing everywhere. A mighty clash between the old ascendancy politics and the new social democracy had to come. When it did come Orange-unionism was found wanting, without a case, virtually without friends, and in the end without power when its government was abolished – ironically by a Tory Prime Minister, Edward Heath. Thus Orange-unionism's minimalist and tribal politics of ascendancy had not only inevitably failed, but had been summarily brought to an end.

Sequel

The disbanding of the B- Specials, the loss of control over the RUC, the ending of fifty years of one-party government, the prorogation of the Stormont parliament, the introduction of direct rule by British ministers, and the concession of reforms that had been demanded by the Civil Rights Movement were all alike repugnant to Orangeism. Taken together, they were seen as catastrophic. It was fully appreciated that Northern Ireland's Orange-Protestant ascendancy had long been under threat. Yet that threat had always been fairly well contained, and so long as there was a unionist government in power the Orange writ could continue to run. But now in a moment, ascendancy had gone and probably forever. Thus the realisation began to dawn, albeit reluctantly on hard-line Orangeism, that the socio-economic and political world had changed irrevocably and that change would also have to come to Northern Ireland. The Catholic minority was now scarcely a minority at all and, because of the Education Act of 1948, it now had a professional middle class, an effective political leadership, and a confidence that, in the new media age, enabled it to articulate its grievances to the world. It was very, very good at it, but it did enjoy a considerable advantage, for a just cause and a good case is the greater part of eloquence. The papists could no longer be kept in their places with impunity, and in this new situation Orange-unionism seemed distracted, divided, and without direction.

A process of schism, due first to unionism's disconcerted reaction to change, and then to its disordered rejection of that change when it came, first began in the 1960s. The schism was sparked off by Ian Paisley's aggressive and ultra-Protestant unionism, and developed throughout the next thirty years to such an extent that unionism fragmented into some half-a-dozen rival political parties. Nevertheless, the Ulster Unionist Party continues to be the main trunk of party political Orange-unionism and still has an official organisational link with the Orange Order. In fact, the Order continues to send one hundred and twenty representatives to the Party's ruling body, the Ulster Unionist Council. For a number of reasons, however, that link is now a very controversial one and is currently under review. Some liberal-minded unionists argue that a party whose leadership has come to espouse the pluralism of the Good Friday Agreement should not have an official link with, and give a privileged place to, the explicitly sectarian and anti-Agreement Orange Order. These liberal unionists would also argue that if any significant numbers of Catholics are ever to be encouraged to support the Union (the only means of saving it in the longer run) the Orange link must be decisively broken. And so the Ulster Unionist Party, like unionism itself, is seriously divided.

There are other anomalies associated with the Orange link. As things stand there is nothing to prevent the Order sending unknown numbers of delegates to the Ulster Unionist Council who may be supporters or even members of the various opposition unionist parties. Many believe that this is in fact now happening. It is not suggested that this is necessarily part of some deeply laid anti-Ulster Unionist plot. Such a plot is quite unnecessary, for the Orange-Unionist organisational arrangements are such that there are no structures or regulations in place to prevent such intrusion. The Ulster Unionist Party remains as it began – a broadly based movement rather than a properly organised political party. Thus the Ulster Unionist leader could conceivably be overthrown by the votes of Orange delegates who are either members or supporters of an opposing political party. This obviously gives cause for concern, especially to the more liberal-minded members of the Party who would seek to foster a distinctively liberal and inclusive politics vis-à-vis Orangeism and the other rejectionist brands of unionism. Greater control and discipline in this area are obviously very important considerations in regard to protecting the 'agreed cross-community politics' of the Good Friday Agreement and to the preservation of the peace it underpins.

There is a second group of Orangemen who also support the breaking of the link between the Ulster Unionist Party and the Orange Order, albeit for a different reason. These hard-line Orangemen believe that the Ulster Unionist Party is no longer sufficiently representative of traditional Orange political thinking to be afforded the privilege of a special relationship with the Order. They argue with a degree of justification that Ian Paisley's Democratic Unionist Party is culturally and politically (though perhaps not religiously) more attuned to Orangeism than is the Ulster Unionist Party under David Trimble. And so it is argued for this different reason that the party political link should be broken.

To confuse the issue further, there is a third position – one that favours the retention of the status quo. There are some senior Orangemen who, although prominent Ulster Unionists, share the Order's anti-Agreement position. These Ulster Unionists wish to keep the link so as to deploy the Order's strength and influence for their own right-wing political ends. These ends include the overthrowing of the Party's support for the Good Friday Agreement – and the leadership of David Trimble with it. The whole question of the Orange link is therefore fraught with considerable difficulty and controversy, and it would be easy to prophesy that any attempt at its resolution in the near future will result in further schism within unionism. It would also be easy to prophesy that any political party that harbours Orange ascendancy ideas will achieve nothing for the development of good politics in Northern Ireland, and still less in the longer run for the preservation of the Union.

Like Britain when it lost an empire and found itself without a role in a new and radically different world, Orangeism with unionism out of power needed to find a new role for itself. And find one it did. This was the role of the watch-dog, one which for the past thirty years has involved opposition to anything that smacks of concession to nationalism or Catholicism, any diminution in security, or any hint of change in Northern Ireland society and its constitutional position within the Union. But whilst keeping a watchful eye on its natural nationalist and republican enemies, and a suspicious eye on certain unionist politicians who so much as hint at reform, the main focus of the Orange Order's attention has been on successive British governments, both Labour and Conservative, whose Northern Ireland initiatives and policies it has almost without exception opposed root and branch.

The earliest and most significant of these initiatives was that of Edward Heath's Conservative government, whose Constitution Act of 1973 was implemented at the end of that year following what became known as the Sunningdale Agreement. This was a tri-partite agreement between British and Irish government delegations and a delegation representing those Northern Ireland political parties that were predisposed to the principle of 'agreement' – agreed cross-community government. The Sunningdale Agreement therefore made provision for power sharing in Northern Ireland, as well as for a Council of Ireland comprising ministers from both North and South. And so the conference successfully brought to fruition many months of hard work, often in the face of fierce opposition from a coalition of unionists and Orangemen who were fundamentally opposed to the very principle of 'agreement' with Catholic nationalists. This was especially because the Agreement for the government of Northern Ireland was based on power-sharing together with cross-border links. Thirty years on it seems that precious little has changed.

The new Northern Ireland power-sharing Executive that took office on 1st January 1974 was comprised of moderate unionists, constitutional nationalists and some liberals and socialists. Its chief executive was the former Orange hard-liner Brian Faulkner who in 1955, as a minister in an earlier unionist government, had attracted some notoriety by participating in a contentious Orange march along the Longstone Road near Annalong in County Down. That march, like the earlier infamous march over the adjacent Dolly's Brae, involved a provocative detour through a Catholic district, and in the three preceding years had been banned by unionist ministers of Home Affairs. On this occasion it was allowed to proceed, but when the road was bombed the night before, the march was deemed to require the support of three hundred policemen. Years later the enigmatic Faulkner could reflect that he no longer needed to participate in Orange marches in order to 'demonstrate his superiority'. In his new non-ascendancy role he had for his deputy chief executive the colourful nationalist and life-long socialist, Gerry Fitt – now Lord Fitt of Bell's Hill. A former merchant seaman who had first been elected to Stormont in 1962, Fitt could likewise reflect on his own early experience of that throwback to Protestant ascendancy. On first attending parliament and surveying the serried ranks of ex-army officers and clergymen who sat on the unionist benches opposite, Fitt exclaimed that he 'didn't know whether to salute or to genuflect'.

For several months the new Faulkner-Fitt Executive worked exceedingly well, despite almost fanatical loyalist opposition, which at times erupted in violence even within the parliamentary chamber itself. Such violence was not new to Irish politics, but the difference now was that this particular batch of parliamentarians included within their ranks many 'fighting Saundersons'. From the very outset the Orange Order – because of its Protestant ascendancy doctrine fundamentally opposed to any form of association with Catholics – arraigned itself with other loyalist groupings against the new power-sharing arrangements. The largest umbrella group for dissident loyalists was unionist MP William Craig's Ulster Vanguard Movement, which had the support of thousands of loyalist paramilitaries and Orangemen, including the paramilitary Orange Volunteers. William Craig, like virtually all the unionist leaders, was an Orangeman. One of his senior Vanguard deputies, Rev. Martin Smyth, was in fact the new Orange supremo, having just been appointed Imperial Grand Master, a position he was to hold for over twenty years.

Vanguard conducted mass open-air rallies to which Craig was driven in an open car, escorted by motor cycle outriders of his own paramilitary Vanguard Service Corps. These rallies, which were widely described as neo-Nazi in character, were marked by massive uniformed paramilitary displays and by violent speeches. At one such rally, attended by crowds variously estimated at up to 100,000, Craig said:

> We must build up a dossier of men and women who are a menace to this country because if the politicians fail us it may be our job to liquidate the enemy.

That the excesses of this speech cannot be put down to the atmospherics of mob oratory becomes evident when compared with another Craig speech, this one to the rather more sophisticated Tory Monday Club in London, when he said:

> We are going to war in Ulster. I can tell you without boasting I can mobilise tomorrow 80,000 men who will not see any compromise in Ulster. I am an ex-officer in the Air Force. I am prepared to come out and shoot to kill. Let us put the bluff aside. I am prepared to kill and those behind me will have my full support.

For a time Craig's rousing mass appeal among loyalists eclipsed even that of Ian Paisley who, because of his clerical evangelicalism, could not publicly emulate Craig's blood-curdling message, even though his virulent anti-Catholicism made him even more opposed than Craig to any compromise or political power-sharing.[21] Thus the combined power of loyalist opposition to the Sunningdale Agreement, together with the violence of the Provisional IRA who vowed to 'blow it out of existence', was directed against the coalition. But despite all this opposition, the cross-community Executive could continue to claim the support of the main centre ground. Indeed, when it was brought to a premature end, this was not occasioned by a democratic, political or parliamentary defeat, but by a *coup d'etat* in May 1974. This sometimes has inaccurately been described as the Ulster Workers' Council (UWC) strike, for although the strike format and mechanism was used this was not an industrial strike in any accepted sense of that term, but an act of naked rebellion.

The UWC was led by a co-ordinating committee, chaired by the young Vanguard politician Glenn Barr, political spokesman for the paramilitary UDA. The committee included loyalist political leaders William Craig, Ian Paisley and Harry West, but when the stoppage was finally arranged Paisley suddenly left for Canada where he remained for most of its duration. Craig, who had placed his Vanguard headquarters at the disposal of the Council, was now the predominant political figure. Crucially, however, the committee had the full support of the Orange Order and also included senior loyalist paramilitaries and loyalist-Orange shop stewards, the latter easily sweeping aside their official trades union leaders. Together, the shop stewards and paramilitaries now controlled the largely loyalist work forces of Northern Ireland's industry, as well as the streets and districts where the workers lived. This was achieved by massively intimidating picketing which, combined with total loyalist control of power stations and fuel supplies, soon brought everything to a standstill. After fourteen days when things teetered on the brink of civic chaos – the British government, army and police incredibly behaving like neutral observers – Faulkner and the unionist members of the Executive resigned, thereby bringing it down. Thus an unopposed *coup d'etat* had overthrown an elected government and smashed for many years Northern Ireland's only hope of an agreed peace. This plunged the country into further terrible violence, and it would be a long and terrible twenty-five years before a similar political opportunity would arise.

Paddy Devlin, who as a working class and anti-sectarian socialist had been a respected and successful minister in the Executive, has pointed out that the Assembly and its Executive had been

> set up along the lines provided for in the Constitution Act, 1973, which was introduced by Westminster as its own special solution to the North's problems. The Executive was elected quite properly according to the terms of the Act and sustained in its existence and agreed policies by a comfortable 20% majority vote in the Assembly. What could be more democratic, legal, more likely to succeed, more worthy of support than a non-sectarian, power-sharing Administration providing the entire Northern community with a service based on an agreed set of fair social and economic policies? Alas, the Orange Card was played once again, as it will be in the future, to prevent a humane and efficient administration from changing the evil, ugly and unacceptable face of the North.[22]

Paddy Devlin was in no doubt that as in 1912-14 the Orange Order, heavily supported by its paramilitary members and their many influential associates from all walks of life, had once again been deeply implicated in subversive activity. Devlin writes:

> The Orange Order, through their Volunteers, gave the stoppage full backing. It was ironic for them that in the aftermath of the stoppage large arms dumps were found in a number of Orange halls while the Order still posed as a corner stone of law and order. Documents found with the arms indicated that the Central Committee of the Grand Orange Lodge of Ireland had issued a directive to lodges to organise a trained and disciplined paramilitary force.[23]

After the failure of Sunningdale, the next substantial political initiative was the Anglo-Irish Agreement of 1985. This was a far-reaching development in which the British and Irish governments pledged themselves to work closely together on Northern Ireland matters, through a joint ministerial conference, with a view to promoting peace, stability, reconciliation and improved security measures. Orange-unionism was shaken to its foundations by what it saw as a sell-out that gave the Republic of Ireland a limited say in the internal affairs of Northern Ireland. A massive 'Ulster Says No' campaign was mounted, and the ranks of the Orange Order were temporarily swollen by loyalist elements in quest of arms to defend the country against an imagined imminent take over. When these elements discovered that the

Order no longer operated ostensibly along paramilitary lines, they quickly learned to go elsewhere. However, as Paddy Devlin found thirty years ago, there is still some spasmodic evidence of Orange paramilitary activity, like that involving the unauthorised possession of papers of British military origin, which were uncovered in November 1999 in Stoneyford Orange Hall. The *Irish News* commented:

> Security sources have linked the material to the group known as the Orange Volunteers, which has been carrying out sectarian attacks on Catholics across Northern Ireland. The Orange Order has angrily denied that it has any connection with the paramilitary group, but the evidence indicates that dissident loyalists have ready access to Orange property. Few observers will have forgotten that senior Orange figures were happy to share a public platform with Billy Wright, the sectarian mass murderer who effectively launched the dissident loyalist movement.[24]

Each year an organisation known as the Orange Volunteers is permitted to place an advert in the Orange Order's official magazine *The Twelfth*, published to coincide with the annual July celebrations. I raised this matter in a recent interview with an Orange spokesman, in the course of which I also mentioned Paddy Devlin's previously quoted reference to the Grand Orange Lodge directive for the creation of 'a trained and disciplined paramilitary force'. This met with the stony silence of Orange secrecy. When further pressed on alleged Orange paramilitary links, the Orange spokesman, far from denying these, reluctantly observed that 'there have been times when we were facing into a doomsday scenario'. He did not demur when I rejoined that Orangeism might regard almost every British initiative – like Sunningdale, the Anglo-Irish Agreement, the Frameworks Documents and even the recent Good Friday Agreement – as constituting a 'doomsday scenario' on which basis, depending on perception, almost anything might go. By his resigned silence he appeared to acquiesce with my comments. Indeed, it seemed that almost anything would go provided it was understood to be in the ultimate defence of 'whatever it was King William established' – a good example of what was described earlier as Orangeism's 'arbitrary attitude towards authority'.

Another residual effect of the Anglo-Irish Agreement was the increased incidence of Orange marching, an increase that could be up to 40 per cent in the years after 1985. As ever, when the enemy was perceived as threatening, the Orangemen increasingly went on the march in order to demonstrate their ascendancy and strength. However, the nationalists and republicans, who had had enough of ascendancy, were now intent upon equality – the very antithesis of ascendancy. They therefore opposed a number of Orange marches through Catholic residential areas on the grounds that these were now regarded as deliberately provocative and disruptive. Confrontations between marchers and residents led to bans on certain marches, notably that from Drumcree Church to Portadown via the Catholic Garvaghy Road after 1995, which in turn led to annual protests by the Orangemen about their right to march the Queen's highway. The subsequent Orange protests at Drumcree have involved much violence, sometimes leading to murder. During the years after 1995 orchestrated protests against the banning of the July march down the Garvaghy Road developed into something of an annual festival of violence. This involved the illegal blockading of roadways that sometimes brought everything to a standstill, and gave rise to vicious arson and to many sectarian killings. Despite all the experience of the past, and the clear inevitability of such terrible consequences, leading Orangemen did not hesitate to call the people on to the streets in their 'hundreds of thousands' during the July 2000 protest. Happily there was no such response – a good example of the people being wiser than their leaders. However, as in previous years since 1995, that ongoing protest situation proved to be particularly dangerous and violent in Portadown, where one Orange leader specifically refused to condemn the violence and welcomed the support of militant loyalist paramilitaries at those protests.[25] That welcome was despite the fact that much of the Drumcree dispute arises from the Orange Order's refusal, for high-minded and allegedly anti-terrorist reasons, to dialogue with the Catholic residents' group – on the grounds that the group is led by a former IRA man. For obvious reasons Orangeism can never be consistent with regard to violence. However, the Drumcree situation will be examined in greater detail when we consider the question of Orange marching in chapter 14.

No reference to Orange violence would be complete without mentioning Orange Lodge 633, the Old Boyne Island Heroes, some of whose members were in the paramilitary UVF and even had links with the notorious Shankill Butchers. Known locally as the 'UVF Lodge', it still commemorates those connections on a bannerette that displays the names of five brethren who lost their lives through UVF involvement in the Troubles. One of these men was a Shankill Butcher. Peter Taylor, who provides a detailed account of this in his book *Loyalists*, says that one senior member of that lodge told him, 'If you hadn't done gaol, you weren't a real member'.[26] It is, of course, relatively easy to condemn or condone violence on either a morally superior or a sectarian basis. Either way there is a strong tendency in Northern Ireland to cast out the other's mote whilst ignoring the personal beam, but my purpose is to show that although the Orange Order is most unforgiving of republican violence, it takes a highly selective and inconsistent stance in regard to its own. This is inevitable given its own long association with paramilitary and terrorist activity throughout its history. So far as can be ascertained, none of the above episodes has resulted in disciplinary action by the Orange Order – hardly the hallmark of an institution that, according to some, is a bulwark of the Christian religion. Ambivalence about violence was never the sole preserve of Irish republicanism. Historically (and also currently, albeit in a confused and ramshackle manner), Orange paramilitarism has a connection with unionism similar to that which the IRA has with Sinn Féin. They are linked but also separate. However, the Orange-loyalist axis is now fragmented, often seeming to operate as loose cannon and on a politically maladroit basis.

For the most part, the Orange Order has endeavoured to keep daylight between its public persona and any paramilitary activity, which more often than not is covert and carried out under separate or individual responsibility. There is no doubt that respectable elements in the Orange leadership would wish to protect themselves against overt involvement with violent elements, and thus avoid the obvious charge of hypocrisy when they criticise the violence of others, and especially the violence of the republican movement. But such Pontius Pilate attitudes do not wash. Some Orangemen admit the existence of paramilitary links, both historical and extant, and regard the Order as the vital manpower resource for future paramilitary activity 'when the time comes'. It is significant that the Orange Order's objection to Sinn Féin's participation in shared government responsibility is not primarily because of IRA violence or its possession of guns. When I pressed an Orange spokesman on this matter he was adamant that the Order would remain implacably opposed to the power-sharing arrangements of the Good Friday Agreement 'whether or not the IRA decommissioned its weapons'. It is therefore clear that Orangeism, which obviously is not at all well-fitted for a high moral stance on the paramilitary or weapons issues, will continue to operate on the old principle that it cannot share fellowship or participate with Catholic nationalists on any basis of political or governmental equality. To do so would be in violation of its Protestant ascendancy principles.

Such a reading of Orangeism would harmonise readily with the views of Robert Saulters who, on succeeding Rev. Martin Smyth as Worshipful Grand Master in 1997, felt constrained to criticise new Prime Minister Tony Blair as disloyal 'because he married a Romanist'. It is clear that the bottom line in Orange philosophy is every bit as anti-Catholic as anti-republican, which should hardly surprise the reader who has followed the story of Orangeism's religio-political principles and objectives since 1795. Nothing has changed. Indeed, the principles and policy objectives that eventually caused the collapse of Orange-unionist power with the prorogation of Stormont in 1972 were the self-same principles and policies that Orangeism posited against the Sunningdale Agreement in 1974. And it was the same story in 1998 when the Orange leadership rejected the Good Friday Agreement and its provisions for parity, pluralism and power sharing – for all these things involve the participation of Catholics. And this despite the fact that the Agreement was democratically supported by a large cross-community majority of the Northern Ireland people in a referendum. Clearly, cross-community majorities do not count. Only the Orange-unionist 'majority of the majority' matters, which is consistent with the well-established fact that Orangeism stands for ascendancy, not democracy.

The conclusion therefore remains inescapable that the ancient doctrine of conditional loyalty to the Crown in parliament, so long as that Crown continues to support undemocratic Protestant ascendancy by keeping the papists in their places, is still the anachronistic watchword of the Orange army with banners. Should the Crown in parliament not do so, Orangeism will consider itself under no obligation to be loyal to that authority. On the contrary, it will regard the British government in exactly the same light as it regards the 'disloyal' Prime Minister Tony Blair – a traitor to 'whatever it was King William established' in long ago 1690.

Section Three:
Ordinances of Orangeism

12.
Orange Religion –
Its Relationship to the Reformed Faith

It is not possible to reach an understanding of Orangeism without knowing something of its religious aspect. This is not to contradict the earlier assertion that the Orange Order is primarily a political institution. Evidence for that has been presented at length, ranging from its paramilitary origins, its political motivation and ascendancy objectives over the two hundred years of its history. It was therefore concluded that the Order was primarily political, although it also contained a religious element. One might think that this would require no further comment were it not for the fact that some Orange apologists, usually from among the clergy, insist on the primacy of the Order's religious aspect. The point at issue therefore concerns that alleged primacy. Our consideration of this will lead to other questions regarding the precise nature of that religion and its relevance to Orange politics. It is hoped that the reader will not be turned off by the 'religious' nature of what follows. This is not intended to advocate any one religious view over another, but to examine the claims that are sometimes made for Orange religion, and also to establish its real nature by means of comparison and contrast with the Reformed Faith.

An Orange clergyman the Rev. Fred C. Gibson has written that

> the supreme purpose of the Order has not primarily been political, but religious – the safeguarding of the religion of the Reformation. The Orange Order is, therefore, essentially an association of Protestants banded together in a great brotherhood for the defence and furtherance of the evangelical principles revealed in the New Testament, and rediscovered and reaffirmed at the Reformation.[1]

On reading that, we may well wonder how the commentators on the Orange outrages perpetrated in County Armagh, Gulladuff, Dolly's Brae, Ballybay, Maghery and many other places in Ireland right up to the Drumcree saga, have so managed like Shakespeare's Cassius to 'misconstrue everything'. And yet we are to believe that all along the Orangemen's real purpose and intention has been the defence and furtherance of the evangelical gospel. It seems that despite their originating purpose, their stated objectives, their often-armed violence and the terrible consequences of many of their actions in Ireland over a period of two hundred years, the Orangemen have been seriously misunderstood and wrongly maligned. All along the line their real objective has been to witness to the Christian gospel of grace, peace, love and reconciliation toward all men – Protestant and Catholic alike.

We have seen that Orangeism's founding fathers had a far different motivation. When James Wilson initiated the first moves that led to the Order's creation, he did not consult with his local church – a strange thing if he were motivated by an evangelical concern for the defence and furtherance of the Christian religion or the Reformed Faith. He consulted with his Masonic lodge in Benburb, a non-Christian and religiously neutral body, because he was very concerned about politics and about civil defence against the Catholic Defenders. And when his Lodge showed no interest in his proposals he solicited the support of publicans, cock-fighters, Peep O' Day militants and other Protestant hard men who would soon provide the nucleus of the incipient Orange Order. And as we have seen, from the beginning that Order was an oath-bound, armed and secret society with an essentially politico-military objective – in the words of the Orangemen themselves, the defence of Protestant ascendancy and the keeping of the papists in their places.

Over time, that objective would remain the same in principle, although in practice it would evolve into the maintenance of a Protestant hegemony under the Union. In principle, therefore, the early Orange objective accords with the previously quoted view of the former Orange Imperial Grand Master, the Rev. Martin Smyth MP, who once said that the Orange Order was a pressure group to ensure that the Unionist Party remained firm on the constitution. The Rev. Smyth is obviously much better placed than most to represent the Orange position on this matter – and his stated position is fully consistent with the findings of this book. The objectives of Orangeism's founding fathers and their successors were not religious, nor was religion ever the predominant feature at any stage in the Order's history – certainly not in that spiritual and evangelical sense postulated by the above quotation from the Rev. Fred Gibson.

It cannot be denied that there are numbers of evangelical Christians and evangelical clergymen in membership of the various orders of Orangeism. We saw earlier that the clergy had a role in reforming the original Orange Order after 1798 in an attempt to give it a more respectable image. It would also appear that from time to time certain allegedly Christian elements have been introduced and admixed with the Orange rituals and ordinances. However, the question is whether these developments were of such a nature or extent as to transform a paramilitary movement for political defence into one for 'the defence and furtherance of the evangelical principles revealed in the New Testament, and rediscovered and reaffirmed at the Reformation'. There is no compelling evidence to suggest that this question should be answered in the affirmative. Indeed, one Orange clergyman recently testified that he was in membership of the Orange Order because of the opportunity that this afforded for evangelising the Orangemen! The clergyman was quite rightly describing Orangeism as a mission field, certainly not as a missionary foundation.

Steve Bruce in his *God Save Ulster! The Religion and Politics of Paisleyism* argues that 'the Northern Ireland conflict is a religious conflict' and that Ian Paisley's success 'can only be understood if one appreciates the central role which evangelical religion plays in Ulster unionism'.[2] This is very hard to swallow. Paisleyism represents only a part of a much divided unionism, but it is arguable that evangelical religion does not play a central role even here. Unionism harbours many variants, ranging from atheism through liberalism and shades of evangelicalism to fundamentalism, but the typical Ulster Protestant is neither religious nor committed to evangelicalism. It would therefore be an exaggeration to ascribe to it a 'central role' in any general area of Ulster's life. Bruce therefore overstates evangelical religion's role in an environment that is predominantly secular. But it is natural for elements of secular Protestantism – which include unionists, Orangemen and loyalists – to find common ground with fundamentalists and evangelicals. However, that shared ground is not the gospel; it is their common Protestant tribalism, which can often be anti-Catholic and sectarian. Surprisingly for one that gives evangelical religion such an exaggerated role in unionism, Bruce makes no such claim for its role within the Orange Order. He merely observes that: 'To what extent the Orange Order, the Apprentice Boys of Derry, and Royal Black Preceptory have ever been thoroughly evangelical is debatable'.[3] Thus, pursuant to his thesis, Bruce wrongly ascribes to unionism what it has never claimed, yet rightly denies to Orangeism what is often attributed to it. Paisleyism is his dubious evangelical touchstone here – as Ian Paisley is the authentic voice of unionism it too must be evangelical; and as he rejected the Orange Order years ago its evangelical credentials have to be very doubtful. We would take issue with Bruce's premises and therefore consider his conclusions a *non sequitur*. However, it must be significant that the one scholar who exaggerates the role of Ulster evangelicalism gives no credence to its salience for the Orange Order, and on this we agree with him.

This is not to say that the Orange Order is no sense religious, for it has been recognised that the Order does have a religious aspect. The philosopher Ninian Smart, an authority on the world's religions, says that there are seven common dimensions that characterise religions – the practical and ritual; the experiential and emotional; the narrative or mythic; the doctrinal and philosophical; the social and institutional; and the material.[4] It is quite clear that, even on a cursory examination, the Orders of Orangeism meet the criteria of all these religious dimensions. In that broad or general sense Orangeism might therefore be regarded as a kind of religion in its own right, as can Freemasonry, which for many valid reasons has often been described as a religion. However, this is very different from saying that the religion of Orangeism is essentially or adequately representative of Christianity or of the Reformed Faith. We would wish to see the evidence of that. Certainly there is evidence to argue that Orange religion, like Masonic religion, could be regarded as a separate or even substitute religious culture. For example, some Christian pastors ministering to the sick and dying have occasionally to their very great dismay found Orangemen and Freemasons placing their faith in the things pertaining to their membership of those secret and esoteric Orders, rather than in the gospel of Jesus Christ.

There are therefore two issues here – first, the extent of Orange religion *vis-à-vis* its political dimension; and second, the nature of Orange religion as compared with the principles of Christianity and the Reformed Faith. The first point has largely been dealt with – compared with the political dimension the religious element in Orangeism is very small indeed. A recent writer on this subject and a former Orangeman, W.P. Malcomson, reckons that whereas there is a small element of 'religious formalism' within Orangeism, quantitatively speaking this amounts only to about five per cent of all the interest and activity of a typical Orange lodge. A very large majority of urban Orangemen are not churchgoers and indicate no personal commitment to religion. In fact, on those occasions when and where there were circumstances in which the evangelical religion was strongly in the ascendant, Orangeism has tended to become muted and to adopt an uncharacteristically low profile. Referring to the Evangelical Revival of 1859, Jonathan Bardon observes that 'the 12 July parades ... were remarkably quiet; in Ballymena there were no uniforms, drums or music'.[5] This was surely a strange reaction on the part of an Order whose demonstrations were supposedly in celebration of Protestantism and the evangelical religion, given that at that time these were in significant revival, and especially if that religion was essentially what Orangeism really stood for and held most dear.

The remaining question is whether, to the extent that it is religious at all, the nature of Orange religion conforms to the beliefs and objectives of Christianity or of the Protestant Reformers. It has been shown that in the immediate context of their new Orangeism the founding fathers did not have this in mind. Indeed, if it be allowed that the original Order was religious in accordance with Ninian Smart's 'seven dimensions' criteria, then it can be asserted that the nature of that religion should be regarded as neo-Masonic rather than Christian. For this is a religion which Orange spokesmen have approvingly described as one of 'rituals, mysteries, crafts, arts and secrets' as will be shown in the next chapter. Some may argue that religious improvements were introduced after 1798, with the setting up of a central authority in the form of the Grand Lodge of Ireland and when Church of Ireland clergymen first came into leadership positions. It is true that at that time Orangeism underwent an 'improvement', its original neo-Masonic ritual being largely jettisoned, albeit temporarily, in favour of a simpler initiating rite and degree system that included some Christian elements. But that change, though not unwelcome from the Christian perspective, was hardly of such significance as to transform the Order into a great brotherhood for the defence of the 'evangelical principles revealed in the New Testament'. The new religious dimension was an add-on, and largely a piece of religious tokenism to be deployed in the opening and the closing of lodge meetings. The most that can be said for the 'improvement' is that it now rendered the Order nominally Christian, albeit more in the well understood politico-Protestant and tribal sense of that term. However, this is a very far cry from asserting that the Order was founded on Christian principles, or that its supreme purpose then or now was to defend and advance the gospel or the religion of the Reformation. Such a claim simply cannot be sustained.

In 1967 the Grand Lodge of Ireland introduced an updated *Constitution, Laws and Ordinances of the Loyal Orange Institution of Ireland*, a document that includes the important 'Qualifications of an Orangeman', together with no less than one hundred and one 'General Laws'. Here was surely the place for Orangeism to set out its alleged evangelical and Reformed position. Yet we find that this substantive document, far from epitomising the religion of the Reformation, makes only a few sparse mentions of God, some brief allusions to the Bible with suggested readings, and a fleeting reference to 'Jesus Christ, the Saviour of Mankind'. This is significant. No evangelical movement, set for the defence of the gospel, could conceivably omit a clear and substantial Christology from its Constitution, Laws and Ordinances. The paucity of solid Christian and evangelical content in these Ordinances is very much in line with W.P. Malcomson's opinion on Orangeism's mere religious formalism, as well as with his low estimate of the extent of its Christian activity. This obvious shortcoming not only reflects the Masonic rather than Christian origins of its formal practices, but is consistent with the fact that its belief system derives primarily from an emphasis on Protestant ascendancy politics and from a negative politico-religious preoccupation with Roman Catholicism. In this writer's judgement Orange religion subsists mainly in the negativity of its anti-Catholicism, as is evident from the whole thrust of its Ordinances.

The lack of evangelical coherence in Orange religion is evident from its Rule 81, which refers to the role of ordained clergymen chaplains. These clergy are defined by reference to a list of Protestant churches that contains the Non-Subscribing Presbyterian Church in Ireland, a church that includes Unitarians within its membership. On the basis of this rule heterodox Unitarians who reject the vital evangelical doctrines of the Trinity, the divinity of Christ and his atoning sacrifice, could conceivably become Orange chaplains. This simply could not happen if Orangeism's Rules and Ordinances were half as concerned about evangelical principles as they are about Rome. Of course it may be argued that there are no Unitarian chaplains in the Order, but it cannot be denied that there are Non-Subscribing Presbyterian Orangemen, in regular church fellowship with Unitarians, who hold very high office in the Orange Order. Thus an Orangeman may share fellowship with Unitarians with impunity, but fellowship with Roman Catholics on peril of expulsion. The supreme irony here is that, in common with evangelicals, the Roman Catholic Church has always stood for those historical doctrines of Christ that Unitarians reject – the virgin birth, the Trinity, the deity of Christ and his atoning sacrifice. But this religious question seems relatively unimportant to Orangeism. It is the political and anti-Catholic aspect of Protestantism that really matters, an attitude that is epitomised by the riposte: 'At least he's a Protestant Unitarian!' In making this point it is stressed that is not my purpose here to denigrate Unitarianism, for my position on the theology of that denomination is entirely beside the point. My task is to demonstrate from Orangeism's own standards the weakness of the claim that it is a defender of the evangelical and Reformed Faith. The Orange Order's extreme position on Roman Catholicism simply cannot be squared with its uncharacteristically liberal and indifferent attitude to Unitarianism. Can a shared Protestantism be more important than a shared Christ?

Orangeism's usual response to the charge that it is anti-Catholic is to quote from its 'Qualifications of an Orangeman' which state that he should ever abstain 'from all uncharitable words, actions or sentiments towards his Roman Catholic brethren'. The Order clearly deserves some credit for this mitigating injunction, and it should be acknowledged that most Orangemen do behave respectfully towards their Roman Catholic neighbours. However, this decency operates largely at the individual level, in the context of which one will often hear the ambivalent expression, 'I know many decent Roman Catholics'. Collectively speaking, however, in the context of community, or of politics, and certainly of church and religion, Roman Catholics are often regarded as a potential enemy, if not the enemy. The overwhelming message of Orangeism's Laws and Ordinances conveys this anti-Catholicism. Its religious preoccupation is therefore a negative one, being almost entirely taken up with its opposition to a Church it regards as pagan, idolatrous and anti-Christian. Orangeism appears oblivious to the fact that for many centuries, and unlike certain Orangemen, the Roman Church has been a fortress in defence of the Christian doctrines of the incarnation, the Trinity, the deity of Christ and redemption – the things that are of the utmost importance both to the Reformed Faith and to Christianity.

The 'Particular Qualifications of an Orangeman' require that 'he is not, and never was, a Roman Catholic or Papist, or married to one (unless in cases under Law 3)'. The exceptions under Law 3 involve fully attested conversion plus other stringent preconditions. We also find under Law 4 that 'any member dishonouring the Institution by marrying a Roman Catholic shall be expelled; and every member shall use his best endeavours to prevent and discountenance the marriage of Protestants with Roman Catholics.' A leading Orangeman once sought to defend this in a televised debate with the writer by quoting St Paul's injunction that Christians should not be 'unequally yoked with unbelievers'.[6] Thus he equated Roman Catholics with pagans, a position consistent with the 'Qualification of Candidates', which requires that the Orangeman 'should strenuously oppose the *fatal* errors of the Church of Rome' (*emphasis mine*). Orangeism believes that Roman Catholics are not Christian, and that they are guilty of fatal and damnable heresies.

Breaches of Orangeism's fearsome and extreme anti-Catholic rules have given rise to many public examples of direct discipline, or of the perhaps more frequent pre-emptive action taken by individual members themselves in order to avoid such discipline. William Fitzsimmons, a long established Unionist MP, resigned from the Order in 1968 because his daughter married a Roman Catholic. That same year Phelim O'Neill, the Unionist MP for North Antrim and cousin of Terence O'Neill, was expelled for carrying out his political duty in attending a Catholic ceremony during a civic week in Ballymoney, a town within his constituency. In September 1969 the Unionist MP for Mid-Antrim, Robert Simpson, felt constrained to resign from the Orange Order when he became

Minister for Community Relations. Simpson's role in fostering better communal relations would have involved him in activities that could have been deemed incompatible with the principles of Orangeism, since they would have included socio-religious contacts with Roman Catholics. But bigoted and narrow-minded as these examples were, they could hardly match the incredible case of James Gyle, an Independent Unionist MP. In January 1934 Gyle visited the home of Nationalist Party leader, the famous Joe Devlin, who was on his deathbed. Whilst Gyle was still present in the room a Roman Catholic priest said prayers, an occurrence that was subsequently reported to Gyle's Orange Lodge. For graciously participating 'by his presence' in that act of human decency and Christian compassion James Gyle was suspended from the Orange Order for seven years. It would be very difficult to find anywhere a rule with concomitant disciplinary action more contrary to the mind and example of Christ. Consider by way of contrast his gracious and welcoming response to the sinner, or the stranger, or the outsider, whether the despised Samaritan or the shunned Gentile, to say nothing of his compassion for the sick and the dying.

These cases illustrate what was stated earlier in the book when responding to Ruth Dudley Edwards – that whereas Orangeism includes many very good people it also holds some very bad sectarian principles. However, there is an impression abroad that public expulsions and suspensions of this kind are much less frequent nowadays and that the Order is now rather more liberal on these matters. When this was put to an Orange spokesman he quite frankly demurred, pointing out that the Rules remained entirely unchanged and that such discipline could and would still happen 'if pressed by the local lodge'. He stressed, however, that in the present fraught circumstances of Northern Ireland there was an increasing degree of self-regulation within the Orange Order. By way of explanation he said 'a brother in breach of the Rules – by marrying a Roman Catholic for instance – might feel so ashamed of himself as to withdraw voluntarily from the Order'. Thus it could reasonably be concluded from this that, far from being more liberal, Orangeism is now so inherently conservative as to render direct and public discipline of this kind almost unnecessary.

There are two important points to note in relation to the Order's strong stance on the 'errors of the Church of Rome'. First, according to Orangeism the Roman Church is guilty of errors so gross as to be spiritually 'fatal', with consequences that are therefore eternally damnable. And second, that since some of those fatal errors are inculcated into Roman Catholic worship such as the Mass, all these ceremonies must never be countenanced in any way, but scrupulously and personally avoided. All Orangemen must therefore physically exclude themselves from Roman Catholic funeral and marriage rites. However, questions arise as to why, and on what biblical or Reformed authority, these errors should be regarded as fatal? And why should such errors be regarded as so much more serious than those which Reformed evangelicals, on powerful biblical authority, have always regarded as the really fatal heresies – those which we have already mentioned with respect to the Godhead, the person of Christ, and his work of redemption. Orangeism's attitude on these matters shows a serious lack of proportion, and seems to indicate a fixation with anti-Catholicism that is at the expense of any balanced regard for the really vital matters of essential Christian doctrine. The Reformers carefully avoided falling into this trap, and never allowed their distaste for what they regarded as the errors of the Roman Church to diminish their acknowledgement of its historic defence of the foundation truths on which their own Christian experience was based. They therefore took a more generous attitude to Roman Catholicism than does the Orange Order. The Reformers could not have been Orangemen.

The early Reformers Martin Luther and John Calvin had been baptised, found Christ, and been clergy in the Roman Catholic Church. On leaving it they were never subsequently re-baptised, and continued to recognise the validity of Roman baptism. They acknowledged that, despite the errors of that Church and the sad state into they perceived it to have fallen in the sixteenth century, the ordinances of God, Christian grace and all the essentials for salvation could still be found within its Christian ministration. As Calvin wrote:

> To the extent that some marks of the Church remain, we do not impugn the existence of churches among them (*Institutes*, 4. 2. 12).

The writer can recall how as a young man and avid reader of Reformed Theology he was intrigued by a significant event that occurred in 1845 – one which is still powerfully relevant to this issue. It is equally intriguing that in his recent *Portrait of Ian Paisley* the Rev. Dennis Cooke refers to that event when responding to Paisley's view that the Roman Church is not Christian.[7] In fact, the episode in question contains many lessons that are applicable to the doctrines and rules of Orangeism. It concerned the General Assembly of the American Presbyterian Church, which had just passed a resolution denying the validity of baptism as administered by a Roman Catholic priest. On learning of that resolution, the then leading Reformed theologian Dr. Charles Hodge of Princeton was at some pains to persuade the General Assembly to reverse its verdict, which he described as being 'in opposition to the principles of the whole Protestant world'. And reverse it the Assembly subsequently did.

Dr Hodge achieved this on foot of a powerful article entitled 'The Validity of Romish Baptism'. In the course of this he pointed out that in accordance with Protestant principles baptism was (1) a washing with water; (2) carried out in the name of the Trinity; and (3) with a view to signifying our engrafting into Christ. Subject to that definition its validity stemmed from the appointment and word of God. This validity did not depend upon the character, faith or orthodoxy of the administrator, either pastor or Church. In fact, to link the validity of baptism to the particular status of a pastor or a Church was coming close to the Roman Catholic position in regard to the vital importance of historical apostolic succession. The validity of Christian baptism depended on the theology and word of God upon which it was based. Charles Hodge ended his case with a quotation from the Protestant Reformer John Calvin who wrote, 'We were baptised not in the name of any man, but in the name of the Father, of the Son, and of the Holy Spirit, and therefore baptism is not of man, but of God, no matter by whom it was administered.' The Princeton theologian therefore concluded by arguing that to say otherwise was to

> pronounce Calvin, Luther and all the men of that generation, as well as thousands who with no other than Romish baptism have since been received into the Protestant churches, to have lived and died unbaptised.

Hodge recognised that this question of baptism couched another related issue. He anticipated that argument – which in principle is also the Orange argument – that 'the Church is a congregation of believers in which the pure word of God is preached; the pure word of God is not preached in Rome, therefore Rome is not a Church'. He rejected this proposition, regarding its prescriptive notion of Church purity as nothing short of sectarian, and rejoining that 'by the same argument the whole world may be unchurched, save our own particular sect'. As Charles Hodge saw it, this argument was as unreasonable as it would be to say that 'a Christian is one who believes the doctrines and obeys the precepts of Christ, therefore no man who is erroneous can be a Christian'. Just as we could not take a definition of a perfect Christian as the absolute standard by which a man is to be regarded as a brother in Christ, likewise we could not take the definition of a pure church as the essential criterion for being a proper Christian church. On such premises there could be no Christians, and no Christian churches. Arguing further from this anti-perfectionism Charles Hodge also asserted that

> any man who professes truth enough to save his soul is not to be denounced as a non-Christian simply because of his other beliefs … Any body of men that professes truth enough to save men cannot on the ground of heresy be denied the character of a Church.

To the mind of this Reformed theologian the essential question, therefore, was whether the Church of Rome had held on to sufficient truth for salvation and thereby retained the character of a Christian church. If it held such truth then its errors could not be of such a nature as to be spiritually and eternally 'fatal' – the pejorative word chosen by Orangeism. Thankfully, the historic Christian position on this matter is much more simple and inclusive. John the Apostle tells us that 'whoever believes that Jesus is the Christ is born of God',[8] on which central theme the Roman Catholic Church and countless thousands of its adherents have been rock solid for centuries. The essence of Christianity is that Jesus is the Christ – a belief that involves his incarnation, his deity, his atoning death and resurrection, and his glorification and return at the end of time to be our judge. Thus to assert, as Orangeism categorically does, that Roman Catholics are unbelievers is preposterous. On the question whether the Roman Catholic Church held sufficient truth for salvation and retained the character of a Christian church, Charles Hodge was quite unequivocal:

> We do not understand how it is possible for any man to answer this question in the negative. They retain the doctrine of the Incarnation, which

we know from the infallible word is a life-giving doctrine. They retain the whole doctrine of the Trinity. They teach the doctrine of the Atonement far more fully and accurately than multitudes of professedly orthodox Protestants. They hold a much higher doctrine as to the necessity of divine influence than prevails among many whom we recognise as Christians. They believe in the forgiveness of sins, the resurrection of the body, and in eternal life and judgement. These doctrines are in their creeds, and however they may be perverted or overlaid, still as general propositions they are affirmed. And it must be remembered that it is truth presented in general propositions and not with subtle distinctions that saves the soul.[9]

Thus one of the leading Protestant teachers of his generation concluded that, in accord with the views of the Reformed theologians and 'the principles of the whole Protestant world,' the Christian status of the Roman Church, despite its imperfections, had to be affirmed. Most of the major Protestant churches, including the Presbyterian Church in Ireland, currently take that view. Such a view of the Roman Church accords with biblical teaching and with the mainstream Reformed Faith that Orange apologists profess to uphold and defend. That Orangeism does not do so is self-evident, and in this important respect it does not properly represent the Reformed religion.

Some fundamentalists would take issue with this view of Reformed theology. They refer us to other authorities such as the seventeenth century Westminster Confession of Faith and the Thirty-nine Articles, which regard the papacy as the antichrist. One could rejoin that 'papacy' and 'church' are not in all respects the same thing, and that in any case these Articles are 'subordinate' documents, but the issue deserves more detailed treatment. It should be borne in mind that on the back of the sixteenth century Reformation came the religio-political crises of the seventeenth century – a time of great revolutionary fervour, national fears and crazy millenarian hopes. This was a time when the antichrist seemed to lurk under every bed – when popes, prelates, presbyters, governments, sects, churches, and even the Westminster divines themselves were in turn castigated as antichrist. It was in this hyper-charged atmosphere that the documents in question were written – they were documents of their own time. It is significant that this atmosphere and its attendant phenomena began to fade in the 1660s when the situation and mood in England was changing because of the evolving separation of religion from politics. This led to a gradual demise of the antichrist scare – a demise that, according to Christopher Hill, probably the best authority on this subject, was commensurate with the trend within religion towards the abandonment of political objectives. However, in the absence of such a trend anywhere or at any time that demise might not be so pronounced. This still applies in Northern Ireland, where fundamentalism and religio-political Orangeism now constitute probably the last significant outposts of the old 'Roman antichrist' theory. Yet even here it is the view of most of the Reformed Churches that the subjective and subordinate confessions of those tumultuous times are not fully relevant or finally authoritative in the world in which we now live. And so it is submitted that these anachronistic antichrist theories cannot overturn our thesis.

Although the separation of religion from party politics is a good thing, Christian citizens of any national polity are, of course, free as individuals to engage in politics to whatever extent this may be possible or deemed desirable. But this is not to say that the Christian community *per se*, or any part of that community, may legitimately seek to represent what is allegedly the essentially true Christian politics. Christianity has no such politics. It therefore cannot constitute any earthly polity, for as the Christian apostle wrote, 'Here we have no continuing city (*polis*)'.[10] This is where the separation of religion from politics comes in, for the Christian polis belongs to a different order of things, and is not delimited by considerations of geography, race, culture, nationality, denomination or party. The City of God is the capital of a kingdom that is not of this world. It belongs to the universe, having gates that are ever open to all from the north, south, east and west so that 'the glory and honour of all the nations are brought into it'.[11] Christ's kingdom is not a party political one.

The universal city is not over-flown by the Union Jack, the Stars and Stripes, the Tricolour, or by any other flag. The glory and genius of Christianity by which it has survived and grown for centuries is that it transcends all the worldly politics of nationality, race, tribe or party and certainly anything that tends to ascendancy or exclusion. Christ's kingdom reaches out to 'all men everywhere' and to 'all the world' – but can only do so precisely because it is 'not of this world'. It was therefore anything but the spirit of Christ's inclusive kingdom that inspired the Ulster Convention, or the Ulster Covenant, or the Ulster Volunteers, by means of which the Orange-unionists laid claim to 'God and Ulster' for themselves, and by force of arms if necessary. Nor could it have been by the laws of Christ's kingdom that the Orange Order suspended James Gyle MP for giving comfort to the dying Joe Devlin. And it could not have been in the name of that kingdom when, amid the encircling fundamentalist gloom that followed the Good Friday Agreement, a Baptist preacher offered a partisan political prayer that God would defend 'our wee Province'. In contrast with the beautiful and universal precepts of Christ, these narrow, self-interested and provincial views seem but a shabby sectarian parody that

... showed the fraud
That preachers to their lasting shame,
Can heap on God.[12]

Concerning the kingdom of Christ, Charles Hodge has written:

It can decide no question of politics ... being designed to embrace all other kingdoms (it) can exist under all forms of civil government without interfering with any. It was especially in this view that Christ declared that his kingdom was not of this world ... His kingdom was of such a nature that it necessitated no collision with the legitimate authority of any civil government. It belonged to a different sphere. It took cognisance of things

which lie beyond the province of secular power, and it left untouched all
that belongs peculiarly to civil rulers.[13]

The Rev. Ian Paisley MP, leader of the Democratic Unionist Party, is a former
Orangeman who, like Orangeism, pursues a religio-political credo that is totally at
variance with this. Recently he was reported in a national newspaper as publicly
advising a political opponent, an Ulster Unionist, to 'move from the darkness of sin
to the restoration of the gospel'. On foot of this extraordinary piece of party-political
evangelism it would appear that Paisley's particular party politics is peculiarly
blessed with divine approval whereas the politics of his Ulster Unionist opponent is
most decidedly not. However, against the background of New Testament teaching
this is utterly off-message. There is no such thing as the politics of the gospel. While
Christian citizens are free to participate in politics they are not entitled to lay claim
to an exclusive political credo in the name of Christ, whose kingdom is not of this
world. And while they may pronounce on the political issues of the day in light of
the applied moral truths of the Christian religion, this application is only practicable
when done in a hermeneutical and dialogical manner. Politics in any case is not a
matter of dogmatics or of absolutism. It is in the nature of politics that it is done
discursively and not dogmatically, for political opinions are as relative, changeable
and transient as is the world that gives them birth – a principle that could easily be
illustrated by reference to the fluctuating vagaries of Paisley's own political career.
Political propositions cannot properly be adopted or argued as though they emanated
from divinely delivered laws based on eternal truths or written on tablets of stone.
If this were so then all our political parties could feel free to wage perpetual holy
war, each striving to authenticate its own particular politics by reference to a so-
called true gospel. Happily, God-given politics does not exist except in the minds of
the sectarian theocrats and the battling demagogues. For this we ought to be
thankful. As Jesus put it: 'My kingdom is not of this world, else would my servants
fight'. Those religionists who fight, or talk about fighting, or who stir up fighting
have the wrong end of the stick – or perhaps they have the wrong kind of stick.
Religio-politics, which is the essence of Orangeism, is the bane of Ulster.

Conclusions

Despite its claims to be a representative and a defender of the Reformed religion,
it has been shown that the Orange Order is something of a parody, only partly and
nominally a religious institution. Essentially religio-political, it is mainly
concerned with what, in contradistinction to the kingdom of Christ, Charles
Hodge describes as 'the province of secular power' – a passable pun for the six-
county province that is Ulster Orangeism's chief preoccupation. For that reason
alone we need hardly be surprised that the Orange Order has so little to say about
Christian citizenship, or the practical principles of Christianity and the Reformed
Faith. Nor, because of its potential association with Unitarianism, which it
tolerates while rejecting Roman Catholicism, should we be surprised that, to
whatever extent it is religious, it is so lacking in both the ability and will to uphold

evangelical standards in a really meaningful way. Orange religion is therefore largely negative, being much more concerned about what it opposes that what it proposes. It subsists almost entirely within the great *sine qua non* of its anti-Catholicism, in the zealous pursuit of which it has gone much too far, transgressing into sectarian territory and well beyond the Reformed theological position. By its intolerant views on the Roman Church it has out-Luthered Luther and out-Calvined Calvin, while at the same time strangely tolerating other heterodox religious views that the Reformers would most certainly have regarded with considerable opprobrium. On that basis Orangeism's position on Unitarianism is too liberal, and its position on Roman Catholicism too extreme. Therefore, like the American Presbyterians of 1845, the Orangemen need to review the peculiar nature of their position in regard to these important issues.

These matters have implications far beyond doctrine. Extreme and excluding judgmental beliefs necessarily impinge on the lives and behaviour of ordinary people. In this case the religio-political doctrines involved certainly impinge on our relations with our Roman Catholic neighbours whom we are enjoined to love as ourselves, to whom we must do good, and with whom as Christian citizens we ought to live in communal equality and peace. It can hardly be conducive to those good neighbourly ends if we insist not only on adopting exclusive, separatist and damning attitudes towards the so-called 'fatal' errors of their religion, but also on marching that sectarian message of theocratic and territorial dominance into their districts and past their doors. The lessons of history have already addressed those dangerous and damaging matters. It is now long past time that the Orange Institution took positive steps to revise its ordinances, rules and attitudes on these questions. And if Orangeism feels in need of help and guidance, and desires to uphold a truly Christian banner, its leaders and chaplains should sit down with mainstream Christian ministers and theologians, to whose churches most Orangemen at least nominally belong, and review their whole position here. There are other important matters that have serious religious as well as political implications, which also need to be reviewed and which are examined in the course of the next two chapters.

13.

Orange Ritual –
The Influence of Freemasonry

D espite its much vaunted claim to be a defender of the Reformed Faith, which is austerely anti-ritualistic, Orangeism is strongly given to what Lord Randolph Churchill described in his famous Ulster Hall speech as 'all those ceremonies and forms which are practised in Orange Lodges'. That ritualism is a major element in Orange religion, and as has already been shown is of a form that clearly owes its origins to Freemasonry. The reader will recall that when James Wilson failed to convince the Freemasons of Benburb of his plan to establish a militia to resist the Catholic Defenders, he angrily mounted his horse and vowed to 'light a star in the Dyan that would eclipse them for ever.' That symbolic star was something with which all Freemasons would have been very familiar. Both the language and its attendant circumstances would have conveyed a clear message to them that Wilson proposed to form an alternative brotherhood along Masonic lines, but one that unlike theirs would be fully amenable to his politico-paramilitary purposes. And as we have seen, that is exactly what he did when he founded the Orange Boys, an organisation that quickly mutated into the Orange Order in the immediate aftermath of the Battle of the Diamond in September 1795. It will also be recalled that all the original initiates to the new Orange Order were Freemasons, and that they soon received specialist Masonic assistance in creating a secret system of ritualistic initiation rites, degrees and recognition signs, all based on adapted Masonic principles.

Originally there were three Orange degrees devised by James Wilson and the other founding fathers between 1795 and 1797. These have been described as 'elaborate', the second and third degrees having been crafted in a Masonic room in Portadown with the help and guidance of a leading Freemason and Orangeman, named John Templeton. Shortly afterwards, however, the incoming new leadership of gentry and clergy had to introduce radical reforms which were designed to curb growing Masonic influence. The reforming leaders therefore abolished the original ritualistic degree system and replaced it by two simple catechetical degrees known as the Orange and Purple. And this remains the official position, for according to the Purple lecture there are 'only two orders recognised by the Grand Orange Lodge of Ireland'.[1] Nevertheless, in what follows we shall see that despite those reforms Orangeism's original ritualistic and neo-Masonic nature would not only survive but would have lasting impact and influence. In the end the new leadership's efforts to reform the Order along more orthodox 'Christian' lines would fail after years of internal conflict and confusion.

Since 1798 the reformed Orange Order has officially operated on the basis of the two simple non-ritualistic degrees known as the Orange and Purple degrees. The word 'officially' is emphasised because the Order eventually succumbed to ways and means around its own rules, which enabled Orangemen again to countenance 'higher' ritualistic and neo-Masonic degrees similar to those of pre-1798. The elaborate degrees of what is sometimes described as the original Diamond System were in structure and method modelled on the first three degrees of Freemasonry, and known as the Orange, the Orange Marksman and the Purple Marksman degrees. These three degrees were abolished and outlawed in the 'improvement' of 1798, which was followed by the dissolution of the Order and the new beginning of 1800. However, the ritualistic dissidents still managed to preserve them by developing and including them in the Royal Arch Purple degree, in which form they survive within Orangeism to this day. Surprisingly, this also applies in the case of the fundamentalist Independent Orange Order, which was founded by strongly anti-ritualistic, ultra-Protestants.

It is evident that the early days of unregulated *laissez faire* Orangeism were marked by a strong preoccupation with ritualism. During this period, and in some cases even before it, there was a mushrooming of secret degrees such as the Knights of the Most Noble Order of the Boyne, the Black, Royal Mark, Scarlet, Blue, Gold, Green and Red Cross – all of which were influenced to a greater or lesser extent by Freemasonry. But Freemasonry had itself been shaped by influences as diverse as the ancient Occult and the mediaeval Orders of the Crusaders that included the Knights of Malta and the Knights of St. John of Jerusalem. This hotchpotch of ancient and arcane ideas was yet again being recycled, this time within the early Orange Order, where its proliferation was giving rise to much confusion and controversy. The Royal Black Preceptory, the most ritualistic of all the Loyal Orders with no fewer than eleven degrees culminating in the Red Cross, eventually evolved out of this admixture. Like the Royal Arch Purple, it too would find ways and means of permanently circumventing the Orange Order's attempted anti-ritual reforms of 1798.

Being neo-Masonic, the original Orange degree principle was based on the concept of measured progress – 'progress by degrees'.[2] These were degrees of spiritual enlightenment and advancement, attained by ritualistic participation and induction into the mysteries and secrets of the Order. This was the means to a notional spiritual and moral improvement that was very far removed from the teachings of the Reformed or evangelical faith. Progress from initiation led through the various stages of the Order's 'mysteries, crafts, arts and secrets' and was facilitated, demonstrated and experienced by means of a degree system that included a complex symbolism. It is not proposed to enter into the detail of Orange symbolism, as it is sufficient to my purpose to touch on the broad principles of the ritual rather than deal with all its tedious minutiae. It may suffice to point out that the origins of the Orange symbols – such as compass, square, five-pointed star, arch, ladder, coffin, skull, sword, hoodwink, sun, moon and stars, all-seeing eye – are just one remove from Freemasonry. And Freemasonry owes much of its own ritual to an extensive plagiarising from the ancient Occult and other archaic Orders.

The rituals of all these Orders, and particularly those of the Loyal Orders, were the outcome of a long drawn-out mongrelising process that eventually produced some very strange offspring. We find, for example, that the members of the Royal Black Preceptory call themselves Knights, wear the chivalric Red Cross and bear the sword, as well as boasting alleged links of rite and tradition with the medieval Christian Crusaders.[3] Yet the Crusaders were those Orders whose military crusades to Palestine were held on behalf of the Holy Roman Empire and instituted by none other than Pope Urban II. It is therefore ironic that, in addition to their neo-Masonic ritualism, the professedly Protestant Blackmen in effect boast association with medieval and papal Rome. It is even more ironic that these chivalric and quasi-papal Knights of Ulster may only attend a Catholic funeral service on peril of expulsion from their Order. There was one Master who might have likened this particular contradiction to 'straining at gnats and swallowing camels'.

My cursory approach to Orange symbolism ought not to suggest that the subject is unimportant, for symbolism has, or should have, significant meaning. It cannot be so vapid that the five-pointed star, for example, 'can mean what you want it to mean and nothing more', as say Orange clergy Meredith and Kennaway.[4] This is the semantics of Humpty Dumpty: 'When I use a word it means what I choose it to mean – neither more or less'. If a symbol can mean what any Orangeman wants it to mean it can also mean nothing, but either way it cannot be an effective symbol. A symbol must have coherent meaning, reached in light of its origins (or plagiarised origins), and consistent with the context of its usage over time. Orangemen who have 'worked' these symbols and degrees for years, and whose own historians acknowledge their Masonic and other connotations, cannot duck, dismiss or demean their meaning when that meaning is found to run counter to Christianity. And if Orangemen do reject an interpretation of their symbolism, then the very least they should do is explain their dissent and proffer a credible alternative interpretation.

Contemporary Orange historians proudly acknowledge that the elaborate neo-Masonic symbolism and ritual of the original Diamond System has been preserved, despite long condemnation by Grand Lodge, and successfully carried forward under the aegis of the Royal Arch Purple Order[5] to which the vast majority of Orangemen also belong. Like its modern counterpart, the original Orange degree system included secret recognition signs and passwords, which provided a sense of arcane political security, brotherhood and bonding. This was inculcated by a dramatised ritual of quasi-biblical events such the Exodus, the wanderings of the Israelites in the wilderness, the crossing of the River Jordan and the entry into the Promised Land. By way of flavour, the following is a short excerpt from the original Purpleman degree of 1796, in which the candidate's response to a question about his buttonhole ribbon of purple, blue and orange develops into a catechetical dialogue:

Q. Why do you wear that?

A. Because I am free.

Q. Free of what?

A. Of the wilderness.

Q. Whence came you?

A. From the Land of Moab.

Q. Whither do you go?

A. To the plains of Jericho.

Q. How do you hope to get there?

A. By a password.

Q. Have you the password?

A. I have.

Q. Will you give it to me?

A. I will divide it with you: The Ark of God.

Q. Why do you make purple your colour?

A. Because the ornaments of the curtains of the Ark of God were purple, blue and red; and I chose purple for mine.[6]

There was obviously much more to the original degree ritual than this, for we know that it was a very lengthy and elaborate process, but unfortunately the detailed material is not available to us. However, the excerpt just quoted clearly indicates that the ritual did not balk at reducing scripture and sacred principles to the esoteric purposes of passwords or badges. For the convenience of its own oath-bound secrecy the open Bible was made to facilitate Orangeism's neo-Masonic secrets and mysteries. It is therefore certain that the crude adaptation that characterised the original Diamond ritual would have appeared irreverent and unseemly to the informed Christian mind, such frivolous misappropriation and admixture being incompatible with the Reformed tradition's reverential attitude to the Bible. Those who would reject this should ask themselves why it was that the new Orange leadership felt constrained to take such strong action in the late 1790s? And what had caused things to develop into such a Babel of confusion that fundamental root-and-branch reform, regulation and control were deemed by the new Orange leadership to have become imperative?

Thomas Verner, who was appointed the first Grand Master of the Grand Lodge of Ireland in 1798, quickly embarked on that programme of reform. It was shown earlier in the book that he tried to root out the original ritualistic Diamond System to the extent of organising an entirely new beginning, which included the re-initiation of all Orangemen into an 'improved' Orange Order in early 1800. We have seen that the improvement introduced a new and simplified two-degree 'New System', which involved a short catechism and address. It abolished the old ritual 'travel' in which the hoodwinked candidate was led around the Lodge-room enduring robust and often rowdy behaviour, giving rise to physical hazard and not inconsiderable trauma. In fact, we now have a much clearer indication of the nature of the old ritual since the Royal Arch Purple Order (which boasts its perpetuation) has now published, albeit on limited circulation, its own official *History*. Readers also now have access to the former Arch Purpleman W.P. Malcomson's book *Behind Closed Doors*, as well as to his pamphlet *The Forgotten History of the Orange Order*, both of them strong critiques written from an evangelical perspective. And so it now possible to outline the various stages and principles of the Diamond system as preserved and adapted within the Royal Arch Purple degree.

The Oath

At the outset, and in a side room, the candidate must swear an oath, the detail of which he is as yet unaware, binding himself to the Royal Arch Purple, its secrets, mysteries and members. He must swear allegiance to the Protestant religion and to the Glorious Constitution of 1688. He must swear to refrain from unlawful carnal knowledge – but, extraordinarily, this is qualified by reference to a specified class of female who are 'near and dear female relatives' of a brother Arch Purpleman. He must also swear to obey the 'five points of fellowship' and keep and conceal the secrets of his Arch Purple brethren, as well as his own, 'murder and treason excepted'. There is therefore potentially much wrong-doing that the Royal Arch Purpleman is obligated to cover up.

The Preparation

After the oath the candidate's clothing is partially removed and adjusted so that'he is neither naked nor clothed, barefooted nor shod, deprived of all monies, means and minerals, blindfolded and led by the hand of a friend to the door'. This state of deprivation and emptiness is designed to bring him to a state of physical and mental readiness to receive an unforgettable initiation, to the end that he will ritually emerge a new man, mystically re-clothed, enriched and enlightened by the mysteries of the Royal Arch Purple degree. This concept of enlightenment through ritual has nothing to do with Christianity, but is patently Occult and neo-Masonic.

The Reception

The blindfolded and semi-naked candidate is then conducted to the Chapter door, which is guarded by a Tyler who is armed with a sword to keep out 'profane or unworthy persons'. Outsiders are therefore regarded as heathen, but on knocking symbolically three times and giving the password the humbled candidate is conducted inside to the sacred precincts of the Chapter room. His advancement toward enlightenment is about to begin.

The Travel

After being branded on his breast by a sharp and heated implement symbolising a pricked conscience should he divulge the secret mysteries he is about to learn, the blinded candidate is suddenly subjected to a loud and unexpected noise that symbolises the thunderous wrath of God against all disobedience. At this point the candidate is compelled to kneel and pray for his deliverance. The long Travel begins as he is 'circumambulated' three times around the Chapter room, the floor of which is strewn with branches, brambles or ashes to ensure physical discomfort to the barefooted traveller. During this protracted part of the ceremony his legs are violently whipped, signifying the serpents and scorpions encountered on the wilderness journey. The Travel evokes boisterous hilarity on the part of the Arch Purple spectators, many of whom bleat like animals in anticipation of the most exciting part of the ritual – that of 'riding the goat'. In the course of all these goings on the candidate is caused to fall and rise on each of the three circuits, this symbolising death and resurrection, all of which, incongruously, is interspersed by several scripture readings and prayers from the Orange chaplain.

Riding the Goat

'Riding the Goat', which is suggestive of a folkloric or saturnalian custom, is regarded as the centre-piece of the ritual and follows an elaborate build-up. After his third and final fall the candidate is raised by the 'five points of fellowship' – a secret ritualised embrace involving five specific points of physical contact. He is then advanced 'two and a half' paces, and elevated by means of a three stepped structure called 'Jacob's ladder', which is said to symbolise faith, hope and charity. However, there is absolutely no biblical basis for this ritualised concept of the typological Jacob's ladder for the symbolic purposes of moral and mystical elevation. The symbol of the two-and-a-half is borrowed from the biblical account of two tribes of Reuben and Gad who, together with the half tribe of Manasseh, led the vanguard of Israel into the Promised Land. Again this is a direct plagiarism from Freemasonry. The symbol is further deployed in the Royal Arch Purple's secret neo-Masonic knock of two long and one short raps. It is likewise found in the Royal Arch Purple's two-and-a-half fingered secret handshake.

At the top of the third step of the ladder is a coffin, symbolising death which the candidate would willingly undergo before divulging the sacred secret mysteries he is now in the course of learning. He then kneels on the coffin, upon which he is encouraged to indicate that he puts his trust in God. Suddenly and without warning he is pushed violently backwards and caught by a canvas blanket held by a circle of several Arch Purplemen, who toss him around in it, generally roughing him up for several minutes amid much boisterous glee on the part of the spectators. The experience is known as 'riding the goat'. Occasionally this and other parts of the ritual have resulted in serious injury, and there have been several recorded instances of death as a result of this traumatic experience.

'Goat' is deliberately intended as a reverse acronym for *The Ark Of God*, the holy receptacle in which Israel's most sacred relics were kept hidden. Through enduring the arduous process of 'riding the goat' the candidate is therefore understood to be processing towards that moral elevation and mystical enlightenment contained within the sacred and hidden mysteries of the Ark of God – all of which are accessed through ritualistic participation in the secret and esoteric Royal Arch Purple degree.

The Blood Curse

When 'riding the goat' is completed the candidate is bundled into a sheet and carried to the north-west corner of the room, where he is advised of the dire consequences of breaking his oath of secrecy. Here he learns of a barbarous three-fold blood curse involving evisceration and bodily dismemberment, the offensive and gruesome details of which we forbear to quote.

The Enlightenment

Shortly after the blood curse the candidate is brought to the climax of the ritual. The chaplain reads several scriptures pertaining to natural and spiritual light, and asks the candidate: 'What do you stand most in need of?' He is prompted to answer 'Light', whereupon his hoodwink is removed. This symbolises his mystical enlightenment on being called out of darkness into marvellous light.

Almost every one of the above-mentioned symbols of the Royal Arch Purple ritual is a plagiarised adaptation from Freemasonry. There is no reason to doubt the Royal Arch Purple's own claim that for the most part its degree preserves and perpetuates the essential elements of the second and third degrees of the original Orange degree system that was known as the Diamond System, which was banned in 1798. It will be recalled that those two degrees were drafted circa 1796 in a Masonic room in Portadown by early Orangemen James Wilson, James Sloan and John Templeton, all of whom were Freemasons.

Reform and Counter-reform

The reasons for Orangeism's post-1798 reforms are therefore obvious. Apart from the unregulated *laissez-faire* approach of the original Order with its neo-Masonic degree system and the proliferation of other degrees, it is clear that Thomas Verner's reform programme was motivated by more than the need for an administrative tidying-up exercise. There had to be something radically wrong with the nature and content of the original Orange ritual to evoke this kind of reform and reconstruction. Now that details of the Royal Arch Purple ritual have entered the public domain we know precisely why reform of the early Orange Order had become imperative. Apart from the political reasons mentioned earlier there were obviously strong religious and moral reasons such as its neo-Masonic origins and degrees, its esoteric mysteries, arts and crafts, and the dangerous horseplay of a traumatic 'obstacle course' ritual. There was also the irreverent, some might say blasphemous, admixture of Occult ideas with the frivolous and foolish misappropriations of Christian scripture. But worst of all to the Christian mind was the concept of 'sublime' enlightenment and moral improvement by means of a mystical ritualism. It is therefore important to note that Orangemen of our own time deny that there was any need for reform, and they go on to describe Verner's actions as 'drastic'.[7] They applaud the fact that the old neo-Masonic ritual, although long outlawed, has been preserved and now survives under the aegis of the 'Order within the Order' – the Royal Arch Purple, of which the vast majority of Orangemen everywhere are now members. It follows therefore that Orangeism is still shot-through with the neo-Masonic practices described above.

It was shown earlier that opposition to Verner's reformed New System soon came from a remnant of Orangemen who insisted on retaining the ritual of the Diamond System. This opposition was neither direct nor open. It was subversive inasmuch as the ritualists ostensibly co-operated with the reforms while continuing covertly to work the old degrees. On Sunday 12th July 1801 Grand Lodge elected a new Grand Master, George Ogle, who defeated Thomas Verner by 14 votes to 12. Ogle was a hard-liner and a staunch supporter of the Protestant ascendancy. But as he subsequently stood by Verner's reforms, it seems likely that the outgoing Grand Master's defeat was not due to those reforms but rather to his support for the recent Act of Union. That Act had weakened the ascendancy much to the chagrin of ordinary Orangemen, all of whom had pledged themselves to its defence. Under George Ogle's leadership Grand Lodge continued to apply the New System, from time to time taking action against those who participated in the 'degree irregularity' of practising the outlawed rituals. In 1801, for example, it was resolved:

> That the Grand Lodge of Ireland does acknowledge no other colour or degrees among Orangemen but Orange and Purple and that all other colours or names of Black, Scarlet, Blue or any other colour are illegal and injurious to the true Orange system, and that if any shall presume after public notice of this resolution to meet in any such Black or other similar Lodge he shall be publicly expelled, and his name sent to every Lodge in the Kingdom.[8]

Similar resolutions had to be promulgated in 1811, 1813, 1814, 1817, 1820 and 1834, which raises the question why Grand Lodge failed to nail down its own reforms. Perhaps it was making only a half-hearted and token stand against the ritualists, but this seems unlikely. It is much more likely that Grand Lodge was fighting a losing battle with something that was inherent in the very nature of Orangeism. In fact this struggle ensued for nearly a century, during which Grand Lodge had to contend with elusive ritualistic opponents who never ceased to dissemble and scheme against the authority and rules of their own Order. Contemporary Orange historians now acknowledge that dissident Orangemen adopted deliberately shadowy and subversive strategies in order to circumvent the anti-ritual rules and oft-repeated resolutions of Grand Lodge.

What was going on, and why was there such a protracted struggle on this issue? Surprisingly, the contemporary historians of the Royal Arch Purple have come out and provided a clear answer in their relatively recent publication:

> Probably in 1802, a new degree was devised by Brethren who valued and loved the old traditions and who were concerned by the turn of events … they realised that with two simple degrees of Orange and Purple there would only be room for one further degree. The Brethren had been accustomed to three elaborate degrees and could still have three even if two of them had been simplified. The third degree would have to include as much as possible

of the travel and ritual of the original three. Instead of being the Purple Marksman's Degree it would be the Royal Arch Purple Marksman's Degree to give it its full style and title. The word Royal, of course relating to the heavenly kingdom. 'Ye are a chosen generation, a Royal priesthood, an holy nation, a peculiar people; that ye should show forth the praises of Him who hath called you out of darkness into His marvellous light' 1 Peter 2:9.[9]

It is quite extraordinary to argue that there was 'room for one further degree' – a third degree. We have shown why Grand Lodge had so sternly resolved that there should only be two. It is equally extraordinary that the Royal Arch Purple historians offer no explanation as to how the Orangemen could 'still have three' degrees, given that the third would 'include as much as possible of the travel and ritual of the original three.' After all, it was the tomfoolery and other excesses of that very travel and ritual which *inter alia* had been deemed to necessitate the reforms in the first place. But the Royal Arch Purple historians and lecturers cannot even acknowledge these contradictions, never mind answer them. The only reasonable explanation for this is that in defying Grand Lodge and its rules the Royal Arch Purplemen were serving what to them was a higher authority – that of the original ritualistic tradition they loved, which was steeped in secret neo-Masonic arts, crafts and mysteries.

The notion of enlightenment that somehow inculcates knowledge of the supernatural through ritualised experience lies on the surface of the Arch Purple historians' statement quoted above. Spiritual enlightenment through ritualism is a concept that is universally common to the ritualistic cults, and is something which has an inordinate appeal for those who, in the words of St. Paul, 'desire to make a fair show in the flesh.' As such it is a kind of gospel or religion in its own right. The Arch Purplemen do not hesitate to couch their mysticism in admixture and misappropriations of the scriptures. By this means they arrogate to their initiates the status of royal priesthood, which allegedly is attained in the 'marvellous light' that is sublimely experienced by being ritually 'made' in undergoing the Royal Arch Purple degree. In a sense, therefore, we need not wonder that Orangemen should describe this formula as the 'sublime degree'. This is widely recognised as the highest of the Orange degrees, despite the fact that under their own rules it remains illegal. The word 'sublime' has the meaning: 'To raise to an elevated sphere or exalted state – to make (morally or spiritually) sublime. To transmute into something higher, nobler, or more excellent' (*Shorter Oxford Dictionary*). But the real wonder is that this moral and spiritual excellence could be magically attained by means of a boisterous ritual involving such rustic tomfoolery as 'riding the goat'. Here we might adapt Winston Churchill's famous wartime retort to the Nazis' threatened wringing of the British chicken's neck – 'Some ritual, some degree!'

One shudders to think what the men of the Reformation would have made of this alternative means of grace, this admixture of mystery and misapplied scripture allegedly designed for moral and spiritual improvement by 'sublime' rite and ritual. It is certain that a Calvin or a Zwingli would have regarded the whole system as tantamount to a pagan temple, and that like Samson of old they would most unceremoniously have pulled it down. Having said that, it must be stressed that this judgement is from the perspective of the Reformed Faith that Orangeism is said to hold. As when we touched upon Unitarianism, it is not our purpose here to attack Freemasonry or the other things with which Orangeism might have association. Rather, the objective is to show that, like the things already mentioned, Orangeism's ritualistic aspect is entirely incompatible with its alleged Reformed and evangelical standards, an argument we shall develop in detail later.

The modern Arch Purple historians freely acknowledge the neo-Masonic nature of the Diamond System and its offspring, the Royal Arch Purple Order:

> Some of those present (when this system was devised) were certainly members of the Masonic Order and would not want to clash with the degrees in the Masonic, and as blue was the colour of the Craft and red was the colour of the Royal Arch only purple would have been seen as available. This is not the only time that the older Order would influence the degrees of the new... the Royal Arch Purple Degree evolved from the pre-1800 Orange and Purple Orders, retaining the original theme and significance with the addition of certain innovations derived from practices introduced by members, some of which may have had their origin in the Masonic Order, and probably introduced by brethren who had dual membership and thus forming a new ritual.[10]

There can therefore be no doubt as to the mixed pedigree of the Royal Arch Purple Order and its 'sublime degree'. Yet for many years past it has been the boast of the Royal Arch Purple that very few Orangemen feel properly initiated until they have received it, and that nowadays almost all Orangemen are in its membership. This is as significant as it is surprising in view of the fact that the Grand Orange Lodge leadership was so vehemently opposed to it. Take for example the conclusion to its annual address on 11th November 1811, which drew attention to 'letters from the North which state that silly, shameful and even idolatrous practices of mystically initiating into Black, Red and perhaps Green Orders still continues'. At their very next meeting Grand Lodge added Scarlet, Blue and Royal Arch Purple to the list. Just one year later a letter was received from the Lifford district complaining that lodges were making men into the Purple Order through a long and 'tedious ritual that involved nakedness and hoodwinking'. In its official response to that letter, the Grand Lodge of Ireland denounced these practices as 'heathenish and indecent ceremonies'. Yet the Arch Purple persisted with its unlawful ritual, despite the damaging admission of its own historians that this ritual had been

> condemned as illegal and injurious in 1811, heathenish and indecent in 1813 and ridiculous, superstitious and spurious in 1814.[11]

In January 1820 Grand Lodge established a Committee of Enquiry to investigate this whole matter. The Enquiry found that the Purple degree – the second of the two simplified degrees of the reformed New System – had been deliberately infiltrated and corrupted by the ritual of the illegal old Purple Marksman degree of the Diamond System. The ritualists, who knew full well that apart from the colour nomenclature the new Purple degree had nothing in common with the old ritualistic

Purple Marksman degree it replaced, took the deliberately simplistic line that 'Purple could still be taken to include Purple Marksman'. This was as deceitful as it was defiant. Yet it was a tactic on which the modern Royal Arch Purple historians have commented with approval.[12] Grand Lodge saw it differently. The Purple degree and its entire membership was nullified, and the concept of Purple Marksman obliterated. As in the year 1800, every Orangeman had to be re-initiated into what was now termed the Plain or Small Purple degree. This issue was therefore neither a trivial matter nor a minor skirmish. It was an undercover power struggle around issues of lawful authority and moral principle, fought out protractedly between the Orange leadership and the illegal neo-Masonic ritualists who, year after year in defiance of authority, persisted in their covert and illegal activity.

Even the purge of 1820 did not end the matter. Years later, in his evidence to the House of Commons Select Committee of Enquiry in 1835, the respected Orange Grand Secretary, Stewart Blacker, described the ritual of the still extant higher orders as 'a mixture of freemasonry with that of the old Orange System, a species of mummery'. In 1878 another Grand Secretary, W.J. Gwynn, could write of the 'heresy of an oral ritual and all fantastic tomfooleries of Arch Purple, Black, Scarlet, Green and the like'. But these practices simply would not go away, despite the condemnations that have already been high-lighted by means of a veritable thesaurus of damning epithets, which includes words like: 'shameful', 'ridiculous', 'tomfooleries', 'mummery', 'superstitious', 'spurious', 'indecent', 'idolatrous', 'heathenish', 'heresy'. Each and every one of these epithets was out of the mouths of the Orange leaders themselves. And yet, despite all this condemnation, neo-Masonic Orange ritualism not only survived, but also quietly established itself to the extent that eventually it would achieve a form of general recognition within all the ranks of Orangeism in Ireland. It would be even more successful throughout the rest of the Orange world.

This Arch Purple achievement was not only by dint of its resistance to authority and rule, but was also by subtle and covert tactics in a long and slow strategic game. The main strength and leadership of those who were sometimes known as 'unlicensed' rebels was in County Armagh where the Order first originated, and from which the other rebel institution known as the Black Order also came. Then as now, County Armagh was the hotbed not only of sectarian conflict, but also of internecine Orange strife. In 1820 the Black Order – a super-ritualist grouping with its own multi-layered degree system – formed its own separate institution and in effect told the Orange Grand Lodge to mind its own business. However, the Black Order succeeded in retaining its membership links with the Orange Order, and especially with its fellow ritualists of the Royal Arch Purple from whom it now draws all its own elite membership by invitation. The arcane Royal Arch Purple took a different course, having a policy of 'keeping out of sight' and of working quietly from within the Orange Order, from which it draws all its membership. And so all Arch Purplemen must first be Orangemen, and all Blackmen must first be Arch Purplemen. Thus despite their original differences, these Loyal Orders have long had a common Orange base and are essentially inter-linked. The Royal Arch Purple historians tell us that:

The loose, flexible structure adopted by the Royal Arch Purple Order and its policy of *keeping out of sight* while staying as close as possible to the Orange organisation, especially at Lodge level ensured that it survived unscathed.[13]

... unlike the Black Order, the Royal Arch Purple, which felt that its original and rightful place had been within the Orange Institution, decided to *shadow that organisation* as closely as possible (emphases mine).[14]

Over the years this covert approach developed into a widespread shadow structure designed to cover as much of the Lodge network as possible, the Arch Purple meeting as convenient before or after the meetings of the regular Orange Lodges to do their own business. This included the conferment of the unlawful and elaborate Royal Arch Purple degree. The success and growth of the shadow structure and the practicalities of its operation necessitated much clandestine infiltration and scheming, and certainly would have required the compliance of senior Orangemen at various levels within the Lodges concerned. It also involved a mechanism known as 'raising the meeting', which in effect meant that at the end of the normal Orange meeting non-Arch Purple brethren left and the meeting was then 'raised' to the so-called higher matters of the Arch Purple. Similarly, where the Arch Purple procedures were carried out first, the meeting would then be 'lowered' and the ordinary Orangemen allowed in.[15]

Was such a hierarchy of higher and lower secret Orders in any way compatible with the broadly egalitarian principles of evangelical religion? Even the separatist Plymouth Brethren, perhaps the strictest evangelical group in the whole of Christendom, have a 'back seat' from which non-members can witness and to a limited extent participate in the service. But the Royal Arch Purple was a secret society, and its secrets were hidden even from its brother Orangemen. The truth is that these practices and arrangements were flagrantly in breach of the very rules the Arch Purplemen had pledged to uphold. Worse than that, they involved a high degree of dissembling that was even more in violation of basic Christian ethics than was the ritualism which that deceit was designed to accommodate. Yet for all that, these historical details would only have been of minor consequence were it not for the fact that, from being a shadowy group within Orangeism, the Royal Arch Purple eventually gained the ascendancy and became by far the largest of all the Loyal Orders.

In 1909 the Arch Purple made application to have its degree integrated into the official Orange system. Had it been successful the Royal Arch Purple would have become the third Orange degree, in line with the Masonic model and with what had happened in Scotland and elsewhere. But surprisingly, and despite all the many previous disavowals of the Arch Purple system by Grand Lodge, the application successfully passed through three official stages and only narrowly failed at the final one. The Royal Arch Purple, far from being dismayed, took encouragement from this and in 1911 decided to form its own Irish institution. Although organisationally separate from the Orange Order, the Arch Purple would remain linked to it by retaining its membership in that Order and by recruiting all its new members from it. Given this dual membership and in view of the fact that ninety-five per cent of all

Irish Orangemen are now in it, the Royal Arch Purple might reasonably regard itself to all intents and purposes as representing the third and highest degree of Orangeism. In drawing that conclusion we are excluding the degrees of the more rigorously independent Black Order. However, the fact remains that the 'third degree' theory is not officially valid, for as we have seen the Orange Order must uphold its own rules which disavow any degrees but two – the Orange and Plain Purple. And yet, for all that, the neo-Masonic 'three degree' model is now universally applied in all but name, for virtually the whole of Orangeism has been initiated into the arts, crafts and mysteries of the long outlawed Royal Arch Purple ritualism.

Some readers may well wonder what was so bad about Royal Arch Purple ritual to justify such a fuss. Others may with greater justification wonder what was so especially good about that ritual as to motivate the Arch Purple to resist its own Grand Lodge's ordinances and rules in a covert rebellion that went on for over a hundred years. We know the answer to the latter question lies in the strange allure that some find in mystical and ritual experience. But can such an allure, however strong and regardless of the rights or wrongs of ritualism, justify the deliberate dissembling and deception that were involved in this whole matter? This is a particularly pertinent question in the context of the claim that the Orange Order stands for the defence of the Christian religion. It becomes even more so when we reflect on the fact that the Reformed Faith is a system of doctrine that takes a strong position on the subject of ritualism. This therefore raises the issue whether the elaborate Orange ritual as practised by the Royal Arch Purple, and even more so by the Royal Black Preceptory, is really compatible and consistent with the standards of evangelical Protestantism that derive from the teachings of the Reformation. In view of what we have just touched upon this seems highly improbable.

Sacrament, Ritual and Ritualism

In addressing the above question we must broadly consider the subject of sacrament, ritual and ritualism. The Reformed Faith regards a sacrament or a sacramental experience as something that in a special way is ordained and used by God to reach our hearts and minds and to evoke a greater understanding and impression of himself. However, it should be borne in mind that according to Reformed principles God reveals himself in ways that are consistent with his Word. Thus a sacrament cannot (1) be the subject of merely human invention; (2) subsist only in ceremonial externalism; and (3) stand alone in the bareness of its own form. Rather the sacrament must be founded on the authority of scripture, be experienced through the power of the Spirit, and lead us to the substance of Christ. Over a century ago W.E. Gladstone, whose passion for politics was matched only by his love for theology, wrote a pamphlet entitled *The Church of England and Ritualism*. This defined ritualism as 'an undue disposition to ritual' and aligned Gladstone with the Church of England's evangelical position *vis-à-vis* the Anglo-Catholic tradition. He was not opposed to ritual, in that he regarded its normal and benign usage as that kind of formalism which in the Pauline sense meant doing 'all things decently and in order'. Seen in that light Gladstone regarded it as 'the clothing which, in some form, and in some degree, men naturally and inevitably give to the performance of the public duties of religion'. However, he believed that those of an undue disposition to ritual tended to carry their rituals so far beyond that natural and normal performance as to turn it into ritualism. William Gladstone therefore regarded ritualism as

> ... obstructive encumbrance; it is departure from measure and from harmony in the annexation of appearance to substance, of the outward to the inward; it is the caricaturing of the beautiful; it is the conversion of helps into hindrances; it is the attempted substitution of the secondary for the primary aim...

The Reformers would have agreed with that analysis. As expositors of the Bible they knew that one of its great themes was the antithesis of shadow and substance – the (fore) shadow of Old Testament ceremonialism *vis-à-vis* the substance that was to come, namely, the full revelation of the New Testament which is Christ. The Reformers believed that pre-Reformation Christianity had in some respects lapsed back into the old Judaeo ceremonial and its ritualistic principles. They knew that Judaeo-Christianity had wrestled with questions about rite and ritual, and that the New Testament scriptures such as the Epistles to the Galatians and the Hebrews had laid down important principles on the subject – principles which had guided them in their own struggle with Rome. They therefore believed that without the authority of the scriptural Word – and the message it entailed as to the substance of Christ received through the Holy Spirit – all mere external rites and sacraments were but 'weak and beggarly elements', or mere shadows without substance. On this basis they believed that much of the elaborate ritual of Christendom had so far departed from the simplicity and spirituality of the gospel as to muffle or even deny the Word, and so had become what John Calvin liked to describe as 'a dumb show'.

In turning away from sacramentalism, the Reformers stressed that the virtue of a sacrament did not subsist in any inherent sacramental power or applied ministerial magic, but was derived from the Word in the sacrament. Thus no sacrament could be truly efficacious if its external nature, its ceremony or its ministration were such as to obstruct or obscure the inner message of the Word. Without the clear message of the gospel there could be neither spiritual meaning nor means of grace, for the efficacy of the sacrament flowed from the authority of the Word within it, conveyed to the heart in the power of the Spirit, and imbibed by grace through faith. The Reformers therefore believed that, in the absence of simplicity and spirituality, external ceremony would become the end rather than the means. The medium would become the message. Thus, in accordance with Gladstone's concept of the 'annexation of appearance to substance', the sacrament could become transubstantiated into sacramentalism and ritual into ritualism. Consequently, the Reformers' pre-requisite for true sacrament, liturgy or ritual was that these things should carry the authority of the Word, convey the meaning of the Word and consecrate the spiritual object of the Word – to the end that Christ may dwell in our hearts by faith.

Calvin, the theologian of the Reformation, believed that 'the simpler the view taken of the sacrament, consistent with the significance attributed to it by Christ and his apostles, the greater would be its potency, and the more it would be a real means of grace'.[16] It was also by such simplicity that we could avoid what Gladstone described as the 'the conversion of helps into hindrances' and the 'substitution of the secondary for the primary aim'. Consequently, it was for spiritual and scriptural reasons that the Reformed Faith placed the emphasis on that simplicity which is found in the Word, the whole Word and nothing but the Word. As one writer put it,

> Calvin drew his whole theology from Scripture. It was a fixed principle with him that he would not go beyond what the express teaching of Scripture authorised... To Calvin the Bible was the perfect and complete rule of righteousness. It specifies exactly in what goodness consists; no item is left out and none should be added.[17]

What is said of Calvin here is generally applicable to the Reformed Faith and to evangelical religion considered as a whole. In broad theological sweep it leaves little or no room for invention or innovation in spiritual things. In fact, the Reformed Faith essentially dislikes any adaptation or admixture, and is instinctively opposed to ritualistic additions to what it believes from the Bible to be 'the faith that was once and for all delivered unto the saints'.[18] There must be no addition to what was delivered 'once for all'. The old Scottish Reformer John Knox was the kind of man one would expect Ulster evangelicals to listen to. Never a man to pussyfoot around an issue, he was extremely explicit about ritualism. Commenting on Deuteronomy 12:32, he said:

> Not that thing which appears good in thine eyes shalt thou do to the Lord thy God, but what the Lord thy God has commanded thee, that do thou. Add nothing to it; diminish nothing from it. Unless you are able to prove that God has commanded your ceremonies this his former commandment will damn you and them.[19]

Conclusions

Having gleaned something of the Reformers' principles on this subject, the important question is whether the ritualism practised by the Orangemen of the Royal Arch Purple (and to a greater extent by the Royal Black Preceptory) is consistent with the standards of the Reformed Faith. We have endeavoured to explain the Reformed and evangelical approach to sacrament, liturgy and ritual. It has been shown how this places the emphasis upon the simplicity, spirituality and substance of the Word of God within these things, so as to ensure that the Christian message is not overlaid by extraneous and distracting encumbrances. It is therefore certain that if the Reformers demanded such scriptural, spiritual and sanctified standards in the ministry of religion, they would have taken a most censorious attitude to Orange ritualism. Far from having any kind of Christian legitimacy, this is a system of alien origin and invention – one that not only superimposes itself upon scripture, but also misappropriates that scripture, and does not hesitate to mix and co-mingle Christian, pagan and occult ideas. The men of the Reformation must have reprobated such a secret, oath-bound and ritualistic politico-religion. Indeed, it beggars description what they might have thought of a degree system that purports to achieve spiritual enlightenment, as well as moral advancement, by means of an arcane ritual that St. Paul would have described as another gospel.

The Royal Arch Purple and the Royal Black Preceptory are the elite Orders of Orangeism, and the vast majority of Orangemen are in one or both of them. Both these Orders continue to practice the rituals that Stewart Blacker once called a 'species of mummery'. These rituals were regularly disavowed by the Grand Orange Lodge many years ago – a position that in principle still obtains and which should still obtain in fact, in accordance with the Orange rulebook. But the rulebook has been ignored, and the position of Grand Lodge utterly swamped by the ritualists. Why is this? The truth is that Orangeism needs its ritualism. True to its arcane origins and principles, it has always had a secretive 'behind closed doors' mentality. The requirement of a separatist neo-Masonic bonding philosophy and a secretive belief system lies at the very heart of its ascendancy nature – a nature that is elitist, exclusive and privilege-seeking. Thus the religio-political beliefs of Orangeism cannot be regarded as innocent or innocuous, for their nature is such that they are bound to impact adversely on the wider society, as in fact they do. Thus the 'lodge' mentality involves attitudinal beliefs and practices that cannot stand in isolation, but spill over into our religion, our politics and the everyday life of our society. Orangeism with all its oath-bound, secretive, exclusive and privilege-seeking principles cannot but have a detrimental effect. Its arcane introspection is the philosophy of the divided Irishmen, the 'brotherhood' that looks after its own to the exclusion of others. It is the very antithesis of that openness and inclusiveness that respects diversity, loves dialogue, encourages pluralism, and which gladly and quite unequivocally extends the principles of liberty, equality and fraternity to all our citizens without exception, and entirely regardless of class, colour or creed.

14.

Orange Rights –
Marching and Civil Liberties

Forty years ago I had a discussion with an older friend on the question of the Orange Order's right to march through nationalist areas in Northern Ireland. My friend, a zealous evangelical Christian of high principle, was ambivalent about certain aspects of such marches, being particularly concerned by their tendency, particularly during the 'mad month' of July each year, to stir the blood and to provoke communal violence. However, he believed that for all its shortcomings Orangeism provided a providential bulwark for what the apostle Paul described as the 'defence of the gospel' – a view that some Ulster fundamentalists who see Rome as the quintessential enemy still hold strongly. Thereupon I suggested to my friend that the gospel was largely of secondary importance to Orangeism, its primary objective being the maintenance of a Protestant political ascendancy, albeit one that could have the secondary effect of ensuring the defence of 'the true religion'. It also seemed to me that Orangeism's particular perception of what constituted the true religion it sometimes purported to defend was open to serious question.

I therefore indicated my profound disagreement with my friend's 'for God and Ulster' philosophy. I found it inconceivable that a secret, paramilitarist-originating society that marched to thundering drums with ceremonial swords and pikes and politico-religious banners celebrating ancient triumphs, could have anything significant to contribute to the furtherance of a religion that was professedly moral and spiritual, and also universal in its outreach. What had the narrow message of Orangeism in common with the Christian message of grace, peace and love to the world? However, my friend continued to insist that the conquests of King William had created what he described as 'the necessary political space for that Protestant liberty which in a special way enabled the true religion to prosper'. For him it followed that Irish nationalism's opposition to Orangeism and its marching practices was symptomatic of Catholicism's rejection of the Protestant principle of civil and religious liberty, as well as of its repudiation of the true gospel of Christ.

I rejoined that the principle of liberty was of its very nature reciprocal, whereas Orangeism's concept of liberty, in the context of Protestant supremacy, was entirely one-sided and exclusive. (I might have added, in the words of John Stuart Mill, that it was like 'the liberty of the pike which means death to the minnow', or like one man's liberty that was another man's bondage.) And so it followed that the opposition this kind of Protestantism incurred was due, at least in part, to its explicitly anti-Catholic and religio-political stress. I felt that this was also due to that equally unnecessary Orange imperative of a politico-religious national environment. Orangemen often accused the Roman Catholic countries of this, yet seemed to regard it as vital to Protestant Ulster. Theocratic ideas of this kind were potentially dangerous, in that they could give rise to various forms of sectarian, totalitarian and racist evils throughout the world – of which Dutch-Reformed *apartheid* was but one example. But it was surely significant that the founders of Christianity had not sought to create any kind of protective or exclusive theocratic polity for themselves. To establish one, whether Protestant or Catholic, and seek to defend it by force of arms, was alien to the way of the cross and to the kingdom that was not of this world, but which was moral, spiritual and inclusive of all the nations.

I therefore suggested that the distaste of those who saw themselves on the receiving end of Orange marching had much more to do with their rejection of what they perceived as the sectarian ascendancy of Orange-unionist politics than with their response to the message of Jesus. No Irish nationalist who knew the history of Orangeism and understood its belief-system was likely to hold it in esteem. But the principles of Christianity were a different matter. By way of example, I pointed to the Salvation Army that was Protestant, evangelical and marched to bands and banners. Yet it was precisely because that denomination was so explicitly universal, non-sectarian, apolitical and overtly charitable in its outreach to the whole of society that, unlike the Orange Order, it could be welcomed anywhere in Ireland. There was something to be learned here.

I was greatly surprised and gratified when this example proved to be the turning point in our discussion, and I shall never forget the profound impression it had on my friend's mind. It seemed to provide a sudden insight that started a process which would later transform him into a much more large-hearted Christian citizen. Such transformations within the ranks of Orangeism are needed in greater measure, and now more than ever before. During the ensuing forty years, the Ulster situation has clearly demonstrated that religio-political movements make for poor religion and even worse politics. Both epitomise much of what is usually perceived to be bad about Northern Ireland – where Orange dominated religio-politics held power for all too long, and which is still capable of exerting an influence that is at variance with democracy, to say nothing of Christian virtue.

My anecdote may explain why the subject of Orange marching has been included under the heading of Ordinances and given a religious connotation. It was stated earlier that although Orangeism is primarily political and not essentially religious in the sense that is often claimed for it, it is nevertheless religio-political and strongly theocratic in nature. It was also shown by reference to history how that, in a society so deeply divided by religion and politics, Orangeism's insistence on religio-political marching inevitably and regularly gives rise to disorder and bloodshed, often leading to government intervention. This is because Orange marching powerfully epitomises the religio-politics of Protestant ascendancy attitudes. Sadly, these attitudes are still very much with us in Northern Ireland. As summer approaches each year something seems to happen to the political atmosphere. Young urban loyalists are already stockpiling huge quantities of felled trees, used tyres and wooden pallets for their bonfires in celebration of the Twelfth of July. Paramilitary flags and other loyalist emblems suddenly proliferate provocatively, sometimes with corresponding activity on the nationalist side. Not surprisingly, sectarian behaviour and outbreaks of communal violence now tend to increase. Tension is palpable, for we are approaching the annual several-months-long Orange marching season, which is now also the annual rioting season. Political leaders recognise that during this time political business, sometimes urgent business, has to be put on hold. It is also a time when hard-won progress can often regress. Can it be that an institution that allegedly was established to further the Christian gospel of peace, is a major contributor to such a state of affairs?

Incredibly, there are nearly three thousand Orange marches in Northern Ireland each year, some of which are to and from annual church functions that are known as 'Orange services'. These sometimes involve Orangemen in full regalia marching their standards into a local church, where they sit together as a large body in the midst of the congregation, the impact of which to some degree changes the ethos and character of the normal church worship in that place. This is inevitable, for such a service is often described and advertised as an 'Orange service'. Many Christian people are now questioning the propriety of these services, given that they tend publicly to identify or associate the whole local congregation with Orangeism, quite regardless of any dissenting views or contrary feelings on the matter. For these and other obvious reasons some clergy are now refusing to facilitate Orange services, while others reluctantly acquiesce with them for fear of giving offence. Those clergy who actually do support Orange services sometimes lamely argue that they cannot prevent people from attending church, and it is a good thing that at least once a year the Orangemen should hear the gospel. They are of course right on both counts, but neither of their two responses really addresses the question of propriety. Like everybody else, Orangemen could come incognito and be welcomed into the Christian congregation as sinners, or worshippers, or both. But within the church of God, given the very nature of its universal and spiritual calling, the Orange Order should be not be allowed any special status as a discrete and identifiable religio-political group or sect. On no account and in no respect should the regular Christian service of the church of God be permitted to be taken over or metamorphosed into an 'Orange service' of any kind.

A small number of these church parades are also politically contentious, notably those to the annual venues of Dunloy and Drumcree, which involve marching through Catholic-nationalist areas. For reasons we shall address later, it is now a fact of life that any Orange march, church parade or not, which essays to enter a predominately nationalist area has the potential to provoke organised opposition. The merest glance at the structural arrangements of the Dunloy and Drumcree church parades will show that, like Orangeism itself, the general character and demeanour of these things is much more religio-political than religious in any normal Christian sense of the word.

Dunloy

Dunloy is a Catholic-nationalist village in North Antrim, to whose outskirts Orangemen from other parts of the county are annually bussed for the purpose of marching in semi-military style up its one street before going into the local church service. We shall later consider the reasons why the Orangemen feel constrained to do so, for the Dunloy church parade involves arrangements and circumstances that far transcend those of ordinary Christians walking incognito to and from their church service in the usual manner. The Orangemen argue unconvincingly that there is perfect equivalence with normal church-going here, whereas the Dunloy Catholic community clearly perceives the parade to be a sectarian demonstration by invading Orangemen – one that, because of the nature of things in Northern Ireland, requires many imposing and socially inconveniencing security measures.

There was confrontation and violence at the 1995 parade, and in the years that followed the police had to intervene and stop the march just outside the village. This led to Orange and loyalist protests that were sometimes violent. These protests included the occasional blocking of the roads that led to Dunloy, and the picketing of several Catholic church services in that area. In June 1997 a policeman, Greg Taylor, whose duty the year before had involved him in a Dunloy parade intervention, was having an off-duty drink in the adjacent town of Ballymoney when he was recognised by a group of Orange sympathisers. They kicked him to death in the street outside. As to the picketing, the worst occurred at the Harryville Catholic chapel in Ballymena. This started in September 1998, when a mixed group of Orange and loyalist pickets targeted the Saturday evening Mass. They took their stand on the basis of a rather warped sense of equivalence. It was argued in effect that if Orangemen in regalia could not march in semi-military fashion to a special church service in Dunloy then ordinary Catholics would not be allowed free passage to walk incognito to their normal church services in Harryville. As a result, Catholic worshippers were picketed, regularly insulted and obscenely abused during a period of nearly two years. To its credit, Grand Orange Lodge gave a lead and officially opposed the picketing, but a number of well-known local Orangemen, some of whom wore their sashes in breach of Orange rules, persisted in their picketing for many months. They did so with apparent impunity.

Drumcree

Much more serious even than Dunloy, the Drumcree parade in Portadown is now an annual crisis. It regularly involves an orgy of upheaval and violence that costs lives and multi-millions of tax-payers' money. At times it seriously threatens Northern Ireland's peace process, and increasingly gives one the impression that it is that very peace, and the equality principle it inheres, which is the real point at issue. There can be no doubt that these annual Drumcree occurrences now involve issues and attitudes that far transcend the normal circumstances of any church parade, even an Orange church parade. Each July thousands of Orangemen march to a service in Drumcree Parish Church – a service that can accommodate just a few hundred people. That fact, and the Orangemen's declared intention to return to Portadown via a different route down the Garvaghy Road, which passes Catholic housing estates, seems to confirm the local residents' belief that the march is a powerful exercise in ascendancy politics. This is inevitable in an area whose history of controversial marching and attendant violence goes back to the beginnings of Orangeism.

Certainly that impression was underpinned by the turbulent events of July 1995, which subsequently became known as 'Drumcree 1' to distinguish it from each successive 'Drumcree' that followed. In the face of the Orange Order's refusal of the offer of consultation, the local residents' association opposed the after-church return march through its area that was planned for Sunday 9th July. They then decided to take direct action and blocked Garvaghy Road, whereupon the police intervened to stop the Orange march. This led to a massive stand-off which continued through that weekend until the following Tuesday. Amid tension that spread far beyond the confines of Portadown, a mediated agreement was reached that, inter alia, provided for a greatly reduced return march, together with a number of other restrictions. The march proceeded as agreed, but the Rev. Ian Paisley and David Trimble, both of whom had been prominently involved in the stand-off, later joined the head of the parade in nearby Portadown after it had passed the Garvaghy flash-point. The now augmented march proceeded to Carlton Street Orange Hall in Portadown, at which point television cameras captured Paisley and Trimble joining raised hands in a rather foolish-looking victory dance. This was widely interpreted as triumphalist, and was made all the worse when Trimble and other Orange leaders denied that there had been any agreement with the residents group. It was as though all that had happened amounted to a belated exercise of the Orangemen's inviolable marching rights, local objections having been swept aside by an Orange victory that was almost as good as the 'double triumph' of Dolly's Brae in 1849. The residents were filled with indignation. Many observers from all walks of life in Northern Ireland realised that things would now worsen and would be even more difficult next time. In fact, even during the hours that immediately followed there were outbreaks of rioting and arson throughout Northern Ireland. Just a few weeks later David Trimble, hitherto a minor contender, was catapulted into the leadership of the Ulster Unionist Party.

Trimble quickly denied all charges of triumphalism, contending that his double act with Paisley was quite spontaneous and therefore simply indicative of their joint relief that the march was safely over. It was as though there could be no such thing as spontaneous triumphalism – which was how the episode was widely understood, and which the well-reported facts strongly support. First, there was the Orange denial, patently wrong, that any agreement had been reached with the residents. Then there was the fact that Trimble and Paisley had not actually participated in the march past the Garvaghy Road residents, and therefore had not experienced that trauma or nervous tension which, at a stretch, might have excused even a silly expression of relief. Finally there was the upbeat Paisley, whose after-taste was certainly very different from that of Trimble, in that he described the episode in terms that justified the triumphalist interpretation of their dancing duo – it was 'the greatest victory during the past twenty-five years for Northern Ireland Protestantism'. Some years ago, in the course of researching the religio-political history of mid-Ulster, political philosopher Frank Wright perused the provincial newspapers over the forty-year period that followed the Irish Famine. His research left him 'with an impression that whenever the name Portadown came before my eyes it was nearly always bad news'.[1] For over two-hundred years Orange marching in the general area of north Armagh and Portadown has been the major source of that 'bad news', even though this is carried out allegedly in furtherance of the 'good news' of the Christian gospel of peace. This is a supreme irony.

Persistently bad news became even more inevitable when Sinn Féin developed a political strategy – one that placed an 'equality agenda' high on its list of priorities. Since equality is the very antithesis of ascendancy it was predictable that politicised republicans would mount a challenge to the small number of particularly contentious Orange marches that go through certain nationalist areas. Organised resistance and protest led to some Orange marches being banned, restricted or re-routed, which in turn provoked counter-protests that were followed by violence. Local opinion on this issue is often deeply intransigent. Protestant understatement wonders what's the big deal – why do Catholics refuse to recognise the Orangemen's right to march for just a few minutes through a Catholic area on their way back from a church service? Some Protestants go so far as to repudiate the very concept of a 'Catholic area' and simply insist on the citizen's right to freely process along the 'Queen's highway'. It is only fair to mention that some liberal-minded and usually uninvolved Catholics can take a rather benign and detached view of Orange marching. On the other hand many Catholics are deeply sceptical about the Orange 'rights' arguments and the motivation they see behind the whole issue. They point to the local people's right to access the public roads of their own district, which should be open at all times for the use of all citizens. They query the choice of certain routes, and ask why Orangemen insist on marching here when it would be much more sensible to march there? They claim that a contentious route inevitably results in closing the road to local citizens and, involving as it does a massive security presence, seriously impinges on their normal lives and sense of well-being. In short, they wonder what happened to their own rights, and believe the Orange marching rights argument to be a lie.

Rights, Liberty and Responsibilities

Orange marching and local objections to it involve many questions to which there can be no satisfactory answer unless and until we examine the nature of and motivation behind that marching, and assess its impingement on the local community. The issue has to do with what the marching signifies. Why it is so important to Orangemen, despite its often terrible consequences of destruction, upheaval and murder? We are told that marching asserts a precious Orange principle – 'the untrammelled right to walk the Queen's highway'. Although this description of a public road as the Queen's highway seems grandiloquent nonsense, it must be borne in mind that the Orange marching culture has a largely symbolic and ritualistic function. It is the acting out of a drama that affirms Protestant identity and territorial authority, demonstrating that 'we are Queen's men; we are still here and we do not intend to relinquish any of our rights, territorial or otherwise'. Certainly that these dramatisations should be so precious as to extend to three thousand parades a year in a Province barely the size of Yorkshire, and which in terms of population is roughly equivalent to Merseyside, suggests that they involve more than the exercise of legal, cultural or festal rights. Obviously there is more to marching than the right to do it. Jeffrey Donaldson, an Orange-unionist MP, has expressed the issue as follows:

> If Portadown District, seen as a bastion of Orangeism, lost out then there
> was little hope for Orangemen in other parts of Northern Ireland where
> there were contentious parades. If republicans could take on the Orange
> Order in Portadown and win then they could win anywhere. The feeling
> was that the real agenda was to drive the Orange Order off the streets. It
> became about much more than a stretch of road in Portadown. Drumcree
> became the symbol of Protestant civil rights. It was regarded by many
> Orangemen as the last stand.[2]

This melodramatic statement is shot-through with exaggeration. It is quite absurd
to equate the minority Orange Order and its marching practices with the general
preservation of Protestant civil rights. The Orange Order, and especially its leadership
in Portadown, does not represent the generality of the Protestant people considered
either in the narrow context of Northern Ireland, or in the proper context of their civil
rights within the United Kingdom. It is also absurd to ascribe to the banning of a mere
handful of contentious marches – among the huge number of Orange marches that
take place every year – the potential for such a spectacular domino effect. In fact, this
is not a civil rights issue. It is an equality issue *vis-à-vis* an anachronistic and arcane
form of ascendancy politics. The residents' groups have indicated their willingness to
dialogue with Orange representatives on the subject of those few disputed marches
through some Catholic areas, but the elitist Orange Order has firmly rejected their
overtures, even as it has refused to have any dealings with the Parades Commission.

The Parades Commission was appointed by the British parliament to deal with
these marching problems. It is therefore an integral part of that sovereign authority
to which Christian citizens are enjoined by the New Testament to submit
themselves. Yet the reasons behind these opposing attitudes are clear. On the one
hand, Orangemen intend to march in order to demonstrate their Protestant rights and
notional ascendancy; but any requirement to discuss and agree (with the residents or
the Commission) the details of a given march would call into question their absolute
right to do so. On the other hand, the residents' group representatives submit that the
very act of Orangemen engaging in dialogue with the local people would *ipso facto*
indicate a relinquishment of the ascendancy attitude. They explain that, should
genuine dialogue occur, this could create an egalitarian ethos in which both sides of
the equality equation would develop mutual respect and, as a consequence, some
form of agreed and controlled marching should become possible. This, however, is
unacceptable to the absolutist and ascendancy-minded Orange Order. As the
Orangemen see it, this would strip them of their rights and their whole marching
culture of much of its point. And so the issue epitomises the clash between
Orangeism's old ascendancy politics and the egalitarian politics to which the now
radicalised nationalist residents lay claim. David Cook, a lawyer of generous liberal
mind who is a former Lord Mayor of Belfast and a former Chairman of the Northern
Ireland Police Commission, has made the following comment:

> The right to free association; the right to free assembly; and the right of
> freedom of speech do not automatically mean that there is a right to march
> in semi-military style. But even if there were such a right, it is clearly not
> absolute. It is clearly subject to the rights of others and it cannot possibly

extend to situations where one of the purposes of some of those involved is to offend and antagonise people. Marching and parading is at best a privilege that may be earned if you behave yourself. And if you behave yourself there may be no reason why you shouldn't march. There may be no end to what could be achieved if more people could bring themselves to say 'please' and 'thank you'.[3]

The absence of an absolute right postulates the existence of other rights, which is why the exercise of mutual respect, tolerance and good manners is so important here. Sadly this liberal philosophy is immediately ruled out by Orangeism's politics of ascendancy. To say 'please' is to sell the pass. To recant the absolute right to march wherever you want in semi-military style is heresy to an organisation that was created to do just that, as the very means of demonstrating its ascendancy. And so it is not surprising when misguided ideas like these give rise to trouble. There was the violence of the Orange supporters on the infamous Lower Ormeau march of 1st July 1991 – misbehaviour which the then Secretary of State Sir Patrick Mayhew likened to that of 'cannibals'. More recently an Orange march was permitted to pass a Catholic chapel, but subject to its loyalist band refraining from playing while it did so. Having been authorised on that basis, the Orangemen proceeded to provide impromptu marching music by a raucous rendering of that most sectarian of Orange songs, 'The Billy Boys'. Like a distant echo of Henry Grattan's reference to that 'army whose idea seems to be blood', this song grotesquely proclaims 'We're up to the neck in Fenian blood / Surrender or you'll die'. Such misbehaviour, whilst not typical of most Orange marches, has a terrible potential to break out from time to time like a recurring disease, for there is a causal link between belief and behaviour. St. Paul once warned that 'evil communications corrupt good manners', which might be paraphrased to the effect that the wrong-headed crowd is the product of a corrupting ethos. Ascendancy attitudes represent wrong thinking, which in the crowd can produce dangerously bad behaviour.

Protestant ascendancy belongs to the past. There is no longer any right to behave in this way. There is no absolute right to march along public roadways in a provocative and semi-military fashion, especially through areas where your arcane religio-political message will be construed as sectarian and insulting, and likely to endanger the peace. Therefore, if Orangemen aspire to be good citizens in a pluralist world they must give serious consideration to these things, for it is a sound principle of natural justice that rights must be balanced. The exercise of one citizen's liberty should not result in another's deprivation. Consequently, given Orangeism's history and the unequivocal nature of its belief system, there are very good reasons to challenge its 'right' to march in certain circumstances and situations. Any disputed march can, at the minimum, result in massive and prolonged inconvenience and trauma, in that the security and policing measures required can impose heavily on the freedom and well-being of all the local people on whom the march inevitably impinges. But the effects of a march can be worse than that, given the possibilities of serious civil disturbance, as history, even recent history, all too amply shows.

The current dispute at Drumcree has deep roots in the earlier violence associated with Orange marches going back two-hundred years, parades to the Drumcree

Parish Church being mentioned in the Report of the Parliamentary Select Committee on Orangeism as far back as 1836. However, its more recent origins lay in the violence associated with Orange marches in the 1980s through the mainly Catholic Obins Street in the Tunnel area of Portadown. Sir John Hermon, who was Northern Ireland's Chief Constable at that time, eventually felt compelled in the interests of public safety to take a firm stand on the issue of Orange marching in the area. Sir John was no soft liberal, but was a tough though fair-minded policeman who, in justification of his forward thinking on the vexed question of marching, stressed the need to take account of the rights and responsibilities of all the people concerned, all citizens being equal before the law. He wryly observed that Orangemen would not be prepared to show reciprocity in tolerating nationalists should they wish to exercise their liberty to march the Protestant areas of the town. He was of course well aware that the police had long recognised the existence of a Protestant veto in Portadown. A Catholic accordion band, for example, had regularly been prevented from parading local nationalist areas because its proposed circular route would encompass a relatively small Protestant enclave. In his autobiography Sir John Hermon has written perceptively of this Orange attitude to these parades:

> These (loyalist parades) had been given a special position in Northern Ireland and appeared to have acquired a sort of temporal sanctity. Participants believed they could parade almost wherever and whenever they chose. Their marches epitomised the right to civil and religious liberty, as long as the religion in question was Protestantism. By a process of evolution, the Orange Order, the Apprentice Boys and the Royal Black Institution had attained positions of privilege within the Protestant 'establishment' in Northern Ireland ... There was, however, no reciprocal right for Catholics; the equivalent Catholic organisations – namely, the Irish National Foresters and the Ancient Order of Hibernians – could not march other than in their own 'non-unionist' areas. They certainly could not have entered any area housing a sizable number of Protestants without unleashing a vicious backlash of loyalist violence. I was not alone in believing that this superior attitude of the loyalists, in respect of their marches, had to be changed.[4]

Liberty, which is one of the really important and more complex principles addressed by political philosophers, is multi-dimensional and therefore gives rise to qualitative differences of approach and emphasis. The issues under consideration here throw up some of the antitheses of that ancient debate. On the one hand, the United Irishmen's idea of liberty, which emanated from the European Enlightenment, took the high ground from which they saw liberty as giving citizens the freedom to shape their political community and exercise a collective direction to their lives. On the other hand, the Orangemen's idea of liberty, practised by the eighteenth century oligarchy in Ireland, took the low ground from which they saw liberty as the right of a privileged few to keep the rest in subjection. Over time, the changing political circumstances that brought an end to ascendancy compelled Orangeism to revise some of its practice, though not its philosophy of liberty. It still believes in a privileged liberty. Sir John Hermon was right. Despite that fact that Orangeism professes to be strong on the principle of civil and religious liberty, it constantly needs to be reminded that is has rather flawed, impoverished and very narrow views on the subject.

Liberty is a two-edged sword. It is not selfish but reciprocal, and someone who loves liberty must also cherish it for their neighbour. It is not absolute but relative, otherwise everyone would be free to do as they choose, despite the consequences. In exercising liberty we must ensure that our actions are not unnecessarily detrimental to others. This is to restate the Christian ethic: 'Do unto others as you would have them do unto you' – an ethic which stresses our responsibilities over our rights, and the duty to respect the dignity of our neighbour, who is also created in the image of God. Citizenship acknowledges that all are created equal, and is expressed in that love which is implicit in shared responsibilities with and towards our fellow human beings. Thus to love our neighbour as ourselves is a duty that far transcends the dry legalism of competing rights. Indeed, to insist on our rights, and especially on such things as our right to participate in military-style marching regardless of the sensitivities of others, or despite its consequences for human life, is an attitude more like that of the Ku Klux Klan than that of our common Christian credo. Liberty is essentially reciprocal and is therefore relative. It is not absolute and does not stand alone. It involves equality, but true liberty and equality will respect human dignity, and thus it will also aspire to the high ideal of fraternity and love, in communal peace.

Fundamentalist Christians who share a religio-tribal Protestant affinity with Orangeism as described in chapter 12, object that this 'idealism' fails to take account of our sinful human condition. This suggests that any aspiration to political reconciliation is just an impossible dream. Yet the fundamentalists, who are also sinners and themselves still possessed of the 'old sinful nature', do not allow their own shortcomings to prevent them striving for the successful realisation of their personal aspirations in all departments of their lives. The question therefore arises whether this objection to the idea of reconciliation is because of its impossibility due to sin, or more pertinently whether those who object are motivated by an opposing agenda. Recently an evangelical group pasted gospel posters all over the North that proclaimed 'Real peace found only through Christ'. No doubt the group regarded this as a legitimate gospel truth claim, but it seems significant that its campaign coincided with fundamentalist opposition to the peace process.

Fundamentalism stresses a vertical relationship with God much more than the horizontal relationships with our fellows, holding that only those who are 'reconciled to God' by conversion can really enjoy reconciliation. Jeffrey Donaldson MP has recently argued along these lines.[5] But even on its own terms this is an inadequate and unbalanced view, missing as it does the reciprocal Christian converse of its own claim, which is that we cannot be reconciled to God if we refuse to be reconciled to our neighbour. Christianity stresses the importance of both horizontal and vertical relationships: 'If a man does not love his brother whom he has seen, how can he love God whom he has not seen?' Reconciliation brings enemies together, but this does not mean the obliteration of difference. It means that difference will no longer be driven to the extremes of hostility, alienation and division – the inevitable outcome of sectarianism, ascendancy, xenophobia and racism. It means that former enemies may now live in tolerance, respect diversity and together enjoy equality and fraternity.

The question now under consideration concerns the possibility of political reconciliation, which not for the first time is being confused with the spiritual imperatives of the kingdom that is 'not of this world', as we saw in chapter 12. When discussing political peace and reconciliation, fundamentalists usually insist on religious answers involving the vertical dimension. Thus reconciliation is only achievable on evangelical grounds – 'Get saved, join us, and then we may be reconciled'. But this is not political reconciliation. In fact, it suggests conquest – conquest by conversion or 'assimilation', as Norman Porter pithily puts it in his recent book, *The Elusive Quest*. Thus the fundamentalist approach rules out reconciliation with Catholics *per se* and is another version of the old Orange ascendancy doctrine now riding on the back of an evangelical horse. But for all its haughty exclusivism, or rather because of that exclusivism, this religio-political philosophy is both negative and defeatist. If reconciliation is only for the 'born again', then fundamentalism must rule out any possibility of reconciliation with or among even those of its own political tribe who do not share its particular religious position. It must also rule out any reconciliation within or between secular groups everywhere, including, incidentally, the very party to which Jeffrey Donaldson belongs. It is therefore much too pessimistic to imply that the application and exercise of the Christian ethic is for evangelicals only. On its own terms it is a general standard of universal application reaching far beyond the Christian community. Its general acceptance as such, and the extent to which it is publicly practised, gives reason to believe that it is an outworking of what theologians call common grace, and which in terms of the political community might loosely be described as civic virtue.

The problem with this pessimistic view of the world is that, apart from being rotten politics, it is contrary to the general tenor of Christian theology as believed and taught by all the mainstream Christian churches, both Roman and Reformed. This teaches that despite human failure, sin does not rule the world, but that all things are under the providential control of a Sovereign who is the God of peace, and who preserves, controls and governs all things.[6] This theology, commonly held by Christians of various denominations throughout the world, proclaims a message of providential hope – that to everything there is a season and there always can be 'a time to dance' and 'a time of peace'.[7] Christians do not regard it as futile to seek and pray for peace, for the ultimate hope of their religion is the eventual dawning of a great cosmic reconciliation and redemption.[8] Christian theologians, both Roman and Reformed, also believe that this providential governance is not confined to the things of history or eschatology, but continually reaches out to the hearts and minds of human beings everywhere – a moral governance called common grace. This restrains and regulates human behaviour. It inspires, enlightens, enables, and ennobles human endeavour, operating on minds and consciences through agencies such as reason, truth, love and moral law. And so, given this commonly held teaching of the whole Christian world on the doctrines of providence and common grace – precepts we might therefore reasonably expect the Orangemen and fundamentalists to believe – peace rather than pessimism should be the great watchword on their banners. Sadly it is not.

Fundamentalists should not repudiate the possibility of peace merely because the principle of that peace or its precise nature is contrary to their own prejudices. The peace and reconciliation that resolves conflict must of its very nature be much greater and more comprehensive than the particular ideas and aspirations of any of the parties to that conflict. The pursuit of peace must involve critical self-examination, and will require that we learn to love our neighbour and our enemies – a love that seeks not its own to the exclusion of others. On these grounds it is evident that notions of ascendancy and self-interest are incompatible with reciprocal liberty, equality and love – the things that make for peace. None of us, whether fundamentalist, evangelical, Orangemen, or whatever is in a position to take up the apparently high moral ground of denying the possibilities for peace because of the failings of others. This is the low ground of pride and prejudice. All of us must accept our own responsibilities for what has gone wrong, and never shirk our duty to love, forgive and reciprocate our neighbours' rights and liberties.

Orangeism and various forms of ultra-Protestantism can only give a heavily qualified acceptance to the principles surrounding the concepts of liberty, equality and fraternity, because it takes a much too narrow and self-interested view on these matters. It believes that Protestantism has a privileged relationship with liberty. This means that liberty cannot be entirely reciprocal because its existence and survival depends on Protestantism, and therefore on Protestant ascendancy. The notion of privileging Protestantism stems from the belief that the Reformation was the chief means by which the principle of civil and religious liberty was established, a principle that Orangeism believes was underpinned by King William's Act of Settlement. Indeed, it is sometimes argued that Protestant liberty is the necessary condition of a free society, an idea that in the ascendancy past was stretched to suggest that civil and religious liberty was really the prerogative of Protestants. The logic runs inexorably: papists are anti-Protestant, the enemies of true liberty, and therefore need to be kept in their places – and, of course, Orange marching is a very useful means of demonstrating if not enforcing this point. As was pointed out in Chapter 7, when sectarian notions such as these are privileged by the theocratic state they can be nourished by crazy theories that provide bogus justifications for the exclusion of the non-covenanted people from citizenship. This means exclusion from equality of rights, civic participation and civil liberties, much of which lay at the root of a divided Northern Ireland's deeply troubled past.

In thus privileging Protestantism, Orangeism makes exaggerated claims on its behalf. Of course the Reformation did make a significant contribution to the growth of individual liberty, and assisted in the development of freedoms such as those of conscience, opinion, assembly and worship, although that is not the whole story. Nevertheless, there was a time when the Orangemen were not so alone in their over-blown praise of the Reformation. Linda Colley has observed in her book Britons that in the eighteenth century an extraordinarily large number of the British people really believed that, under God, their Protestant nation was peculiarly free and prosperous. This was an exaggeration. As Colley goes on to show, the British at that time were much more heavily taxed than many of their Continental counterparts. They were also subject to a very harsh and often arbitrary criminal code, with as many prisons in London as in the rest of the capital cities of Europe put together. Thus like other familiar notions of British superiority, the emancipating power of Protestantism needs to be kept in some perspective. As Norman Porter has pointed out, Protestantism was but one influence among others contributing to the liberalising of Western society.

Even though exaggerating that influence, Orangeism refuses to recognise that as a consequence of modernisation and reformation change continues to occur throughout the world and within Catholicism itself – the new freedoms, openness, pluralism and egalitarianism that characterise the liberal democracies, to say nothing of the change in religious attitudes. As to the latter, we might cite the example of the late Cardinal John Heenan who once took a television opportunity to praise the Reformed theologians whose hermeneutical works had been of such assistance to him when a young theological student. Thus if Orangeism exaggerates the role of the Reformation in the early development of liberal-democracy, it also denies its extended impact in the context of the real reform which is increasingly evident within Catholicism. It refuses to accredit even the impact of its own Protestantism where this might involve recognition of any consequential change in modern Catholicism. Instead, Orangeism prefers living in its own caricatured eighteenth century world in which an unchanged and unchanging enemy must ever be denigrated and kept in his place. Such a reactionary reading of the situation is so much more convenient when it comes to justifying Orange and Protestant ascendancy politics. Thus as Ian Paisley uncompromisingly sees it, we must ever be on our guard in defence of

what our forefathers won through the Reformation and enshrined in British constitutional law – the principle of Protestant ascendancy over papal supremacy.[9]

The concept of Protestant ascendancy, however illusory or impractical nowadays, is obviously still very much alive in the Orange mind. It is an attitude and rationale that in the main is privately held, but seldom publicly articulated when issues such as liberty, the right to march, or not to be marched upon are under public discussion. Apart from references to tradition, Orange spokesmen never explain why they march, for it would now be much too politically incorrect to proclaim or to publicise their doctrine of Protestant supremacy. Only a turbulent Ian Paisley, or a tee-shirted 'simply the best' Ulster loyalist could hope to get away with that kind of attitude. Instead, the Orangemen protest about their rights and their liberties, ignoring the rights of others in what are always unimpressive performances. Rights and liberties are instrumental. They are the means by which we are free to do things, but they cannot explain why we do those things, nor of themselves can they really justify the things we do. So we still have to explain and answer the question posed earlier – what does Orange marching signify and what gives rise to the Orange imperative to do it? In answering these questions we may also learn why many Catholics and liberal Protestants object to it so strongly.

Militarism

When discussing the origins of Orangeism, reference was made both to the Williamite ex-servicemen's clubs and to the colonialist, loyalist, and imperialist attitudes of the 'Anglican' (Church of Ireland) planters of mid-Ulster. Mid-Ulster was a place of growing Catholic population, where the clash of rival socio-economic interests gave rise to the sectarian tensions that led to the creation of the Orange

Order. Given such origins, and bearing in mind that the Order was established for paramilitary defence purposes, it was inevitable that it would quickly develop a substantial British military connection and ethos. It will be recalled that many military men involved themselves in the early leadership, and that the young Order became the recruiting ground for the new Yeomanry, which by 1798 was 66,000 strong. Over time a significant Orange military tradition was to develop. Commanders, captains, colonels and other ranks of the British armed forces joined in numbers, and Orange lodges were even illegally established within the British Army. Thus by 1882 Colonel Edward Saunderson could say with justification that the Order in Ireland bore 'very much the position the army does to the citizens of England'. At that time Colonel Saunderson was about to become the leader of the Orange-unionists, and he soon saw the opportunity to deploy the Order as an armed force that might resist the Land League and later Home Rule. Events would show that the fighting colonel had called it correctly, for by the time of Edward Carson and Captain Craig the marching Orange army with banners would readily provide the manpower for the Ulster Volunteer Force and subsequently for the Ulster Special Constabulary – the B- Specials. Militarism is a major source of the Orange marching ethos.

It is therefore significant that in the Orange Exhibition of March 1998 in Belfast's Waterfront Hall the Order's military connection was given pride of place. As one Orangeman recently put it, 'marching is in our blood'. Marching is a military concept, being defined by the Chambers Etymological English Dictionary as meaning: 'to walk in a markedly rhythmical military manner'. In the strict military sense, marching or drilling is designed to achieve discipline and control so as to facilitate the expeditious logistics and disposition of the forces under command. But in the politico-military sense of the term, politicians can deploy marching forces to dramatise and demonstrate conquest. They do this by marching their victorious army through the defeated or subject territory. It is in this latter sense, or as a symbolic adaptation of it, that Orange marching is largely to be understood in the context of Northern Ireland. It is also why it is of a characteristically 'swaggering' nature, as Jeremy Paxman and even Ruth Dudley Edwards have observed. David Miller has explained it as follows:

> Orange parades assumed the function of marking out Protestant territory. A recent historian (the unionist Conor Cruise O'Brien) has translated the message of the drums as, 'We are your superiors: we know you hate this demonstration of that fact: we dare you to do something about it: if you don't, you ratify your own inferior status' (bracketed insert mine).[10]

Jonathan Bardon writes in similar vein, suggesting that in the Ulster situation these 'parades and demonstrations were bound to be regarded as assertions of, or challenges to, the territorial imperative of one side or the other'.[11] As the political academics Bew, Gibbons and Patterson bluntly express it: 'To march in or through an area is to lay claim to it'[12] – a particularly significant view given that nowadays Bew and Patterson are not without sympathy towards the unionist position.

David Miller and Conor Cruise O'Brien's 'message of the drums', draws attention to the most intimidating aspect of all the Orange demonstrations – the drumming parties. Some Orangemen point out that interest in the fife and big drum is an important part of their cultural and musical heritage. But that is not the whole story.

Loud drumming, still an integral part of the larger Orange marches, is a derivation from battles long ago when this simulated the noise of distant gunfire. Now less common, Orange drumming parties involve drummers in unison frenetically thrashing huge chest-carried 'Lambegs' with short canes in a thunderous rhythm that can be heard miles away. These parties were very popular in the nineteenth century, being deployed to circumvent the Party Processions Act at times when marching was banned. Instead of marching, the drumming party and its camp followers would casually swagger along with ill-concealed intent to 'pay attention' to such targets as Catholic missions, chapels, convents, priests' homes or housing enclaves. These would then be subjected to several hours of intimidating thunder from the 'war drums of the Orange Order', which could be followed by an attack on the targeted property, ending in riot. This sometimes led to legal proceedings. On one such occasion a drumming party 'beat its way' to Banbridge Courthouse, where its thunder prevented the magistrates from hearing the case until the accused Orangemen were permitted to go outside and negotiate a cessation to the drumming. The militant message of the Orange big drum is one of unashamed intimidation, ascendancy and dominance.

Denial

In the course of a recent conversation with a political philosopher who had been an Orangeman in his youth, I enquired as to his impressions of Orange marching and asked what had been his personal attitude when participating in it. His answer was quite unequivocal: 'I felt I was putting it up to the Catholics, saying in effect, "We are right and you are wrong; we won and you lost; so in your face!"' Some Orangemen would dismiss this analysis and deny that they personally hold any notions of ascendancy. This might imply that they have renounced some of the major tenets of Orangeism, but this is highly doubtful. Whatever the personal views of these apparently liberal Orangemen, it is evident that they have not made any meaningful impact on the Order as a whole. In fact their position seems very unconvincing. Logic would seem to demand that they should deny, or dissociate themselves from the whole tradition of ascendancy marching and the sectarian attitudes that have been the pith of Orangeism from the beginning. But they do not do so. So we are left wondering how they can still insist on marching through disputed territory, with all the nastiness and dangers that this entails, and yet maintain that somehow their marching is different from that of their ascendancy forefathers.

There has been no appreciable change in Orange marching attitudes or in their often-disastrous consequences, even though some ascendancy-denying Orangemen do struggle to screen out of their minds the obvious content of the traditional marching package. They certainly struggled with their consciences at the height of the annual Drumcree protest in July 1998 when three Catholic children, the Quinn brothers, were horrifically murdered as their home was fire-bombed by loyalists. The boys perished in what Ulster poet Tom Paulin was to describe as 'orange flames' – imagery he might have borrowed from a British cartoonist's depiction of Belfast's Orange pogroms eighty years before. It was stated at the time of the Quinn murders that their housing estate had been 'in a state of tension because of Drumcree', a connection only a few would have doubted. Indeed, in the immediate wake of the murders, a leading Orange chaplain had such a change of heart on the whole Drumcree affair as to publicly lament that 'no road is worth a life'. It occurred to many people at the time that the Orange clergyman should have realised the clear potential for catastrophe that was inherent in Drumcree. It was common knowledge that the heightened sectarian tension had in the recent past given rise to several tactical and locally orchestrated murders of innocent young Catholics. There was that of Michael McGoldrick in 1996. Just the following year, Robert Hamill was savagely kicked to death by a loyalist mob as it howled 'die Fenian, die', and then teenager Bernadette Martin was shot dead in her sleep by the same gun that was used in the slaying of Michael McGoldrick. Marching the Garvaghy Road never was worth a life, nor should it have taken the awful Quinn murders to bring a man of God to that conclusion. But this was not the end of the story. A year later, when the probability emerged that no Orangeman had actually perpetrated the Quinn murders – something never seriously alleged – the Orange chaplain cravenly apologised to the Order 'if there was any misunderstanding' arising from his earlier comments.

It is tragic that such ambivalent and equivocating attitudes can obtrude on the minds of good men and get in the way of straight thinking. The chaplain's earlier comments left no room for subsequent doubt or misunderstanding about the marching in question, the dangers of which had always been well-known, even if all too easily forgotten. It had long been established from the history of Orange marching and the actions of its camp followers that the consequences which can arise from the marching and/or the activity of its followers are not necessarily the work of Orange people themselves, and hardly ever ostensibly so. Yet this cannot remove the responsibility that, in the first place, belongs to those whose whole marching package has the clear potential to set up very dangerous situations. The findings of the Committee of Enquiry into Orange marching (1857) are still entirely apposite. Those marches 'were plainly and unmistakably the originating cause' from which the awful consequential actions of that time eventually flowed. Will they ever learn? Orange marching has been the cause of much of the sectarian murder and mayhem that has occurred in the course of the past two hundred years. If detailed research were carried out it would be found that, directly or indirectly, hundreds of lives have been lost because of it. It is surely time to call a halt to this state of affairs.

An honest assessment

The Rev. John Brown, for many years a leading Orange historian who clearly was not given to dissembling or spin-doctoring techniques, has made some transparently honest comments on the reasons behind Orange marching. Referring to the situation after 'the failure of 1849' – shorthand for the Dolly's Brae debacle – a time when Orange leaders were engaged in damage limitation and endeavouring to improve their PR image, Rev. Brown observed that:

> These things were not realised by many of the ordinary members, who often, if they could not parade, looked on the lodge as a kind of social club and little more.[13]

This is the institution that allegedly was established to advance the doctrines of the gospel and the Reformed Faith. The unvarnished truth, as recognised by Orangeism's own historian, is that it was an organisation which was regarded by many of its members as a social club whose primary purpose was that of providing them with the opportunity to march. But why did these young men so relish the opportunity to march? The answer to that will be found when we consider questions concerning the precise nature of Orange marching and its historical purpose. Several explanations and answers from a whole variety of sources have already been suggested, but in old-fashioned Protestant style, and unlike the modern dissemblers, the Rev. John Brown again provides us with the refreshingly unequivocal and definitive answer:

> Ordinary Orangemen joined in lodge and walked defiantly as an assertion of old rights, and to keep Papists in their places.[14]

The Rev. Brown then graphically describes how the ordinary rank-and-file Orangeman set out to achieve those powerfully assertive objectives, and how the process actually worked.

> On the 12th of July, and on other occasions, he marched with his lodge behind its flag and drums and fifes, wearing his regalia . . . and armed with his yeoman gun, to show his strength in the places where he thought it would do most good. *Where you could 'walk' you were dominant, and the other things followed (emphasis mine).*[15]

Thus in two pithy sentences the Orange historian has synthesised the whole business, and in a manner fully consistent with the findings of this book. Orange marching is by its very nature and design a demonstration of strength, of Protestant ascendancy, domination and anti-Catholic triumphalism. It is fundamentally an exercise in unashamed sectarianism – all of which, it is submitted, is borne out by ample evidence. Can we wonder then that some Catholics should decide that they are having no more of it in their own areas? Should it be contended, despite Dunloy, Drumcree and Harryville, that this evidence is drawn from old sources and reflects old-fashioned attitudes (even though John Brown wrote as recently as 1967), the reader is referred to an official decision of the Northern Ireland Parades Commission dated as recently as 12th June 1998. This important decision was in respect of a proposed Orange march via a circuitous route through North Belfast, which had become a highly contentious annual affair widely known as 'The Tour of the North'. The following is a short but significant excerpt from the decision:

> The parade clearly has a symbolic significance for the Protestant community in the area. We are aware that there is a sense of contested territory created by the significant population shift over the past years and that a concession by the Orange Order not to parade in the contested area would be seen as the loyalist community ceding further territory to nationalists. We are told that, as in other locations, the parade was seen as a coat-trailing triumphalist display. Stephen McAllister, one of the parade

organisers, said on the recent BBC 'Spotlight' programme: *'I can't really see any reason why we should parade round in circles within, you know, a 100% Protestant area. There would be no reason for the parades'*. It seems to us that those words can only have confirmed the validity of that perception (*emphasis mine*).

The position could hardly have been stated in starker terms. To the Orange mind, there is no real point in this kind of demonstration unless the Orangemen can uninhibitedly march where they choose, and particularly through Roman Catholic areas. It is only on this basis that marching Orangemen can effectively deliver their assertive message of Protestant ascendancy designed to 'show them who's master'. Sadly, the Orange mind on this matter is sharply at variance with the mind of Christ, who gave specific instructions to his disciples on how to behave themselves if, when on their mission tours, they found themselves in places where they and their message were not welcome. There was to be no question of confrontation or resistance; they were to shake off the dust from their feet and leave in peace.[16]

Conclusions

By proclaiming itself and its message in the manner it regularly does every year, Orangeism presents itself to the Catholic-nationalist community with an arrogant, bigoted and intolerant face. For over two hundred years Orangeism's semi-military attitudinal message, dramatised by 'those booming, swaggering marches', has been a trigger for some terrible sectarian violence. There have been many bloody landmarks along the way – from the Armagh outrages, Dolly's Brae, the Orange riots in Belfast and Derry in 1969 that sparked off the Troubles, through the Tunnel at Portadown during the 1980s and on to Dunloy and Drumcree – to name but a few. Even if we exclude the hatred, mayhem and murder this marching can in certain circumstances generate, it is patently ridiculous nowadays to expect the Catholic-nationalist community always to show tolerance and forbearance to something that was designed 'to keep the papists in their places' and 'to show them who's master'. The politics of ascendancy is both foolish and dangerous. It is an anachronism that is totally impracticable in an age of developing democracy, socio-political egalitarianism and human rights. The attitudes behind such politics are morally if not legally wrong, to say nothing of how they run counter to the moral and spiritual standards of Christ and Christianity.

Bearing in mind Orangeism's claim, albeit a dubious one, to be truly representative of the Protestant religion and the Reformed Faith, the following observation by an Irish Presbyterian clergyman about his fellow Presbyterians could be applied even more appropriately here:

> We have not understood that the other side of the Battle of the Boyne has been a history of dispossession and humiliation for our neighbours and we do not seem to see that you cannot love your neighbour and celebrate his defeat at the same time.[17]

Endgame

15.

Marching Backwards from the Future

This book began with the hope that Orange-unionism, instead of being preoccupied with the shortcomings of others, might address its own problems and reflect on its own contribution to what became known throughout the world as the Northern Ireland tragedy. That hope carried the clear implication that Orangeism was not alone in its failings – a point that has to be made in view of the tendency on all sides to evade hard issues by defensive 'what-aboutery'. We cannot escape our own responsibilities by complaining about what others have done. We must all bear our own burden. Obviously this book is a polemic and contains a strong critique. But its message must not be construed to mean either that Orangeism is exclusively culpable, or that the 'accusing eye' could not with justification be fixed upon others. There is no monopoly here, for there is a societal sense in which we are all guilty. But the book is about Orangeism. Its message is that Orange-unionism carries its own particular responsibility – a burden that is by no means light – for what has happened in Ireland, and latterly in Northern Ireland, where for fifty years it was the sole party of power. Evidence has been adduced, which has occasionally been acknowledged even by some Orange-unionists, that its stewardship was both inefficient and unjust. We saw that that stewardship ended in a violent and disastrous collapse, the result of failure in all aspects of its governance – social, economic and political. Thus the memory of Protestant ascendancy has been neither glorious nor immortal, and this should candidly be admitted. To do so would be a substantial step along the road to reconciliation.

Instead of perpetuating what Gladstone described as 'the bitter memories of ascendancy', Orange-unionists must look to the future. They must help to build a non-sectarian society based on the fundamental principles of citizenship – a shared sense of civic belonging, involvement and responsibility. Only this can provide liberty, equality and fraternity for Protestant, Catholic and Dissenter alike. It will be tragic if they do not, for the endgame of our politics will result either in equal citizenship, or yet more 'blood and destruction and fierce civil strife'. It follows that if Orangeism is to contribute to an egalitarian society it must jettison those doctrines of Protestant ascendancy it was created to defend – the first of the four 'General Principles' of Orangeism proclaimed by James Sloan in 1797. Orange-unionist leaders from the progressive Terence O'Neill to the reactionary Ian Paisley have long acknowledged the existence of the ascendancy principle that has always been Orangeism's *raison d'être* – that of 'showing them who's master' and of 'keeping the papists in their places'. However obvious it is that such vain supremacist notions can serve no useful purpose in the politics of a twenty-first century liberal democracy, they still lie at the root of many of our political problems as Terence O'Neill foresaw they would.

The now disenchanted Orange-unionists, who once regarded themselves as privileged members of the ascendancy class, consider the achievement of equality by the formerly underprivileged nationalists as at best a dangerous concession and at worst a humiliating defeat. The mantra is that 'we are giving them everything, but we are getting nothing from the so-called peace process'. This is the nonsense of the ascendancy attitude. It is the inevitable conclusion of zero-sum politics – if you do not win you must lose. The politics of equality means that nobody loses but that we can all win, and that together we all can enjoy the fruits of peace and prosperity in a diverse, just and peaceful society. This is the only workable or worthwhile endgame.

Orangeism's religio-politics is not in accord with good religion, and certainly not with Christianity. The teachings of Christ and his apostles leave no room for the privileging of one class, or race, or nation over another. All of us equally are the 'offspring of God' who is 'no respecter of persons' – the God who 'has made of one blood all nations of men to dwell on all the face of the earth'.[1] And so it follows that it is the Christian citizen's duty to love his neighbour as himself, rather than to seek privilege and subjugate that neighbour. God's kingdom, like his love, is universal. Orange-unionism was therefore arrogant and wrong in purporting to make a theocratic, but divisive covenant with God in respect of a selfishly selected piece of earth, whilst ignoring the dignity and rights of the other half of the Christian people who also lived there. This was not only the minimalist 'worm's eye view' politics of the narrow ground, it was also deeply sectarian. We saw that it is the Christian citizen's duty to 'render unto Caesar' and to obey lawful government as ordained of God – not to resist such a government by threatened rebellion through force of arms, as in 1912. In fact Orangeism's claim to defend the gospel and to represent the Reformed Faith has been examined and found wanting on several grounds. Could it have been otherwise given that the Orange Order was not established for any ostensibly religious purpose? There were no later developments such as would suggest that its subsequently acquired smattering of religion was other than for the purposes of a much-needed gloss of formal respectability. The matter may be summarised by stating that Orangeism's rules, standards and general practices are not typically Reformed or evangelical for the following reasons: First, by their exclusive and sectarian Protestant ascendancy ethos; secondly, by their paucity of biblical and doctrinal content, as demonstrated by the Order's lack of involvement in evangelical outreach; thirdly, by their recognition of Non-Subscribing Presbyterianism, which countenances links of fellowship with heterodox Unitarianism; fourthly, by their total reprobation of Roman Catholicism despite the Roman Church's historical adherence to the fundamental doctrines of Christ - as was and is still recognised by the mainstream Reformed Churches; fifthly, by their permitting in private ceremonies the practice of the oath-bound, Occult-inspired neo-Masonic ritualism that lies at the very heart of its arcane mentality, and which in origin and content is alien both to the Reformation and to Christianisty

As was demonstrated time and again, Orangeism's peculiar approach to politics and religion stems from its doctrine of conditional loyalty – a loyalty subject to the Crown defending and maintaining 'whatever it was King William established'. We saw, however, that the British constitution has ever been in an ongoing process of change, and that progress required much seventeenth and eighteenth century legislation to be amended or repealed. Yet more often than not, this progress was right in the teeth of bitter Orange-unionist opposition. Lord Salisbury once made a wry though facetious remark that he had 'spent a lifetime in politics, suffering defeat'. With considerably more truth that remark could be applied to Orangeism, which remains probably the nearest Irish equivalent to right-wing Salisburian politics. Much more than Lord Salisbury, Orange politics regularly suffered defeat on the great issues of the day. The Orangemen usually found themselves on the losing side, often wondering why their 'opportunist' political friends and mentors had deserted them. They could never understand that politics was not a product delivered once and for all by 'our William', but an ongoing negotiable process in a transient and changing world. Change is the very stuff of politics. Any party or institution that glories in the immutability of its ultra-conservatism will soon find itself caught in a time warp, and eventually must become an anachronism and die. Orange-unionism is now in dire danger of this.

It is extremely doubtful whether William of Orange could have supported that which Orangeism has come to regard as his immortal legacy. We saw that by the standards of his time the King was a liberal-minded advocate of civil and religious liberty. But when even to a limited extent he sought to apply those benefits to the Irish Catholics and Dissenters, the corrupt and self-seeking Protestant ascendancy frustrated all his efforts. It will be recalled that in chapter 1 his biographer was quoted to the effect that when the disgruntled King left Ireland he 'began to give up hope of the crazy island'. For the next two hundred years Orangeism would do much to accentuate that craziness, and ironically it still does it in the King's good name.

Orangeism could glory in its fidelity to William of Orange whilst at the same time pursuing policies that would make him turn in his grave. It could also glory in its loyalty to the British Crown whilst in the very act of rebelling against elected British parliaments. But such inconsistencies never seemed to faze Orangeism. Whatever the circumstances, it would continue to regard itself as totally steadfast both in its loyalty and in its Britishness. It could do this for two reasons: first and most importantly because of the conditional nature of that loyalty; and secondly, because it conveniently understands loyalty to the Crown as meaning loyalty to the Monarch, rather than to the Crown in parliament. On these two grounds all responsibility for any breakdown in Orangeism's loyalty has always been laid at Britain's door, and blamed on her backsliding from what allegedly are the true Williamite standards. Thus the great Gladstone was disloyal for disestablishing the small minority and, at that time, corrupt Church of Ireland. The Duke of Wellington was disloyal for introducing Catholic Emancipation and for resisting the nefarious activities of the Orange Imperial Grand Master, the 'Damnable Duke' of Cumberland. Asquith was disloyal for pressing ahead with Home Rule – even though this later produced the Stormont parliament – and for resisting the 'complete Grammar of Anarchy' in the mutinous behaviour of the Orange-inspired Curragh army officers. This book contains many such examples, but for sheer effrontery few can surpass the most recent specimen provided by the current Orange Imperial Grand Master when he described Prime Minister Tony Blair as 'disloyal for marrying a Romanist'.

Despite its much vaunted loyalty and pride in its Britishness, Orange-unionism has regularly been at loggerheads with British governments, but more especially with Liberal and Labour administrations. Significantly, it has been particularly uncomfortable with the more visionary and forward-looking British statesmen – men like Gladstone, Asquith, Lloyd George and Winston Churchill. The first and last of that impressive cadre were incontestably the greatest British statesmen of the last two hundred years, and yet their Irish policies were utterly reviled by Orangeism. It is equally significant that prior to the 1970s Orange-unionism had relatively little difficulty when the Tories were in power. During the nineteenth century it did not really matter if the Tory leadership of the day was 'opportunist' and playing Lord Randolph Churchill's exploitative Orange card, or whether it was going through a fundamentalist 'die hard' phase, faithfully following the cynical and ultra-conservative ascendancy doctrines of Lord Salisbury. Either way Orangeism could expect a reasonably fair wind. And obviously for much of the next century things were even more to its pleasing when it got its own unencumbered hands on the Stormont tiller.

Such a state of affairs could not last. The great sea change of the First World War meant that even the Tories gradually had to bend before the strengthening imperatives of democracy, which eventually would render inevitable the end of empire and ascendancy. Now the winds of change would blow ever more strongly, to the point where the old Tory politics of opportunist exploitation and supremacist privilege would be driven hard on to the rocks of history. From then onwards Orange-unionism could no longer count on a special relationship with the Tories. Indeed, it would be the administrations of Edward Heath (who collapsed the old Stormont parliament in 1972) and Margaret Thatcher (who signed the Anglo-Irish Agreement in 1985) that would cause Orangeism its greatest pain. This was a pain made all the more acute by its almost total incomprehension of the reasons behind the Tory actions that gave rise to it.

Orangeism's arcane introspection, combined with its dogmatic and inflexible religio-political belief system, has induced a blindness both to the realities of modern politics and to the impact and implications of its own past actions. Consequently, it is now disillusioned with Britain and in despair of Ireland. In lamenting what it perceives to be the currently disastrous state of affairs in Northern Ireland, it unhesitatingly lays most of the sins involved on the head of the republican scapegoat. It believes naively that a major part of the solution to our present problems would be to drive that scapegoat into the political wilderness forever. Fixated as it is with the sins of the IRA, Orangeism is blind to its own negative role in the situation both before and after the creation of Northern Ireland. It has no real perception of its own impact as the terrible ascendancy army which to that great Protestant Irishman Henry Grattan was one 'whose idea seemed to be blood'. It has screened out its gunrunning and rebellion, and all the repression, sectarian discrimination and exclusion that followed in its wake. Orangeism is therefore quite impervious to the fact that it was its own example which 'opened the way' for the republicans of 1916, as Patrick Pearse and Eoin MacNeill fully acknowledged, and which made it a mid-wife at the birth of the IRA.

As to its role in the events of more recent times, Orange-unionism is in almost total denial and cannot see that it provided much of the tinder and the spark that fired the long-running republican campaign in Northern Ireland, triggered as it was by the loyalist marching season in 1969. Indeed the annual marching season that used to be called 'the mad month' is now also the rioting season that still continues to fan what one hopes are the dying embers of our troubled times. Thus Orangeism has no reason for self-righteousness, and no grounds for any holierthan-thou attitudes of condemnation or exclusion. Like those other parties and organisations that had or have roles in the tragedy, it needs to acknowledge its own particular sins, and reach out to its enemy in a spirit of mutual forgiveness and reconciliation. Without this there can no true or well-founded peace.

Over the years the Orange Order has officially opposed virtually every political initiative for peace in Northern Ireland. This certainly applies to the recent Good Friday Agreement that was supported by 71.6 per cent of voters, a figure that included many individual Orangemen who exercised admirable independence by voting 'Yes'. However, the unionist 'Yes' vote was virtually matched by the extended Orange-unionist family that voted 'No'. This family largely comprises those who adhere unflinchingly to the Orange belief system, which still holds to notions of Protestant ascendancy, remains unambiguously sectarian and still opposed to any agreed system of shared political responsibility commanding the allegiance of all our citizens, Catholic and Protestant alike. Orangeism sadly still stands for the minimalist politics of majoritarian tribal rule, and in a poignant way remains a malign influence on the politics of Northern Ireland. It offers nothing other than the failed beliefs and exclusionist politics of the past, and consequently it can offer no hope to the people, and certainly none to our children.

It is perplexing to find that so many unionists are at best ambivalent about the Good Friday Agreement, and that both Yes and No unionists still share so much common ground. It has to be symptomatic of something that almost all shades of unionism still seem to retain at least a tint of Orange. These blend together and can unite, for example, on the right of Orangemen to march in quasi-military style through Catholic areas, quite regardless of the wishes of the residents upon whom that marching impinges. And in insisting on this right they can unashamedly cite the example of the Ku Klux Klan and the American Nazi Party. This could indicate that as yet even the best of unionism has not quite dislodged the worst of Orangeism, and that it still cannot bring itself to resist the old devil called sectarianism that would march roughshod over Christian neighbourliness and equal citizenship. Far too many unionists are not yet imbued with the egalitarian spirit of the Good Friday Agreement, given their admiration and support of 'those booming swaggering marches' that are clearly designed to 'keep the papists in their places' and to 'show them who's master'.

It is sometimes argued that in the Northern Ireland situation anyone if not everyone can be infected by sectarianism. This is an excuse, for sectarianism is not a virus but an attitude. It is notable that in the case of Orangeism, outbreaks of sectarianism are neither incidental nor occasional episodes, nor are they the result of a series of unfortunate accidents. Orangeism owes its very existence to a nakedly sectarian purpose – to maintain the interests of a privileged Protestantism – which it seeks to achieve by means that are shot through with anti-Catholicism. Orangeism therefore represents that which lies at the root of unionism's problems. Both seem incapable of learning from past mistakes. As a political party interested in power, the Ulster Unionist Party can no longer afford to harbour these sectarian attitudes, for the future of the Union will in the end be determined by Catholic votes. Unionism therefore must face up to the current challenges of pluralism and egalitarianism, and must cut off the dead hand of Orange prejudice if it is to have a future.

What of Orangeism? In their book *Moving Beyond Sectarianism*, Joseph Liechty and Cecilia Clegg debate the questions whether the Orange Order is (1) sectarian, and (2) redeemable. As to the first issue, they conclude that the Order is sectarian.

This is not because of what they regard as Orangeism's legitimate 'truth claim that the Roman Catholic Church is radically (*sic*) in error'. It is because of Orangeism's negative mixing of religion and politics that conjoins 'the defence of the Protestant religion with the upholding of a particular political loyalty'.[2] Thus whilst their conclusion that the Orange Order is sectarian accords with the position taken by this book, neither their premises nor arguments for that conclusion are fully in line with my own. The Order's apparently legitimate religious truth claim, which they misquote, is not that the Roman Church is radically in error, but that it is fatally so – see chapter 12. This judgmental claim is utterly damnatory. Its motivation is so alien to Christian ethics and doctrine, including that generic to the Reformation, that by any definition Orangeism has to be regarded as religiously sectarian.

Sectarianism does not respect or tolerate diversity and difference. Instead it exploits difference by disfiguring it into dangerous and nasty division. It does so by means that often fall short of that ultimately overt hatred and violence which constitutes the more readily identifiable face of sectarianism at the top of a pyramid of negative attitudes and actions. That pyramid is therefore based on a religio-political division that reflects itself in many consequential responses. Some of these may seem relatively innocuous, but none of them stands alone. They are inter-linked and incremental. Even those near the base of the pyramid make their own contribution to the sectarian pyramid that peaks in violence.

VIOLENCE

separation - exclusion - hatred

ignoring - belittling - demonising - rejection

prejudice - suspicion - fear - intolerance - bigotry

DIVISION BASED ON EXTREME RELIGIO-POLITICAL ATTITUDES

In contradiction to the ideals of the United Irishmen, the Orange Order was founded to maintain Protestant ascendancy and privilege. The product of a deliberately divisive policy to create and to perpetuate divided Irishmen, Orangeism is inevitably sectarian. Does this explain why its attitudes and actions, like those of others, so often appear to epitomise those illustrated by the sectarian pyramid?

As to whether the Orange Order is redeemable, Leichty and Clegg say 'there are some sufficiently strong positive elements in the founding identity of the Orange Order that have the potential to be redeemed'. These are said to include 'upholding the Protestant religion, in particular the place of the Bible'. This sentiment is misplaced. The reader will recall our scepticism as to the reality of such positive and redeemable elements in Orange religion. The Crown placed on top of the Holy Bible is a well-known Orange symbol. However, this dual symbol may no more indicate Orangeism's loyalty to the Bible as the rule of life than signify its loyalty to the Crown as the rule of British parliamentary government. It has often been demonstrated that in Orangeism's case both these loyalties are selective and heavily qualified. In fact, to suggest that the Orange Order stands foursquare for biblical truth and that, therefore, it should concentrate on its religious and biblical elements is massively to beg the question. If the assumption implicit in this were remotely true, one wonders why Orangeism has had such a bloody and rebellious history and why we have to suffer a 'Drumcree' every year. It has been established that evangelical religion formed no part in the 'founding identity' of the Orange Order in 1795. It has also been established that this has never been a salient feature of its two hundred year history, during which it has paid scant regard to the teachings of the New Testament, especially those with respect to the altruistic and beneficent nature of true Christian citizenship.

Orangeism is a mission field; it is by no stretch of the imagination some kind of incipient missionary foundation. Its religio-political element – wherein Liechty and Clegg identify and also delimit the sectarianism it must jettison if it is to be redeemed – ever was and remains the essential reason for its existence. The Rev. Martin Smyth MP, a former Imperial Orange Grand Master, far from making biblical claims on behalf of Orangeism, was quoted in chapter 12 as saying that the Orange Order was 'a pressure group to ensure that the Unionist Party remained firm on the constitution'. We can take his word for it. Thus it seems pointless to enquire whether the Order could be redeemed if redemption requires that it jettison the principle to which, in various forms, it has owed its very existence. In fact, to renounce what Liechty and Clegg quite rightly, albeit too narrowly, regard as its religio-political sectarianism, would involve such a metamorphosis as to render it no longer the Orange Order as we know it.

Like Northern Ireland itself, Orangeism is also in a kind of endgame. But unlike Northern Ireland the Orange Order has started out on that endgame in a condition of steep decline. That decline is not only because ascendancy politics is now increasingly seen to be an anachronism, but because its whole ethos and tradition are inherently inappropriate to an environment of political reform and religious rapprochement. Eoghan Harris, an Irish political journalist who is sympathetic to unionists, had a point when he tried to persuade them that they lacked a theory of change because they regarded politics as a product rather than a process. What Harris fails to add is that traditional unionist politics is derived from the inflexible doctrines of Orangeism. This is probably true of most unionists, but it is more obviously the case with anti-Agreement unionists. Far more than lacking a theory of change, the Orange-unionists who continue to cling to 'whatever it was King William established' are implacably resistant to the very principle of change implicit in political process. Ascendancy politics is incompatible with that flexibility and compromise which are the very stuff of pluralism and equality. The old 'not-an-inch' Orangeism still longs for its supremacist past and, to borrow words that Aneuran Bevan once used of a political opponent, it 'marches backwards with its face to the future'. For so long as it continues to oppose change, its own intransigent and inherently conservative attitudes must ensure that it can never begin to perceive the need for self-reform. If it ever did, and if it jettisoned its anti-Catholic religio-politics in order to embrace the pluralist future that is Northern Ireland's only hope for peace and stability, this would indicate that what until now has been the very reason for its existence had gone, and gone for ever.

In the event of the Orange Order rejecting its now impractical politics and revising its sectarian form of religion, it would be very difficult to envisage it taking on a new role. This is because it is singularly ill-equipped for anything other than what it was created to do and which in another time it once did very effectively. In the view of the writer such a development would herald the approaching end of Orangeism. Yet in the circumstances described this demise would create exciting new possibilities for the formerly 'divided Irishmen' to experience the inclusive and progressive politics of liberty and equality of citizenship for all. In such a society Protestant, Catholic and Dissenter, and those of no religion at all, could participate in an enriching diversity and pursue their lives in progressive peace and community. And wonder of wonders, it would be found that none of these transforming experiences would involve the sacrifice of a single Christian or truly Protestant principle. Hasten the day!

Endnotes

Foreword

1. Somewhat semantically, the Order prefers to describe itself as 'a society with secrets'.
2. Ruth Dudley Edwards, *The Faithful Tribe* – see author's Introduction, pp. xii, xvi.
3. Ibid, p. 293.
4. Edna Longley, quoted in Susan McKay, *Northern Protestants: An Unsettled People*, p. 289.

Introduction

1. Michael Farrell, *Northern Ireland, the Orange State*.
2. Referendum on the Good Friday Agreement, providing pluralist structures of government.
3. Luke's Gospel, 9:5.
4. *The English*, p, 20.
5. Quoted by Bill Rolston in David Miller (ed) *Rethinking Northern Ireland*, p. 254.

Chapter 1

1. Thomas McLoughlin, *Contesting Ireland*, p. 95
2. *Writings and Speeches of Edmund Burke*, ix. p. 615.
3. Nesca A. Robb, *William of Orange*, vol. 2, p. 418.
4. *Works*, iii, p. 343.
5. Finlay Holmes, *The Presbyterian Church in Ireland*, p. 68.

Chapter 2

1. John Byrne, *Impartial Account*, doc. 4 - see David W. Miller, *Peep O' Day Boys*.
2. Letter to Earl Fitzwilliam, p 24.
3. David W. Miller, *Queen's Rebels*, p. 53.
4. Kevin Whelan, *The Tree of Liberty*, p. 119.
5. ATQ Stewart, *The Narrow Ground*, p. 108.
6. Armagh, Monaghan, Tyrone, Fermanagh, Londonderry and Donegal.

Chapter 3

1. Announced in a *Belfast Newsletter* advertisement, 1 February 1793.

Chapter 4

1. Dewar, Brown and Long, *Orangeism*, pp. 96-7.
2. Ruth Dudley Edwards, *The Faithful Tribe*, pp. 174; 187.
3. Kilpatrick, Murdie and Cargo, *History of the Royal Arch Purple Order*, p. 32.

4. *The Faithful Tribe*, p. 188.
5. Quoted by Finlay Holmes, *The Presbyterian Church in Ireland*, p. 71.
6. David W. Miller, *Peep O' Day Boys*, p. 15
7. Ibid, p 55.
8. Edited Papers of Col. William Blacker and Col. Robert Wallace, p. 109.
9. Ibid, p. 50.
10. *Orangeism in Ireland and Britain*, p. 40.

Chapter 5

1. Quoted in Steve Bruce, *God Save Ulster!* p. 251
2. Norman Porter, *Rethinking Unionism*, pp. 109-125.
3. Ibid, p. 121.
4. A piece of Orange jargon often used by Orangemen to describe their traditional beliefs.
5. Prof. Tohill, quoted in John F. Harbinson, *The Ulster Unionist Party*, p. 89.
6. David W. Miller, *Queen's Rebels*, p. 60.
7. Violet Bonham Carter, *Winston Churchill as I Knew Him*, p. 287.
8. Stanley Ayling, *Edmund Burke*, p. 236.
9. *Works*, ii, p. 478.
10. Kevin Whelan, *The Tree of Liberty*, p. 116.
11. David W. Miller, *Queen's Rebels*, p. 56.
12. Kevin Whelan, *The Tree of Liberty*, p. 119.
13. W.E.H. Leckey, *History of Ireland*, ii, pp. 432-5.
14. *The Orange Citadel*, p. 3.
15. Richardson is quoted in David W. Miller, *Peep O' Day Boys*, p. 136.
16. Kevin Whelan, *The Tree of Liberty*, p. 120.
17. John Brown, *Orangeism*, p. 127.
18. Kevin Whelan, *The Tree of Liberty*, p. 126.
19. Ibid, pp. 124-125.
20. *Memoirs of the Various Rebellions in Ireland*.
21. David Trimble, *The Foundation of Northern Ireland*, p. 3.

Chapter 6

1. Jonathan Bardon, *A History of Ulster*, p. 246.
2. Ibid, p. 247.
3. Kevin Haddick-Flynn, *Orangeism*, pp. 230-1.
4. J.L. Porter, *The Life and Times of Henry Cooke*, p. 77.
5. John Brown, *Orangeism*, p. 127.
6. Kevin Haddick-Flynn, pp. 266-270
7. John Brown, *Orangeism*, p. 131.
8. Ibid, p. 132.
9. *Berwick Report on Occurrences at Dolly's Brae*, 12th July 1849.
10. Jonathan Bardon, *A History of Ulster*, pp. 302-304.
11. John Brown, *Orangeism*, p. 138.
12. Jonathan Bardon, *A History of Ulster*, p. 306.
13. John F. Harbinson, *The Ulster Unionist Party*, p. 88.

Chapter 7

1. Jonathan Bardon, *A History of Ulster*, p. 357.
2. James Winder Good, *Irish Unionism*, p. 61.
3. David W. Miller, *Queen's Rebels*, p. 63.
4. S.E. Long, *Orangeism*, p. 151.
5. Asquith regarded Parnell as 'one of the half-dozen great men of action of this century'.
6. John F. Harbinson, *The Ulster Unionist Party*, p. 130.

7. Ibid, p. 131.
8. Roy Jenkins, *Gladstone*, p. 537.
9. Roy Jenkins, *The Chancellors*, p. 28.
10. Henry Pelling, *Winston Churchill*, p. 24.
11. S.E. Long, *Orangeism*, p. 149.
12. James Winder Good, *Irish Unionism*, p. 196.
13. Robert Taylor, *Lord Salisbury*, p. 118.
14. Robert Kee, *Ireland*, p. 146.
15. Jonathan Bardon, *A History of Ulster*, p. 378.
16. Roy Jenkins, *Gladstone*, p. 543.
17. Jonathan Bardon, *A History of Ulster*, p. 440.
18. James Winder Good, *Irish Unionism*, p. 186.
19. Roy Jenkins, *Gladstone*, p. 606.

Chapter 8

1. James Winder Good, *Irish Unionism*, p. 209.
2. Ibid, p. 209.
3. *Queen's Rebels*, p. 98.
4. R.M. Henry, *The Evolution of Sinn Fein*, p. 2.
5. The Orange records were lost when their Dublin HQ was destroyed by the IRA in 1921.
6. Councillor Chris McGimpsey was given this impressive eye-witness account.
7. Violet Bonham Carter, *Winston Churchill as I Knew Him*, p. 216.
8. R.M. Henry, *The Evolution of Sinn Fein*, p. 146.
9. Ibid, p. 137.
10. Jonathan Bardon, *A History of Ulster*, p. 442.
11. A.T.Q. Stewart, *The Ulster Crisis*, p. 58.
12. Ibid, p. 229.
13. Carson's words in his acceptance speech at Craigavon on 23rd September, 1911.

Chapter 9

1. Yeats' poem, *Easter 1916*.
2. Jonathan Bardon, *A History of Ulster*, p. 461.
3. Michael Farrell, *Arming the Protestants*, p. 287.
4. Reported in *Belfast Newsletter*, 13th July, 1921.
5. Reported in *Northern Whig*, 15th October, 1920.
6. Michael Farrell, *Arming the Protestants*, p. 29.
7. Jim McDermott, *Northern Divisions*, p. 36.
8. G.B. Kenna, *The Belfast Pogroms*, pp. 100-114.
9. Ibid – the entire account contains many such British press reports.
10. *The 'B' Specials*, an Orange educational pamphlet
11. Jonathan Bardon, *A History of Ulster*, p. 476.
12. Michael Farrell, *Northern Ireland, The Orange State*, p. 95.
13. Ibid, p. 51.
14. *The 'B' Specials*, an Orange educational pamphlet.
15. *A History of Ulster*, p. 490; cf. Michael Farrell, *Arming the Protestants*, for details.
16. Henry Patterson in Arthur Aughey and Duncan Morrow (eds), *Northern Ireland Politics*, p. 5.
17. ATQ Stewart, *Edward Carson*, p. 134.
18. Ibid, p. 125.

Chapter 10

1. Jonathan Bardon, *A History of Ulster*, p. 484.
2. Ibid, p. 506.
3. John F. Harbinson, *The Ulster Unionist Party*, p. 93.
4. Jonathan Bardon, *A History of Ulster*, p. 678.

5.   Ibid, p. 680.

Chapter 11

1.   Michael Farrell, *Arming the Protestants*, p. 190.
2.   By the Committee on the Administration of Justice 1996.
3.   *A History of Ulster*, pp. 530-533 and 716-717.
4.   Quoted in Robert Kee, *Ireland*, p. 229.
5.   *Irish Times* article, 19th October, 1999.
6.   Jonathan Bardon, *A History of Ulster*, p. 714.
7.   Ibid, p. 529.
8.   Paddy Devlin, *Yes We Have No Bananas*, p. 77.
9.   Jonathan Bardon, *A History of Ulster*, p. 498.
10. Paul Bew, Peter Gibbon & Henry Patterson, *Northern Ireland: Political Forces & Social Classes*, p. 57.
11. Ibid, p. 57.
12. Robert Kee, *Ireland*, p 228; Jonathan Bardon, *A History of Ulster*, p. 538.
13. Michael Farrell, *Northern Ireland the Orange State*, p.. 85.
14. Ibid, p 120.
15. Bew, Gibbon and Patterson, *Northern Ireland*, pp. 114; 138.
16. Ibid, p. 138.
17. Reported in *Belfast Telegraph*, 5th May, 1969.
18. *Minority Verdict*, p. 5.
19. Bew, Gibbon and Patterson, *Northern Ireland*, p. 139.
20. ATQ Stewart, *Edward Carson*, p. 120
21. Paisley believes 'the R C Church is behind the Troubles in Northern Ireland'.
22. Paddy Devlin, *The Fall of the N. I. Executive*, pp. 72-3.
23. Ibid, p. 81.
24. *Irish News*, Editorial, 5th November 1999.
25. Statements by Harold Gracey and David Jones, Press Reports circa 5th July 2000.
26. For greater detail see Peter Taylor, *Loyalists*, pp. 150-2.

Chapter 12

1.   *Orangeism*, a pamphlet written jointly with Rev. Rupert Gibson.
2.   Steve Bruce, *God Save Ulster!* p. 249
3.   Ibid, p. 251
4.   Ninian Smart, *The World's Religions*, pp. 11-22.
5.   Jonathan Bardon, *A History of Ulster*, p. 344.
6.   2. Cor. 6:14
7.   Dennis Cooke, *Persecuting Zeal*, pp. 41-68.
8.   1st John 5:1
9.   Charles Hodge, *The Church and its Polity*, pp. 191 ff.
10. Hebrews 13: 14
11. Rev. 21:26
12. Dominic Behan, *On the Birthplace of Louis MacNeice*.
13. *Systematic Theology*, vol. ii, p. 601.

Chapter 13

1.   W.P. Malcomson, *Behind Closed Doors*, p. 11.
2.   Cecil Kilpatrick, *History of the Royal Arch Purple Order*, p. 172.
3.   Kevin Haddick-Flynn, *Orangeism*, pp. 355 ff.
4.   Pamphlet *The Orange Order, An Evangelical Perspective*, p. 12.
5.   Cecil Kilpatrick, *History of the Royal Arch Purple Order*, p. 59.
6.   From the evidence of Dean Holt Waring to the Parliamentary Enquiry of 1825.
7.   See *History of the Royal Arch Purple Order*, p. 56.

8.   Ibid, p. 58.
9.   Ibid, p. 59.
10. Ibid, pp. 175 and 183.
11. Ibid, p. 70.
12. Ibid, p. 91.
13. Ibid, p. 91.
14. Ibid, p. 75.
15. Ibid, pp. 113, 118.
16. A. Mitchell Hunter, *The Teaching of Calvin*, p. 81.
17. Ibid, pp. 45, 73.
18. Biblical reference: Jude 3.
19. Quoted by W.P. Malcomson in *The Forgotten History of the Orange Order*, p. 46.

Chapter 14

1.   Frank Wright, *Two Lands on One Soil*, p. 401.
2.   Chris Ryder and Vincent Kearney, *Drumcree*, p. 102.
3.   Evidence to the Northern Ireland Affairs Committee, 28th January 1998.
4.   Sir John Hermon, *Holding the Line*, pp. 171-2.
5.   Discussion on BBC radio programme *Sunday Sequence*, 19th January, 2003.
6.   Biblical references: Heb. 1:3; Col. 1:17.
7.   Ibid: Eccl. 3:8
8.   Ibid: Col. 1:20
9.   Quoted by Norman Porter in *Rethinking Unionism*, p. 99.
10. *Queen's Rebels*, p. 68.
11. *A History of Ulster*, p. 653.
12. *Northern Ireland 1921-1926*, p. 155
13. Dewar, Brown and Long, *Orangeism*, p. 138.
14. Ibid, p. 126.
15. Ibid, p. 118.
16. Luke 9 : 5.
17. John Dunlop, *A Precarious Belonging*, p. 61.

Chapter 15

1.   St. Paul in Acts 17: 24 – 29.
2.   Joseph Liechty and Cecilia Clegg, *Moving Beyond Sectarianism*, pp. 113, 126.

Select Bibliography

Aughey, Arthur and Morrow, Duncan (eds). *Northern Ireland Politics*, Longman, 1995

Ayling, Stanley. *Edmund Burke*, John Murray, 1988

Bardon, Jonathan. *A History of Ulster*, Blackstaff Press, 1992

Bew, Paul, Gibbon, Peter and Patterson, Henry. *Northern Ireland: Political Forces and Social Classes*, Serif, 1996

Blacker, William, and Wallace, Robert H. *The Formation of the Orange Order, 1795-1798: the edited papers of Colonel William Blacker*, Education Committee of the Grand Orange Lodge of Ireland, 1994

Bonham Carter, Violet. *Winston Churchill As I Knew Him*, Eyre, Spottiswoode and Collins, 1965

Brewer, John D. *Anti-Catholicism in Northern Ireland, 1600-1998*, Macmillan, 1998

Bruce, Steve. *God Save Ulster! The Religion and Politics of Paisleyism*, Oxford University Press, 1986

Burke, Edmund. *Works*, London, 1899

Burke, Edmund. *Writings and Speeches*, Oxford, 1973

Calvin, John. *Institutes of the Christian Religion*, Westminster Press, 2000

Colley, Linda. *Britons*, Yale University Press, 1992

Cooke, Dennis. *Persecuting Zeal: A Portrait of Ian Paisley*, Brandon, 1996
Curtin, Nancy J. *The United Irishmen*, Clarendon Press, 1998
Devlin, Paddy. *The Fall of the Northern Ireland Executive*, Blackstaff Press, 1975
Devlin, Paddy. *Yes We Have No Bananas*, Blackstaff Press, 1981
Dewar, M.W., Brown, John and Long, S.E.. *Orangeism*, Grand Lodge of Ireland, 1967
Dudley Edwards, Ruth. *The Faithful Tribe: An Intimate Portrait of the Loyal Institutions*, Harper Collins, 1999
Dunlop, John. *A Precarious Belonging: Presbyterians and the Conflict in Ireland*, Blackstaff Press, 1995
Farrell, Michael. *Northern Ireland: The Orange State*, Pluto Press, 1976
Farrell, Michael. *Arming the Protestants*, Pluto Press, 1983
Gibson, Fred and Gibson, Rupert. *Orangeism,* Christian Irishman, c. 1960
Gladstone, W.E. *The Church of England and Ritualism*, London, 1875
Good, James Winder. *Irish Unionism*, Kennikat Press, 1920
Haddick-Flynn, Kevin. *Orangeism: The Making of a Tradition*, Wolfhound Press, 1999
Harbinson, John F. *The Ulster Unionist Party, 1882-1973: Its Development and Organisation*, Blackstaff Press, 1973
Hayes, Maurice. *Minority Verdict: Experiences of a Catholic Civil Servant*, Blackstaff Press, 1995
Henry. R.M. *The Evolution of Sinn Fein*, Kennikiat Press, 1920
Hermon, John. *Holding the Line*, Gill and Macmillan, 1997
Hill, Christopher. *Antichrist in Seventeenth-Century England*, Verso, 1990
Hodge, Charles. *The Church and its Polity*, Paternoster, 1879
Hodge, Charles. *Systematic Theology*, 1871-3, reprinted by Eerdmans, 1989
Holmes, Finlay. *The Presbyterian Church in Ireland*, Columba Press, 2000
Holmes, Finlay. *Persbyterians and Orangeism, 1795-1995*, Presbyterian Historical Society of Ireland, 1996
Hunter, A. Mitchell. *The Teaching of Calvin*, Clarke, 1950
Jenkins, Roy. *Asquith*, Collins, 1964
Jenkins, Roy. *Mr Balfour's Poodle*, Collins, 1968
Jenkins, Roy. *Gladstone*, Macmillan, 1995
Jenkins, Roy. *The Chancellors*, Macmillan, 1998
Jones, R. David et al. *The Orange Citadel*, Portadown Cultural Heritage Committee, 1996
Kee, Robert. *Ireland*, Abacus, 1991
Kenna, G.B. *The Belfast Pogroms*, (Dublin) O'Connell Publishing Co., 1922
Kilpatrick, Cecil, Murdo, William and Cargo, David. *History of the Royal Arch Purple Order*, Royal Arch Purple Research Group, 1997
Leckey, W.E.H. *A History of Ireland*, University of Chicago, 1972
Liechty, Joe and Clegg, Cecilia. *Moving Beyond Sectarianism*, Columba, 2001
Lyons, F.S.L. *Ireland Since the Famine*, Fontana, 1973
McDermott, Jim. *Northern Divisions*, Beyond the Pale Publications, 2001
McKay, Susan. *Northern Protestants: An Unsettled People*, Blackstaff Press, 2000
McLoughlin, Thomas. *Contesting Ireland: Irish Voices against England in the 18th Century*, Four Courts Press, 1999
Malcolmson, W.P. *Behind Closed Doors*, Evangelical Truth, 1999
Malcolmson, W.P. *The Forgotten History of the Orange Order*, Evangelical Truth, 2000
Meredith, Ian and Kennaway, Brian. *Orangeism: An Evangelical Perspective*, published by the authors, 1993
Miller, David W. *Queen's Rebels: Ulster Loyalism in Historical Perspective*, Gill and Macmillan, 1978
Miller, David W. *Peep O' Day Boys and Defenders*, Public Record Office of Northern Ireland, 1990
O'Neill, Terence. *Ulster at the Crossroads*, Faber and Faber, 1969
O'Neill, Terence. *Autobiography of Terence O'Neill*, Hart-Davis, 1972
Pelling, Henry. *Winston Churchill*, Macmillan, 1989
Pattterson, Henry. 'Northern Ireland, 1921-1968', in Arthur Aughey and Duncan Morrow (eds). *Northern Ireland Politics*, Longman, 1995
Paxman, Jeremy. *The English: A Portrait of a People*, Penguin, 1999
Porter, J.L. *The Life and Times of Henry Cooke*, Ambassador, 1999
Porter, Norman. *Rethinking Unionism: An Alternative Vision for Northern Ireland*, Blackstaff Press, 1996
Porter, Norman. *The Elusive Quest*, Blackstaff Press, 2003
Robb, Nesca A. *William of Orange: A Personal Portrait*, Heineman, 1962

Rolston, Bill. 'What's wrong with multiculturalism? Liberalism and the Irish conflict', in David Miller (ed), *Rethinking Northern Ireland*, Longman, 1998

Routledge, Paul. *Public Servant, Secret Agent: A Biography of Airey Neave*, Fourth Estate, 2002

Rowen, Herbert H. *The Princes of Orange: Stadtholders in the Dutch Republic*, Cambridge University Press, 1988

Ryder, Chris and Kearney, Vincent. *Drumcree: The Orange Order's Last Stand*, Methuen, 2001

Smart, Ninian. *The World's Religions*, Cambridge University Press, 1998

Senior, Hereward. *Orangeism in Ireland and Britain, 1795-1836*, Routledge and Kegan, 1966

Sibbett, R.M. *Orangeism in Ireland and Throughout the Empire*, Thynne, 1914

Stewart, A.T.Q. *Edward Carson*, Blackstaff Press, 1981

Stewart, A.T.Q. *The Ulster Crisis*, Blackstaff Press, 1997

Stewart, A.T.Q. *The Narrow Ground*, Blackstaff Press, 1997

Taylor, Robert. *Lord Salisbury*, Allen Lane, 1975

Trimble, David. *The Foundation of Northern Ireland*, Ulster Society, 1991

Whelan, Kevin. *The Tree of Liberty*, Cork University Press, 1996

Wright, Frank. *Two Lands on One Soil*, Gill and Macmillan, 1996

Other Sources

Constitution, Laws and Ordinances of the Loyal Orange Institution of Ireland, unpublished, Grand Lodge of Ireland, 1967

Review of the Parades Commission in Northern Ireland: Submission by the Ulster Unionist Party, 2002

Steadfast for Faith and Freedom: 200 Years of Orangeism, commemorative brochure edited by Billy Kennedy, Grand Orange Lodge of Ireland, 1995

Westminster Confession of Faith, 1643

Government and Parliamentary Reports on Orangeism

Report from the House of Commons Select Committee to Inquire into the Nature, Character, Extent and Tendency of Orange Associations of Ireland, 1835

Berwick Report – An Investigation into Occurrences at Dolly's Brae on 12th July 1849, House of Commons, 1849

Government Committee of Inquiry into the Belfast Riots, 1857

Acts of Parliament Legislating Against Orangeism

Unlawful Oaths Act, 1823

Unlawful Societies Act, 1825

Party Processions Act, 1832

Reply by King William IV to an Address from the Commons, 1836

Party Processions Act, 1850

INDEX

Acton, Lord 10

Agar-Robartes MP 78, 81

Aldermen of Skinner's Alley 19

American census (1790) 12

American immigration 12

American Presbyterian Church 12, 134, 139

American Revolution 9

Andrews, John MP 110

Anglicans 17, 33-4

Anglo-Irish Agreement 121-2, 180

Anglo-Irish Treaty 94-5

Anti-Catholicism 67, 119, 123, 129, 132-5, 138-9, 182

Antichrist 136-7

Apartheid 4, 157

Apprentice Boys of Derry vii, 19, 100-1

Arlott, John 111

Armagh 14-17, 25, 36, 44

    Anti-emancipation rally 44

    Grand Orange Lodge 48

    Outrages 36

Arms, quest for 15

Ascendancy ideas, attitudes 102, 107, 114, 162-4, 169-70, 172, 177-8, 183

    see also Protestant ascendancy

Asquith, H.H. xiii, 33, 74, 77, 78, 80-1, 83, 86, 179, 180

Augustine, St. xi

Balfour, Arthur 75-6, 78, 82

Ballybay murders 43

Balmoral, loyalist rally (1912) 78-9

Banbridge, drumming party 170

Baptism, the Reformed view of 134-5

Bardon, Jonathan 22, 52, 64, 102, 108, 130, 169

Barr, Glenn 119

Bates, Sir Dawson 105, 108, 110

Beers, Francis and William 49, 50

Behan, Dominic 18

Belfast Agreement (1998)

    see Good Friday Agreement

Belfast Poor Law Guardians 109-110

Belfast Riots 52, 65, 173

Benburb 19, 128

Bentham, Jeremy 12

Beresford, John 36, 38, 55

Berwick Report (Dolly's Brae 1849) 50-1

Bevan, Aneurin 183

Bew, Giddons and Patterson 169

Bible, the 143, 182

Black and Tans 87

Black Order, degrees, etc.

    see Royal Black Preceptory

Blacker, Stewart 150

Blacker, William 46

Blair, Tony 123, 180

Bloody Sunday 102

Bonham Carter, Lady Violet 75, 78

Bonar Law, Andrew 78, 97

Boundary Commission 96-8

Boycott, Captain 57-8

British Army 47, 80, 90, 92, 101, 102

British Constitution 32-3

Brooke, Sir Basil

    later Lord Brookeborough 86, 89, 92, 99, 108, 110

Brown, Rev. John 22, 26, 46, 49-50, 171-2

Bruce, Steve 129

Brunswick Clubs 44

B-Specials

    see also Ulster Special Constabulary 87, 90-3, 100-1, 106, 116

Buckingham Palace Conference (1914) 83

Burke, Edmund 10, 11, 16, 27, 33, 39,

Calvin, John 20, 73, 134-5, 139, 148, 153-4

Camden, Earl 34, 36-7

Carson, Sir Edward

    later Lord Carson 52, 71, 73, 75-84, 85-6, 92-5, 97, 115

Carlton Street Orange Hall 160

Casement, Sir Roger 81

Castle junta (Dublin) 10, 27, 34, 37-8

Catholics 1, 5, 9, 10-11, 13, 14, 17, 27, 33-4, 36, 37, 39, 51, 67, 72, 131-6

Catholic Emancipation 13, 15, 39, 40, 42-3, 44-6

Chamberlain, Joseph 60, 65, 96

Chamberlain, Austen 96-7

Chaplains (Orange) 131, 171

Chichester-Clark, James

    later Lord Moyola 102

Christianity 130-3, 133-6, 137-8, 156-7, 173

    and citizenship 3, 138-9, 162, 165-8, 178

Churchill, Lord Randolph 58, 61-2, 76-7, 95, 140, 180

Churchill, Winston xiii, 90, 180

Church of Ireland 1-2, 10, 27, 33, 36, 51, 56-7, 59, 130

City of God 137

Civil Rights 100, 114, 115, 162

Clergy viii, 26, 35, 68, 128

Colley, Linda 1, 167

Common grace, doctrine of 166

Conditional loyalty 2, 31, 32, 43, 63, 77, 115, 123, 178

Conservative Party 53, 57, 58-9, 60-1, 71, 72, 78, 87, 95, 97, 117

Constitution Act, Northern Ireland (1973) 117

Constitution, Laws and Ordinances of Orange Order 131

Contractarianism 31

Cook, David 162-3

Cooke, Rev. Dennis 134

Cooke, Dr. Henry 45-6, 52, 55-6, 66, 99

Cornwallis, Lord 38-9, 42

Council of Ireland 93, 118

Covenant, theory 31-2, 99

Covenant, Ulster 31, 79

Craig, Sir James

    later Lord Craigavon viii, 73, 76, 87, 88, 90-3, 96-8, 105, 110, 111-3

Craig, William 118-9

Crawford, Fred 66, 75, 79, 80, 81

Crawford, Lindsay x, 72

Cromwell, Oliver 36

Crown in Parliament 31, 33, 48, 76, 79, 98, 103, 111, 178-81

Crusaders (Medieval)

    and Royal Black Preceptory viii, ix, 142

Culture, Protestant 3-4

Cumberland, Duke Ernest 44-5, 47-8, 179

Curragh Camp 'Mutiny' 80

Curran, L.E. 111

Demographics

    in 18th century Ulster 17, 51

Defenders, Catholic vii, 9, 14, 18, 21, 49

Degrees, rituals

    of Loyal orders 25-6, 140,

    see also Diamond System

Democratic Unionist Party (DUP) 117, 138

Derry, or Londonderry vii, 100-1, 112, 173

De Valera, Eamonn 94, 98

Devlin, Joe MP 82, 91-2, 133, 137

Devlin, Paddy MP 109-10, 120

Dewar, Rev. Dr. M.W. 25

Diamond, battle of the 21-2

Diamond System 25-6, 35, 141-4, 147

Disestablishment, Church of Ireland 55-6

Die-hards (Tory) 75-6, 97

Discipline, in Orange Order 132-3

Dissenters 1, 10, 11-2, 73

Dissolution of
original Orange degrees (1798) 35, 140
original Orange Order (1800) 35, 141, 143
the Order of 1800 (1820) 150
the Order of 1820 (1836) 48

Divided Irishmen 16, 41, 182

Donaldson, Jeffrey MP 162, 165

Dolly's Brae 49-51, 160, 171, 173

Drennan, Dr. William 12, 15

Drumcree (Portadown) 4, 20, 106, 121, 158-60, 162-3, 170-1, 172

Drums and drumming 169-70

Dublin Castle 16, 19, 27, 32, 36-7, 38, 45

Dudley Edwards, Ruth xi, xii, xiii, 22-3, 133

Dunloy 158-9, 172

Easter Rising (1916) 85

Economic policies of unionists 107-111

Employment of Catholics 88-9, 110-11

'Encroacher' Catholics 15, 18

Enlightenment, the 9, 12

Equality, principle of 162-5, 181-2

Evangelical religion
and the Orange Order 128-9, 130-2, 138-9, 152-4, 156-7, 178
see also Reformed Faith

Evangelical Revival (1859) 130

Errors of the Church of Rome 131-6, 138-9

Faction fighting, country sport 14

Fair Employment 110

Farrell, Michael 99

Faulkner, Brian MP 102-3, 118, 120

Fianna Fail Party 98

Fisk, Robert 108

Fitt, Gerry MP now Lord Fitt 118

Fitzsimmons, William MP 132

Fitzwilliam, Earl 33-4, 37

Freeland, General 101

Freemasonry 18, 23, 24, 25-6, 128, 140-6, 147-152
see also Masonic, Masonry

Fundamentalism, religious 129, 165-6

Garvagh, battle of 42

General Elections
in 1885 57, 59
in 1892 66

in 1910 74
in 1918 87

Gentry, new leaders
of the Orange Order viii, 26, 34-5

George III 34, 42

Gerrymandering
of electoral districts 111-112

Gibson, Rev. Fred 127, 128

Giffard, Captain John 24, 25, 34

Gladstone, W. E. 20, 39, 51, 53, 55, 57, 58, 61, 62, 64, 65-6, 68, 80, 91, 152-3, 179, 180

Good Friday Agreement (1998) 5, 107, 117, 121, 181

Government Inquries into Orange Order
in 1836 47
in 1849 50-1
in 1857 52, 171

Government of Ireland Act (1921) 92-3, 96

Grand Orange Lodge of Ireland 26, 35, 65, 70, 81, 120, 130, 140, 147, 149

Grattan, Henry 33, 37, 163, 180

Gulladuff 46, 127

Guns and gun-running 75, 80-1

Gwynn, W. J. 150

Gyle, James MP 133, 137

Haddick-Flynn, Kevin xi, 47

Hamill, Robert 171

Hanna, Rev. Hugh ('Roaring') 56, 66

Harris, Eoghan 183

Harryville chapel 159

Hayes, Maurice 114

Heath, Edward 102-3, 115, 117, 180

Heenan, Cardinal John C. 168

Hermon, Sir John 164

Hill, Dr. Christopher 136

Hillsborough, Loyalist demo (1834) 46-7

Historia 2

Hodge, Dr. Charles 134-6, 137-8

Holmes, Dr. Finlay 46

Home Rule 33, 56-7, 70
electoral mandate for 61
right-wing opposition to 63-4
Gladstone's definition of 64
Gladstone's determination 68
Home Rule/Rome Rule 57, 64, 66-7, 73
Robert Kee and Jonathan Bardon on 64
Parnell's position on 65
not anti-union 64-5
1st Home Rule Bill (1886) 65
Ulster Unionist Convention (1892) 66, 68
Thomas Sinclair on 66-7

2nd Home Rule Bill (1892) 68
anti-Irish attitudes 73
David W. Miller on 74-5
3rd Home Rule Bill (1912) 74, 78-9
Ulster Crisis 79-84
'political passion' 82-3
Buckingham Palace Conference 83
exclusion of Ulster 82, 84, 86
variations on 92-3

Hope, Jemmy 23

Housing, slum 108

House of Lords 68-9, 74, 79

Hume, David 12

Hume, John MP 100-1

Hume, Joseph MP 43, 47

Hunt Report 101

Hutcheson, Francis 12

'Imperial Province' of Ulster 73

'Improved' Orange Order 35, 140, 143

Independent Orange Order ix, x, 72, 141

Industrialisation 51, 72-3

Internment 102

Irish Republican Army xii, 81, 87, 89, 92, 102, 105, 122, 180

Jenkins, Roy 61, 62, 69, 95, 97

Jesus, on being unwanted 3

Jacobin threat 34

Johnston, William MP 53, 72

Kee, Robert 64, 108

Kingdom of God 137-8, 165-6

Kitchener, Lord 85

Knox, Thomas MP 34, 36

Knox, John (General) 34, 36, 38

Knox, John (Reformer) 154

Ku Klux Klan 4, 165, 181

Labour Government 97, 100, 101

Labour Party (Northern Ireland) 114

Land
ownership of 11
sectarian rent issue 15

Land Acts 51, 57, 58, 70

Land League 57-8, 59, 60

Landlordism 59-60, 66, 70-1, 77

Law, Orange attitude to 32, 121

Leckey, W. E. H. 36

Legislation, anti-Orange Order 42
Unlawful Oaths Act (1823) 43
Unlawful Societies Act (1825) 43
Party Processions Act (1832) 46
King's Reply to Commons (1836) 48
Party Processions Act (1850) 51

Lemass, Sean 114

Liberal Party 52, 53, 58-9, 60-1, 66, 82, 11
Liberal Unionism 65, 68, 69
Liberty 156, 164, 165, 167-8
Liechty, Joe and Clegg, Cecilia 182-3
Lifford, Co. Donegal 149
Linen industry 15-16
Lloyd George, David xiii, 74, 82, 86-7, 92-3, 96-7, 180
Local Government (Northern Ireland) 111-2
Londonderry, or Derry vii, 100-1, 112, 178
Long, Rev. S. E. 56, 63
Long, Walter MP 70, 75
Longstone Road 118
Loughgall, Co. Armagh 21
Loyalists 72, 100, 101, 114, 119, 122
Luther, Martin 133-4, 139
Lynch, Jack 114
Lyons, F. S. L. 108

McDermott, Jim 89
MacDonald, James Ramsay 97-8
McGoldrick, Michael 171
Mackemie, Francis 12
Macmillan, Harold 115
MacNeill, Eoin 81, 180
'Mad month', of July 156, 181
Maghery 46
Malcomson, W. P. 130, 131, 144
Marching 4, 37, 44, 101-2, 118, 121, 156
why march? 170-3
marching season 88, 89, 100, 101, 156, 181
Mardi Gras 4
Martin, Bernadette 171
Masonic 12, 23, 129, 131, 140, 142, 146, 149, 151
see also Freemasonry
Mayhew, Sir Patrick 163
Militarism, and Orangeism 4, 104, 162-3, 168-9
Mill, John Stuart 156
Miller, David W. 35-6, 51-2, 74-5, 169
Milton, John 68
Mitchelbourne, Colonel vii
Monday Club 119
Multi-culturalist claims 3-4
Musgrave, Sir Richard 38

Nationalism 61, 100
Nationalists 82, 87, 107, 111-2, 157
Naziism, American 4, 165, 181
Neave, Airey 76
Neo-Naziism 119
Newtownbarry, violence 46

Nixon, John W. 106
Non-subscribing Presbyterians 131
Northern Ireland, creation of 93-4

Oath, Orange 144
O'Brien, Conor Cruise 79, 169
O'Connell, Daniel 43, 45, 46
O'Neill, Phelim MP 132
O'Neill, Terence 100, 113-14, 177
O'Shea, Kitty 65
Occult 141, 146
Ogle, George 147
Opportunism, Tory 62, 78, 180
Orange Boys 19, 23, 25, 26, 140
Orange clubs 18, 19
Orangemen viii, ix, xii, xiii, 2, 27, 33, 40
Orange Order vii, xi, 1, 2, 3, 13, 16, 22, 24, 25, 27, 32, 36, 38, 43, 47, 73
Orange army xiii, 37, 59, 69
'Orange big drum', the 97
'Orange card', the 62, 65
Orange culture 4
Orange halls xiii, 71, 87, 120
Orange lodge(s) xiii, 20, 26, 35-6, 46, 48-9, 65, 70, 71, 88
Orange religion 3, 129-130, 178
see also Religion
'Orange riots' 52-3, 54
Orange (church) services 158
Orange state, the 2, 99, 104
Orange violence
see Armagh, Ballybay,
Belfast riots, Diamond,
Derry, Dolly's Brae,
Drumcree, Tunnel, Dunloy,
Garvagh, Harryville,
Maghery, Newtownbarry,
Shankill
Orange Volunteers xiii, 118, 120-1
Orangeism viii, xiii, 5, 17, 19-20, 46, 48, 52-3, 56

Paget, General Sir Arthur 80
Paisley, Rev. Dr. I. R. K. vii, xi, 52, 72, 116, 117, 119, 138, 160, 168, 177
Paisleyism x, 72, 129
Parades Commission 4, 32, 162, 172, 181
Parliament Act (1911) 74, 75
Parliamentary Select Committee (1836) on Orangeism 47, 164
Parnell, Charles Stuart 57, 58-9, 60-2, 65-6, 92
Patten, Chris (Report on Policing) 107
Paulin, Tom 170

Paxman, Jeremy 3, 168
Peace, Reconciliation and Protestant fundamentalism 165-7
Pearse, Patrick 81, 180
Peel, Sir Robert 42, 45
Peel Orange Lodge (RUC) 105-6
Peep O'Day Boys vii, 14, 15, 17, 18, 21, 22, 35, 128
Penal Laws 11, 15, 77
Phoenix Park murders 58
Pitt, William 33-4, 42
Plantation of Ulster 15
Pluralism 3, 173, 182
Plymouth Brethren 151
Pogroms, Belfast 90, 92
Politics 2, 27, 63, 103, 111-115, 136-7
Pope, the ix, 11, 20
Portadown 25, 26, 36, 140, 159-60, 162, 164
Porter, Norman 31-2, 166, 167
Powell, Enoch MP 33, 93
Presbyterians 1, 2, 10, 12, 17, 18, 26, 38, 46, 47, 56, 139, 173
Presbyterianism 12, 27, 46, 178
Protestant Ascendancy,
and the Act of the Union 38-9
constitutional aspects of 63, 99
relationship with Orangeism 25
Terence O'Neill on 114
Carson's prescient advice 115
Rev. Ian Paisley on 168
a supremacist ethos 56, 64, 67, 100, 102, 156, 164, 167, 172, 177
Protestant defence tradition 19, 59
Protestantism 1, 129, 134, 156, 167
Protestant parliament for a Protestant people 2, 32, 98, 103
Press, British 90
Property, land and Orangeism 111
Providence, doctrine of 166
Proportional representation 111
Provisional IRA 101, 119
Public banding 52

Qualifications of an Orangeman 131-2
Quinn brothers, murders 170-1

Radicalism 9
Rebellion of 1798 38, 41
Reconciliation 165-7
Redmond, John 81, 83, 85
Reform(s) of Orange Order 26, 35, 140-3, 150
Referendum on the Good Friday Agreement 3

Reformation: Reformed Faith xiii, 127, 129-30, 132-7, 148, 152-5, 166-7, 178
Republicanism 20, 81, 85, 86, 89, 180
Rights, right to march 11-5, 167-8
Revisionism xii
Revival, religious (1859) 130
Ribbonmen 42-3
Richardson, Dr. William 35
'Riding the goat' (Arch Purple ritual) 145
Ritual, ritualism viii, ix, x, 140-155
Robb, Nesca 11, 179
Roden, Lord 46, 49, 50
Roman Catholic(ism) 1, 131-6, 139, 168, 182
'Rome rule' 67, 73, 75
Routledge, Paul vii, 26, 35, 141
Royal Arch Purple 143-6, 147-52
Royal Black Preceptory viii, 26, 35, 141-2, 150-1
Royal Irish Constabulary (RIC) 105
Royalty, British Royal House 27
Royal Ulster Constabulary (RUC) 100, 101, 102, 105-7

Sacrament, sacramentalism 152-4
Salisbury, Lord 58, 62, 63-4, 76, 82, 179
Salvation Army 157
Saulters, Robert 123
Saunderson, Colonel Edward ix, 58-60, 61, 63, 66, 71, 72, 75, 118, 169
Secrecy xi, 36
Sectarianism xiii, 14-15, 60, 67, 70, 72, 88, 90, 103, 109, 112, 113, 129, 135, 159, 165, 180-1, 182-3
Sectarian pyramid 182
Security policy, unionist 104
Senior, Hereward 27
Settler, colonialist attitudes 17
Scarva, sham fight 19
Scotch-Irish 12
Social Democratic and Labour Party (SDLP) 102
Shankill 'butchers' 122
Shipyard, Belfast ix, 88
Simpson, Robert MP 132
Sinclair, Thomas 56, 66-7, 68, 73, 79
Sinn Féin 87, 89, 123, 161
Sloan, James 24-6, 146
Sloan, Tom ix, x, 72
Smart, Ninian 129
Smith, F. E. (Galloper), later Lord Birkenhead 78, 79
Smyth, Rev. Martin MP 99, 118, 123, 128, 183
Socialists, Belfast 73, 112
Somme (1916) 86

Special Powers Act (1922) 105-6
Stewart, A. T. Q. 17, 82, 95
Stormont Parliament (pre-1972) 2, 98, 102, 106, 112, 118, 123, 180
'Sublime' (Royal Arch Purple) degree 148
Sunningdale 118, 123
Symbols, symbolism 142

Taylor, Greg 159
Taylor, Peter 122
Taylor, Robert 64
Templeton, John 140, 146
Tenant Right 51
Thatcher, Margaret 180
Thirty-nine Articles 136
Tithes 55
Times, the (London) 88
Tone, Theobald Wolfe 12, 23
Tories, Tory party 33, 61-2, 76, 95, 115, 180
    see also Conservative Party
Tour of the North, (Orange march) 172
'Travel' (Royal Arch Purple ritual) 144
Trimble, David MP 2, 4, 39-40, 117, 160
Troubles, the 99, 101, 105, 107
Tunnel, the (Portadown) 164, 173
Twelth of July 3, 4, 46, 52, 86, 157
'Two-nations' theory 40, 67

Ulster 13, 14, 15, 17, 26, 39-40, 41, 43, 59, 61-2, 68, 76-7, 80-3, 90
Ulster Covenant 67, 79, 81
Ulster Defence Association (UDA) 119
'Ulsterisation' process 45, 65, 67, 71
Ulster Liberal Unionist Association 66
Ulster Special Constabulary 90-2, 98, 104
Ulster Unionist Convention (1892) 66, 68
Ulster Unionist Council xiii, 71, 75, 79, 80, 86, 87, 93, 99, 116
Ulster Unionist Labour Association 73
Ulster Unionist Party 5, 70, 87, 99, 116
Ulster Volunteer Force (UVF) viii, 40, 79, 80-1, 86, 87-8, 89, 90, 104, 122
Ulster Worker's Council (UWC) 119-20
Unemployment in Northern Ireland 109-10
Union, the Act of (1800) 37-8, 42, 46, 147

Unionist Government (Northern Ireland) 98-9, 104-15
Union, unionism 60, 116-17, 128-9
Unitarianism 131, 138, 149
United Irishmen 9, 13, 16, 17, 26, 34, 37-8, 40, 41, 67

Vanguard unionist paramilitarism 118-19
Verner, Thomas 35, 39, 46, 143, 146-7
Victoria, Princess and later Queen 47, 57
Volunteers (18th century) 12-13, 22-4
Vorster, Henrik 105

Wallace, Colonel 26
War (1914-1918) 83, 84, 85-7, 88
Waterloo (1815) 15, 45
Whelan, Kevin 16, 34
Wellington, Duke of 15, 44-5, 179
Westminster Confession of Faith 136
William III, Prince of Orange vii, 10, 13, 19-20, 32, 167, 179
    'whatever he established' 32, 56, 84, 115, 121, 123, 183
William IV 47-8
Wilson, Harold 100
Wilson, General Sir Henry 80, 91
Wilson, James 18, 21, 22, 23, 24, 26, 35, 128, 140, 146
Winter, Dan 21, 22, 23, 24, 26, 35
Wright, Billy 121
Wright, Frank 160

Yeates, William B. 85, 97
Yeomanry viii, 19, 36, 37, 44, 46, 47, 81, 91, 169

Zwingli 148